The Death and Resurrection of the Beloved Son

The Death and Resurrection of the Beloved Son

The Transformation of Child Sacrifice in Judaism and Christianity

Jon D. Levenson

Yale University Press   New Haven and London

Designed by Sonia L. Scanlon.

Set in Janson type by Rainsford Type, Danbury, Connecticut.

Printed in the United States of America by Vail-Ballou Press, Binghamton, New York.

Library of Congress Cataloging-in-Publication Data

Levenson, Jon Douglas.

    The death and resurrection of the beloved son : the transformation
of child sacrifice in Judaism and Christianity / Jon D. Levenson.

      p. cm.

    Includes bibliographical references and indexes.

    ISBN 0-300-05532-3 (alk. paper)

    1. Child sacrifice in the Bible. 2. Child sacrifice—Judaism.
3. Child sacrifice—Christianity. 4. Judaism—Doctrines.
I. Title.

BS680.C45L48   1993

220.6'4—dc20   93-7545

              CIP

A catalogue record for this book is available from the British Library.

The paper in this book meets the guidelines for permanence and durability of the Committee on Production Guidelines for Book Longevity of the Council on Library Resources.

10 9 8 7 6 5 4 3 2 1

To Sam Jaffe
and to the memory of
Sara Walkinshaw Hazel

But we are Your people, the members of Your covenant, the children of Abraham who loved You and to whom You swore an oath upon Mount Moriah; the descendants of Isaac his only son, who was bound on the altar; the community of Jacob Your first-born son, whom You named Israel and Jeshurun because of Your love for him and the delight You took in him.

Jewish Daily Liturgy

Contents

Preface

The idea for this book came to me in connection with my preparation for a course entitled "The Joseph Story and its Rabbinic Exegesis," which I taught in the winter quarter of 1986–87 at the University of Chicago Divinity School. It occurred to me that the loss and restoration of Joseph to his father constitutes an analogy in narrative to the several Israelite rituals that substitute for the literal sacrifice of the first-born son. In the Joseph novella, as in those rituals, the father's choicest son receives his life anew, and the man who, one way or another, gave him up or should have done so, gets back the offspring who had been marked for death. Further reflection led to the conclusion that the analogy holds for other important sons in Genesis as well—Ishmael, Isaac, and Jacob—and for the man the Church believes to be the son of God.

The prominence of this theme of the near-death and miraculous restoration of the first-born son (or of the late-born son promoted to that exalted rank) led me to question the universal assumption that the great prophets of the late seventh and sixth centuries B.C.E. had eradicated the scourge of child sacrifice from Israelite culture. Both the rituals and the narratives that articulate this theme suggest that though the *practice* was at some point eradicated, the *religious idea* associated with one particular form of it—the donation of the first-born son—remained potent and productive. Indeed, it proved central to Israel's efforts to render account of its origins and character, and it was, again with modification, to prove at least as central to the efforts of the early Church to do likewise. Similarly, the rabbinic and Christian tendencies to celebrate Abraham for his willingness to obey the gruesome command to slay and immolate his beloved son Isaac demonstrate that the matter is more complicated than the language of eradication allows. My term "transformation" is intended to imply that the strangely persistent impulse in question remains alive as a driving force behind the subtle and easily misunderstood theologies of chosenness that, again in their different ways, undergird both Judaism and Christianity.

I gladly acknowledge that I regard this transformation as highly positive, one that metamorphosized a barbaric ritual into a sublime paradigm of the religious life. Some will doubtless think that by drawing attention to the barbaric roots, I mean to deny the sublimity of the developments. I trust that discriminating readers who follow the argument through to its conclusion in part III will not make this mistake. Indeed, I dare to hope for something more: that my readers' appreciation of the later developments will be enriched rather than undercut by an awareness of the continuing influence of the old ideal of child sacrifice upon the classic articulations of the Jewish and the Christian traditions.

Radically transformed but never uprooted, the sacrifice of the first-born son constitutes a strange and usually overlooked bond between Judaism and Christianity and thus a major but unexplored focus for Jewish-Christian dialogue. In the past, this dialogue has too often centered on the Jewishness of Jesus and, in particular, his putative roles of prophet and sage. In point of fact, however, those roles, even if real, have historically been vastly less important in Christian tradition than Jesus' identity as sacrificial victim, the son handed over to death by his loving father or the lamb who takes away the sins of the world. This identity, ostensibly so alien to Judaism, was itself constructed from Jewish reflection on the beloved sons of the Hebrew Bible, reflection that long survived the rise of Christianity and has persisted into the post-Holocaust era. The bond between Jewry and the Church that the beloved son constitutes is, however, enormously problematic. For the longstanding claim of the Church that it *supersedes* the Jews in large measure continues the old narrative pattern in which a late-born son dislodges his first-born brothers, with varying degrees of success. Nowhere does Christianity betray its indebtedness to Judaism more than in its supersessionism.

16 Shevat, 5753
February 7, 1993

Acknowledgments

Several scholars were kind enough to read large parts or even all of my manuscript in various redactions and to offer me their advice. Gary Anderson, Robert Cohn, Arthur Droge, Kimberley Patton, Lester Segal, Lawrence Sullivan, Ronald Thiemann, and Edward Tripp deserve my gratitude and undoubtedly also my apologies for not following their counsel in every instance.

On January 25–27, 1993, I was honored to make use of parts of this book for the Sprunt Lectures at Union Theological Seminary in Richmond, Virginia. I offer my gratitude to the entire seminary community for the extraordinary hospitality that I was shown, with special thanks to President T. Hartley Hall IV and Professors James L. Mays, S. Dean McBride, W. Sibley Towner, and William Brown.

Larry Lyke has performed a number of editorial tasks essential to the publication of this study. He, too, has earned my thanks. So has Noreen O'Connor, my editor at Yale University Press, whose care and judicious advice has helped me to produce a better volume.

Quotations from the Hebrew Bible are taken from *Tanakh* (Philadelphia: Jewish Publication Society, 5746/1985), unless otherwise noted. I refer to this translation as NJPS (New Jewish Publication Society version). As in the NJPS, chapter and verse follow the Hebrew rather than the traditional English enumeration. Passages from the Apocrypha and the New Testament are taken from the *Catholic Study Bible* (New York: Oxford University Press, 1990), which uses the New American Bible translation. (Scripture quotations taken from the *New American Bible* Copyright © 1970, 1986, and 1991 by the Confraternity of Christian Doctrine, 3211 Fourth Street, N.E., Washington, D.C. 20017-1194, and are used with permission. All rights reserved.) Passages from the Hebrew Bible quoted in the New Testament follow the *Catholic Study Bible*.

I have rendered the tetragrammaton without vowels, even in quoting authors who vocalized it.

Several typists have aided me in the production of this volume, no small task given my illegible hand and propensity for endless revision. Hearty thanks are owed to Brian Murphy, Andra Hollis, Sarah Koolsbergen, Margaret Studier, and most of all Sara Hazel, who served as my secretary from my arrival at Harvard in 1988 until her sudden and unexpected death on May 21, 1991, just as I was beginning part III of the manuscript. I am privileged to have afforded her support at the end of her life and even afterward and to include her now in those to whom *The Death and Resurrection of the Beloved Son* is affectionately dedicated.

Abbreviations

Rabbinic, Mishnaic and Related Literature, and Other Ancient Sources
(M = Mishna; b = Babylonian Talmud)

Bek.	*Bekorot*
Ber.	*Berakot*
Bib. Ant.	Pseudo-Philo, *Biblical Antiquities*
Exod. Rab.	*Exodus Rabbah*
Gen. Rab.	*Genesis Rabbah*
JA	*Jewish Antiquities*
Jub	Jubilees
Lev. Rab.	*Leviticus Rabbah*
1 Macc	First Maccabees
4 Macc	Fourth Maccabees
Meg.	*Megillah*
Mek.	*Mekilta de-Rabbi Ishmael*
Mo`ed Qut	*Mo`ed Qaṭan*
Pesaḥ.	*Pesaḥim*
Pirqé R. El	*Pirqé Rabbi Eliezer*
Qidd.	*Qiddušin*
Roš. Haš.	*Roš Haššana*
Šabb.	*Šabbat*
Sanh.	Sanhedrin
Sir	Wisdom of Joshua ben Sira
Tanḥ.	*Tanḥuma'*
Tg. Neof.	*Targum Neofiti*
Wis	Wisdom of Solomon

Secondary Literature

AB	Anchor Bible
AnBib	Analecta Biblica
ASORDS	American Schools of Oriental Research Dissertation Series
BARev	*Biblical Archeology Review*
BHT	Beiträge zur historischen Theologie
BJS	Brown Judaic Studies
CBQ	*Catholic Biblical Quarterly*
CRAI	*Comptes rendus de l'Académie des inscriptions*
HBT	*Horizons in Biblical Theology*
HTR	*Harvard Theological Review*

HUCA	*Hebrew Union College Annual*
JAOS	*Journal of the American Oriental Society*
JBL	*Journal of Biblical Literature*
JJS	*Journal of Jewish Studies*
JNES	*Journal of Near Eastern Studies*
JPS	Jewish Publication Society
JR	*Journal of Religion*
JSOT	*Journal for the Study of the Old Testament*
JSOT Sup	Journal for the Study of the Old Testament Supplement Series
JTC	*Journal for Theology and the Church*
JTS	*Journal of Theological Studies*
NAB	New American Bible
NJPS	New Jewish Publication Society version (*Tanakh*)
NTS	*New Testament Studies*
OBO	Orbis biblicus et orientalis
OBT	Overtures to Biblical Theology
OTL	Old Testament Library
RB	*Revue biblique*
RevistB	*Revista Bíblica*
RHR	*Revue de l'histoire des religions*
UF	*Ugarit–Forschungen*
VT	*Vetus Testamentum*
ZAW	*Zeitschrift für die alttestamentliche Wissenschaft*

Part I
A Father's Gift

As everyone knows, nothing could be more repugnant to the God of Israel than human sacrifice. Judah Goldin

Rabbi Phinehas said in the name of Rabbi Benaiah: [Abraham] prayed: "Master of the Universe, regard it as though I had sacrificed my son Isaac first and only afterwards sacrificed this ram." Midrash

Chapter One
Child Sacrifice in the Hebrew Bible: Deviation or Norm?

[28] You shall not put off the skimming of the first yield of your vats. You shall give Me the first-born among your sons. [29] You shall do the same with your cattle and your flocks: seven days it shall remain with its mother; on the eighth day you shall give it to Me. (Exod 22:28–29)

Of all the passages in the Bible that have been deemed offensive, none has been deemed so more often than this one, and none has generated greater resistance to a literal interpretation. That the God of justice and mercy should demand the first-born of herd and flock is a common stumbling-block for moderns. That he should demand the same of human families has been judged an offense much longer, indeed from biblical times themselves.

Among critical scholars of the Bible—that is, scholars who are prepared to interpret the text against their own preferences and traditions, in the interest of intellectual honesty—there is no consensus as to how to understand the second clause of Exod 22:28: "You shall give Me the first-born among your sons." But most would surely accept the reasoning of Roland de Vaux that "it would be absurd to suppose that there could have been in Israel or among any other people, at any moment of their history, a constant general law, compelling the suppression of the first-born, who are the hope of the race."[1] And, indeed, as he states it, de Vaux's position is almost impossible to impugn. Were the norm constant and general, the Bible would surely provide ample testimony, in both law code and narrative, to its existence, and we should not be left guessing. But de Vaux goes further, denying that the biblical writers ever mandate or even accept child sacrifice. Rather, according to de Vaux and the majority of scholars, the gift of the son to YHWH, God of Israel, in Exod 22:28b and similar passages is really not the same as the gift of the first-born male of the cattle and the flocks. The latter are to be sacrificed; the former are to be redeemed, as specified in several passages in the Pentateuchal law codes, for example: "¹⁹Every first issue of the womb is Mine, from all your livestock that drop a male as firstling, whether cattle or sheep. ²⁰But the firstling of an ass you shall redeem with a sheep; if you do not redeem it, you must break its neck. And you must redeem every first-born among your sons" (Exod 34:19–20). In sum, that shocking last clause in Exod 22:28 only states the general principle, that the first-born son is to be given to God. The particulars as to how this is to be done appear later, in the separate legal corpus of Exodus 34.² It is to be done through redemption, with a sheep perhaps replacing the doomed son.

De Vaux's argument against a literal reading of Exod 22:28–29 would be stronger if those verses were followed by a provision for redemption on the order of Exod 34:20. This is, in fact, the case in Exodus 13, which begins with a demand that every first-born son of man and beast among the Israelites be consecrated to YHWH (v 2) but includes soon thereafter the requirement to "redeem every first-born male among your children" (v 13). Though Exodus 34 and 13 thus show faithful YHWHists how they might—indeed, *must*—evade the sacrifice of their first-born sons, these texts also point up by contrast the *absence* of any such provision in the corpus of law in which Exod 22:28–29 appears.

If it is, in fact, a mistake for us to read the requirement to sacrifice the first-born son in Exod 22:28–29 independently of the provisions for redemption that appear in other textual units, it is a mistake of a sort that numerous Israelites seem to have made. For prophetic literature, at least in the late seventh and early sixth centuries B.C.E., is vehement in its opposition to child sacrifice, which it sees as emblematic of idolatry, for example:

> ⁵They have built shrines to Baal, to put their children to the fire as burnt offerings to Baal—which I never commanded, never decreed, and which never came into My mind. ⁶Assuredly, a time is coming—declares the LORD—when this place shall no longer be called Topheth or Valley of Ben-hinnom, but Valley of Slaughter. (Jer 19:5–6)³

That YHWH did not command his people to offer sacrifices to his great rival Baal need hardly have been mentioned.⁴ The point, rather, seems to be that child sacrifice is something that YHWH finds unacceptable, so that those who indulge in the practice must be worshiping another god. The threefold denial of the origin of the practice in YHWH's will—"which I never commanded, never decreed, and which never came into My mind"—suggests that the prophet doth protest too much. Could it be that Jeremiah's hearers saw themselves not as apostates or syncretists but as faithful YHWHists following the ancient tradition of their religion? If the practitioners of child sacrifice, unlike Jeremiah, thought that YHWH did indeed ordain the rite, then we may have here some indirect evidence that the literal reading of Exod 22:28b ("You shall give Me the first-born among your sons") was not absurd in ancient Israel, as de Vaux and most modern scholars think, and that the practice in question was not always idolatrous, as Jeremiah insisted it was. To be sure, *'ăšer lō'-ṣiwwîtî* ("which I never commanded") does not necessarily imply that the audience thought the practice in question to have been ordained by YHWH. John Day points to the same expression in Deut 17:3 in connection with an astral cult as evidence that it is better rendered as "which I forbade."[5] If so, then Jeremiah provides no evidence, even obliquely, for an Israelite belief that it was YHWH and not some other deity who instituted child sacrifice in Israel. But the last of the three denials in Jer 19:5 ("which never came into my mind," *wĕlō' 'ālĕtâ 'al-libbî*) would be pointless if the author intended to say only that YHWH forbade the rite in question. It appears, instead, that Jeremiah's attacks on child sacrifice are aimed not only at the practice itself, but also at the tradition that YHWH desires it. Jeremiah wanted child sacrifice to be considered idolatrous in every instance, and, as the majority opinion of scholars shows, history has abundantly granted him his wish.

A passage in Ezekiel can be adduced in further support of our contention that only at a particular stage rather late in the history of Israel was child sacrifice branded as counter to the will of YHWH and thus ipso facto idolatrous:

> [25]I, in turn, gave them laws that were not good and rules by which they could not live: [26]When they set aside every first issue of the womb, I defiled them by their very gifts—that I might render them desolate, that they might know that I am the LORD. (Ezek 20:25–26)[6]

At first blush, the meaning of these verses seems clear: the sacrifice of the first-born is indeed an abomination, just as Jeremiah thought. But, whereas Jeremiah vociferously denied the origin of the practice in the will of YHWH, Ezekiel affirmed it: YHWH gave Israel "laws that were not good" in order to desolate them, for only as they were desolated, only as they were brought to humiliation, could they come to recognize YHWH and obey his sovereign will. Here, as often in the Hebrew Bible, God's goodness conflicts with his providential designs: he wills evil in order to accomplish good. The evil that he once willed is the law that requires the sacrifice of the first-born. The good toward which this aims is Israel's ultimate recognition and exaltation of him as their sole God.

That human sin can play a positive role in the larger providential drama is a difficult notion at best. Combining this with the blunt statement that

YHWH did indeed ordain child sacrifice, Ezek 20:25–26 has over the centuries had most exegetes running for cover. The simplest way out of the embarrassment is to downplay or explain away the words "I, in turn, gave them laws that were not good" (*wĕgam-'ănî nātattî lāhem ḥuqqîm lō' ṭôbîm*). The trend starts already in antiquity. Targum Jonathan, an Aramaic translation of the prophets, renders Ezek 20:25 as follows:

> I, in turn, when they rebelled against My word and refused to accept My prophets, put them far away and handed them over to their enemies. They went after their own foolish inclination and adopted decrees that were not good and laws by which they could not live.

In other words, God did not give them bad laws at all, but only punished them for their rebelliousness by allowing them to follow their own base instincts. With various minor modifications, this interpretation comes as close to being standard as any position in the history of interpretation ever does. Its enduring appeal lies in its shifting of ultimate responsibility for the sacrifice of the first-born from God's decree to Israel's rebellion.

Among modern scholars, the dominant tendency is to associate the disquieting assertion of Ezek 20:25–26 with texts that both condemn a person for his behavior and yet attribute that behavior to God. Most famous among these are those passages in Exodus in which God is said to harden Pharaoh's heart so that Pharaoh will fail to heed the very demand that God bids Moses to make of him.[7] The theological point here is that God is even behind Pharaoh's resistance to God; nothing is outside divine control. The goal is remarkably close to that of Ezek 20:25–26: through the succession of plagues that God inflicts upon Pharaoh, whose obstinacy he has himself decreed, Pharaoh—and the whole world with him—will be brought to a recognition of YHWH: "[16]I have spared you for this purpose: in order to show you My power, and in order that My fame may resound throughout the world" (Exod 9:16). As de Vaux puts it, in speaking of Ezek 20:25–26, "all the actions of men, even bad actions, enter into the plans of God, to whom they have a reference as to the first cause."[8] The problem, in short, is solved by resort to a theory of double causality. The ultimate cause is God, whose plans are good; the proximate cause is the human agent, whose deeds are evil. How the two levels of causation can be reconciled is a theological conundrum that exegetes usually do not address.

Though this understanding of Ezek 20:25–26 has much to commend it, there is one aspect of the text to which it does not do justice. The anomaly is nicely stated by one of the most recent proponents of this most common interpretation, Ronald M. Hals:

Further, it is starkly idiosyncratic that God responded to his people's subsequent disobedience of his commandments by giving them bad laws as a punishment. Where else are God's laws ever seen in such a light? One can only conjecture that the mistakenly and syncretistically literal interpretation of such commands as Exod 34:19, "All that opens the womb is mine" (see also Exod 22:28), which ignored the subsequent clarification, "All the first-born of your sons you shall redeem" (Exod 34:20), was viewed as some kind of divine hardening of Israel's own heart, a shockingly bold affirmation of divine all-causality outdoing even Micaiah ben Imlah (see 1 Kgs 22:19–24) in seeing no problem in a false word from YHWH which aimed at Israel's doom.[9]

"Where else are God's laws ever seen in such a light?"—this is exactly the problem. It is also the reason that efforts to assimilate Ezek 20:25–26 to the model of the hardening of the heart are less than convincing. For the assertion in Ezekiel 20 is not that God left a wayward Israel to their own devices, or that he froze them in a posture of defiance like that in which he froze Pharaoh. Rather, the point is that because the people in their rebellion refused to obey YHWH's life-promoting laws (especially those governing the Sabbath [vv 21–24]), he, in turn, saddled them with bad laws that would, nonetheless, ultimately serve his sovereign purpose. The product of his punishment is not a perverted will, as in the case of Pharaoh, or a deceitful oracle, as in the incident about Micaiah to which Hals refers, but rather *the laws themselves.* In a sense, the best way to understand Ezekiel's point is by inverting the theory of double causality: the ultimate cause of the "laws that were not good" was Israel's rebellion; the proximate cause was divine revelation.

Hals misses the key point that the laws referred to in Ezek 20:25 were God's quid pro quo for Israel's apostasy and disobedience. Instead, he constructs a scenario in which God punishes Israel by perverting the Israelites' hermeneutics. As a result, they devise on their own the putative "mistakenly and syncretistically literal interpretation" of the laws of child sacrifice, missing altogether the provisions for redemption of the first-born. But Ezekiel never mentions those provisions, either, and there is no reason to think that he regards the practice of the sacrifice of the first-born as contrary to God's will in the time for which God ordained it. In other passages, in which the target of Ezekiel's preaching is child sacrifice in general, he sees the recipient of the offering as other deities.[10] But here in 20:25–26, where the subject is specifically the offering of the first-born, there is no reason to believe that its recipient was anyone other than the God who gave them the "laws that were not good" in the first place. Those laws are YHWH's retaliation for idolatry, but they are

not in themselves idolatrous, only lethal, "rules by which they could not live,"
"the condign punishment" (in Moshe Greenberg's phrase[11]) for a people that
has turned away from the rules "by the pursuit of which man shall live"
(v 21).

In Greenberg's judgment, however, Ezek 20:25–26 condemns only those
who practiced the popular rather than the normative religion of Israel. Though
there is, according to Greenberg, "outside of our passage no evidence" that
anyone interpreted laws such as Exod 22:28b as requiring "making over all
firstborn males as sacrifices to the deity," still, "at least from the time of the
last kings of Judah it was popularly believed that YHWH accepted, perhaps
even commanded, it."[12] What is curious in Greenberg's comment is his certainty that popular practice was so radically separate from the normative
religion. Why, if there is no evidence in the Bible (outside of Ezek 20:25–26)
for the sacrifice of the first-born son to YHWH, did so many Israelites come to
adhere to such a practice? And conversely, why, if we know there was a
popular belief "that YHWH accepted, perhaps even commanded" such offerings,
should we retroject the provision for redemption even onto Exod 22:28b,
where it is absent and contradicts the implication of the subsequent verse?
The more natural conclusion, it would seem, is that what Greenberg brands
as popular religion is simply the continuation of an older normative tradition
against which the two great prophets of the late monarchy and early exile,
Jeremiah and Ezekiel, turned with passion and vehemence. Because Greenberg
follows Jeremiah's view that God never commanded child sacrifice (Jer 19:5),
he has no choice but to brand the rite as popular and "pagan" and to rely on
the conventional analogy of Pharaoh's divinely hardened heart to explain
Ezekiel's opposing opinion. But it is the latter opinion that better fits the
biblical data: YHWH once commanded the sacrifice of the first-born but now
opposes it. Without recourse to modern historical reasoning, the only explanation for this that preserves the continuity of YHWH's will is the one that
Ezekiel, in fact, offers: YHWH's command and Israel's obedience to it were in
the way of punishment, a means to bring about the death of those who had
turned away from the means to abundant life.

One argument against the literal interpretation of Exod 22:28–29 remains
to be addressed. This is the common argument, advanced, for example, by
both de Vaux and Greenberg, that there is no evidence for "a constant general
law, compelling the suppression of the first-born" (de Vaux) by "making [them]
over . . . as sacrifices to the deity" (Greenberg). That this is so should be readily
conceded: neither the archaeological nor the textual data suggest any such
widespread practice. We need not, however, consign Exod 22:28–29 to some
sort of minority tradition, popular or other. There is a third possibility—that

Exod 22:28b articulates a theological ideal about the special place of the first-born son, an ideal whose realization could range from literal to non-literal implementation, that is, from sacrifice to redemption, or even to mere intellectual assent without any cultic act whatsoever. If this sounds strange today, it is only because we think of law in terms rather different from those of the ancient Near East. The legal thinking of the latter is nicely highlighted by the oft-remarked lack of evidence in contracts and the like for the implementation of the Old Babylonian legal corpus traditionally known as the Code of Hammurabi (mid-eighteenth century B.C.E.). "The code is not binding," I. Tzvi Abusch observes, "and does not necessarily reflect actual practice; it is, however, a literary and intellectual construct that gives expression to legal thinking and moral values."[13] This is, ironically, how de Vaux himself sees the biblical law of the Jubilee Year (Lev 25:8–17, 23–55). "The Law of the Jubilee," he holds, "appears to set out an ideal of justice and social equality which was never realized . . . it was a Utopian law and it remained a dead letter." In truth, a fertile seed would be a better metaphor than a dead letter, for rabbinic literature indicates that, eventually, such provisions did indeed become matters of practice as opposed to utopian idealism. But that was in a later era. In the Hebrew Bible, there is no evidence for the implementation of the Jubilee.[14]

The ideal character of a provision such as that of the sacrifice of the first-born son in Exod 22:28–29 need not imply the historical accuracy of either Jeremiah's or Ezekiel's negative view of the practice.[15] Indeed, Paul Mosca and others have pointed to a number of texts that can be construed, with varying degrees of plausibility, as describing child sacrifice without pejorative intent. According to Mosca, "the earliest datable reference to the rite" is this difficult and perhaps garbled oracle from Isaiah:[16]

[30]For the LORD will make His majestic voice heard
And display the sweep of His arm
In raging wrath,
In a devouring blaze of fire,
In tempest, and rainstorm, and hailstones.
[31]Truly, Assyria, who beats with the rod,
Shall be cowed by the voice of the LORD;
[32]And each time the appointed staff passes by,
The LORD will bring down [His arm] upon him
And will do battle with him as he waves it.
[33]The Topheth has long been ready for him;
He too is destined for Melech—

His firepit has been made both wide and deep,
With plenty of fire and firewood,
And with the breath of the LORD
Burning in it like a stream of sulfur. (Isa 30:30–33)

The Tophet(h) (v 33) we have already encountered in Jer 19:6. It was the site in the Valley of the Son of Hinnom (Gehinnom), just south of Jerusalem, at which a cult of child sacrifice was carried on. It would therefore seem natural to associate "Melech" in the same verse in Isaiah with the "Molech" to whom or to which the Torah forbids Israelites to sacrifice their offspring (Lev 18:21; 20:2–5).[17] The identity of Molech—indeed, even the historical accuracy of the *o* in the first syllable—has long been a matter of sharp controversy and, as we shall see, remains so today. What does not seem controversial is that in these verses from Isaiah 30, it is YHWH rather than some deviant Israelites who utilize the Tophet, consigning Assyria to its firepit. To Mosca, this means that the Tophet in this period—about a century before Jeremiah—constituted "part of the official YHWHistic cultus" and that "Isaiah himself seems to have had no particular objection to YHWHistic 'passing into the fire,' "[18] though, of course, he would not have tolerated such rites practiced for the benefit of another deity. This may well be the case, and, in combination with the other texts about to be presented, the grisly oracle of Isa 30:30–33 may indicate a place for child sacrifice in YHWHism before Jeremiah's time. The problem, however, is that the oracle in question really does not speak about child sacrifice at all. It talks only of the gruesome death of a hated foe, and it could be argued that the death is the more gruesome, and the punishment thus condign, because of its association with an abominated cult-place belonging to the mysterious and abominated Molech. The use of sacrificial terminology to describe YHWH's punishment visited upon an enemy of Israel, by no means unique to this passage,[19] does not suffice to indicate the acceptability of human sacrifice in YHWHism and offers no evidence whatsoever that such practices formed "part of the official YHWHistic cultus."[20] The most that can plausibly be inferred from Isa 30:30–33—and even this is, as I have indicated, not beyond doubt—is that at the time of this oracle, the Molech cult at the Tophet had not yet become emblematic of idolatry.

Mosca makes a stronger case on the basis of an oracle from another eighth-century prophet, Micah:

⁶With what shall I approach the LORD,
Do homage to God on high?
Shall I approach Him with burnt offerings,
With calves a year old?

[7]Would the Lord be pleased with thousands of rams
With myriads of streams of oil?
Shall I give my first-born for my transgression,
The fruit of my body for my sins?

[8]"He has told you, O man, what is good,
And what the Lord requires of you:
Only to do justice
And to love goodness,
And to walk modestly with your God." (Mic 6:6–8)

To de Vaux, the progression of theoretical offerings in vv 6–7 demonstrates the impossibility of the sacrifice of the first-born.[21] "In their disarray," he writes, "the people pass from possible offers to impossible offers, from ordinary holocausts to rams by thousands and torrential libations, and, to continue the progression, the last offer must appear even more impossible—the sacrifice of the first-born." But Mosca reads the progression differently, "from valuable to more valuable to most valuable," and sees the people as repentant, rather than in disarray as de Vaux would have it.[22] Thus, for Mosca, Mic 6:6–8 reinforces the conclusion he drew from Isa 30:30–33, that child sacrifice was at one time part of the official cultus of yhwh. To this George Heider, in turn, objects, pointing out that "what makes this passage so difficult to employ historically is the underlying contrary-to-fact mood established by the context: *none* of the sacrifices is desired by yhwh without the virtues summarized in v 8, so that the prophet has no reason to distinguish otherwise desirable from undesirable offerings."[23] But if Heider has aptly stated the point of the oracle, that sacrifices without the virtues listed in v 8 are bootless, then it would seem strange for Micah to combine an abominated offering with those that yhwh desires. If the sacrifice of the first-born son mentioned in v 7 is offensive to yhwh, then presumably so are all the offerings that lead up to it—the calves, the rams, and the oil. But the language here and elsewhere in Micah (and generally in the Hebrew Bible) does not suggest such a wholesale condemnation of the cultus. More likely, offering of the first-born is grouped with animal sacrifice either because it is on a par with them or, as Mosca argues, it is the most valuable sacrifice and therefore the grand finale of v 7. Evidence from biblical narrative to be analyzed below suggests that Mosca's view is the more probable: the first-born son is the most precious offering.

One other point about Mic 6:6–8 must not go unmentioned. Like Exod 22:28b, Jeremiah, and Ezekiel, Micah knows nothing of a redemption of the first-born son by a sheep or any other means. Micah's language is, in fact, closest to Exod 22:28b, much closer than to those texts that allow or require redemption (such as Exod 34:19–20). "Shall I give my first-born for my transgression?" (*ha'ettēn bĕkôrî piš'î*) is not far from "You shall give Me the first-born among your sons" (*bĕkôr bānêkā titten-lî*). Moreover, mention of the first-born son in each pericope occurs alongside mention of animal sacrifice (Mic 6:7; Exod 22:29). This makes it all the less likely that we are to retroject the provisions of redemption of Exodus 34 and elsewhere into the law of the first-born son in Exodus 22. Rather, what the latter articulates is an ideal of sacrifice, the Israelite father's offering to God of what is most beloved to him, his first-born son, the first fruit of his body presented lovingly to his lord.

There is one text in the Hebrew Bible in which an Israelite father—indeed, the father of all Israel, the Patriarch Abraham—is commanded to offer his son—Isaac, the first-born of Sarah and sole heir to the covenant with YHWH. This text, Gen 22:1–19, will occupy our attention in chapters 11 and 12. Here the point to be made is that whatever the ambiguities of the legal and prophetic materials on child sacrifice, Gen 22:1–19 is frighteningly unequivocal about YHWH's ordering a father to offer up his son as a sacrifice: "And He said, 'Take your son, your favored one, Isaac, whom you love, and go to the land of Moriah, and offer him there as a burnt offering on one of the heights that I will point out to you' " (Gen 22:2). For scholars like Moshe Greenberg, who paraphrases Ezekiel's view of child sacrifice by calling it "at once a murderous pagan practice and an abomination worthy of severest condemnation,"[24] the story of the near-sacrifice of Isaac ought to be a major challenge. For here it is not the wayward people but the faithful God who demands the immolation of the favored son, and not as a punishment in the manner of the hardening of Pharaoh's heart, either, but *as a test of true devotion*. Were the practice of child sacrifice always so alien to YHWH, so "worthy of severest condemnation," would there have survived a text in which it is this act and no other that constitutes YHWH's greatest test of his servant Abraham? If, as Jeremiah puts it, "burn[ing] their sons and daughters in fire" is something which YHWH "never commanded, which never came to [His] mind," then how shall we explain the *aqedah*, the binding of Isaac in Genesis 22?

One solution commands a consensus of extraordinary breadth: that the point of the story is seen not in the initial command to Abraham but in the rescission of it relayed by the angel of YHWH from heaven itself: "Do not raise your hand against the boy, or do anything to him. For now I know that you fear God, since you have not withheld your son, your favored one, from Me" (Gen 22:12). As Shalom Spiegel puts it, "the primary purpose of the Akedah story may have been only this: to attach to a real pillar of the folk and a revered reputation the new norm—abolish human sacrifice, substitute animals instead."[25] Oddly, Mosca, who sees child sacrifice even in Isaiah and Micah,

Jephtah
Judges 11:29-40

agrees with Spiegel on the aqedah. "Its original purpose," he writes, "may well have been to explain why YHWH no longer—or never—*demanded* the sacrifice of the first-born son."[26]

As an etiology of the redemption of the first-born son through the death of the sheep, however, the aqedah is, it seems to me, most ineffective. For although Abraham does indeed spot and then sacrifice a ram just after hearing the gruesome command rescinded (Gen 22:13), he is never actually commanded to offer the animal, as he was commanded to sacrifice his only beloved son, Isaac. And, in fact, so far as we know, Israelite tradition never explained the substitution of the sheep for the first-born son by reference to the aqedah; it was the tenth plague upon Egypt that served that role, with the paschal lamb spelling the difference between life and death for the Israelite first-born males (Exodus 12–13). The sacrifice of *that* sheep is commanded emphatically and repeatedly. But more importantly, it is passing strange to condemn child sacrifice through a narrative in which a father is richly rewarded for his willingness to carry out that very practice. If the point of the aqedah is "abolish human sacrifice, substitute animals instead," then Abraham cannot be regarded as having passed the test to which Gen 22:1 tells us God is here subjecting him. For Abraham obeys the command to sacrifice Isaac without cavil and desists—knife in hand, Isaac bound on the altar over the firewood— only when the angel calls to him from heaven. And the burden of the angelic address is not that the slaughter of Isaac is offensive or that the ram is a preferable victim, but that it is Abraham's *willingness to sacrifice his son* that verifies his fear of God. A second angelic address then specifies the reward for having passed the test with flying colors:

> [16]By myself I swear, the LORD declares: Because you have done this and have not withheld your son, your favored one, [17]I will bestow My blessing upon you and make your descendants as numerous as the stars of heaven and the sands on the seashore; and your descendants shall seize the gates of their foes. [18]All the nations of the earth shall bless themselves by your descendants, because you have obeyed My command. (Gen 22:16–18)

No interpretation of the aqedah can be adequate if it fails to reckon with the point made explicit here: Abraham will have his multitudes of descendants only because he was willing to sacrifice the son who is destined to beget them. Any construal of the text that minimizes that willingness misses the point.

The aqedah is often associated with Judg 11:29–40, which tells of the military hero Jephthah's vow to sacrifice, again as a burnt offering,[27] whatever comes out of his door to meet him if he returns in safety from combat with his Ammonite foes. To Jephthah's shock, it is none other than his daughter, like Isaac his "only child,"[28] who greets him, with timbrel and dance no less, upon his return in triumph. Vows being irrevocable, Jephthah carries his out. And so Jephthah is both like and unlike Abraham. Like the great patriarch, he is willing to sacrifice his "only" child. But whereas Abraham was commanded to do so and then spared, Jephthah was never commanded but actually performed the horrific act.

Among the features of the aqedah unparalleled in the tale of Jephthah's daughter is the lucidity of the former. Many critical features of Judg 11:29–40 remain unclear and therefore subject to continuing scholarly controversy. Some have even doubted that Jephthah sacrifices his daughter there at all, preferring to see in her request to "bewail [her] maidenhood" (v 37) a different form of donation to the deity—consecration as a lifelong celibate priestess.[29] Though it must be conceded that the prominence given the daughter's virginity in vv 37–40 is problematic, it remains true that Jephthah vowed to bring a burnt offering and carried out by means of her just what he vowed.[30] Less clear is the narrator's attitude toward the act in question. Rabbinic tradition sees in Jephthah's sacrifice a punishment for his rashness in making the vow, and not without grounds in the text.[31] We can all wish that the hero had formulated his vow more precisely, taking into account that it might be his own daughter who would come out of his house to greet him, as he was to find out too late. But what is missing in this story is any indication that child sacrifice, painful to father and offspring alike, was inappropriate from *God's* standpoint. Quite the opposite: Jephthah's actions are intelligible only on the assumption that his daughter—he had no son—could legitimately be sacrificed as a burnt offering to YHWH. Had she not been fit to sacrifice, the vow would have been unfulfillable, as he obviously wishes were the case (v 35). The tone of the narrative thus is one of great pathos rather than moralistic judgment. Jephthah and his unnamed daughter are figures reminiscent of the great protagonists of Greek tragedy (Euripides' *Iphigeneia in Aulis* comes to mind immediately). If he has a flaw, it is the rashness and imprecision with which he pronounces his vow, not his willingness to carry it out by sacrificing his daughter to the God who delivered the Ammonites into his hands.

If the tale of Jephthah provides some support for the existence of child sacrifice within the YHWHism that left us the Bible, though less than the aqedah, the story of Mesha is more problematic than either text. King of Moab in the mid-ninth century B.C.E., Mesha finds himself on the losing end of a war with the Kingdom of Israel:

[26] Seeing that the battle was going against him, the king of Moab led an attempt of seven hundred swordsmen to break a way through to the king

of Edom; but they failed. [27]So he took his first-born son, who was to succeed him as king, and offered him up on the wall as a burnt offering. A great wrath came upon Israel, so they withdrew from him and went back to their own land. (2 Kgs 3:26–27)[32]

For those who see child sacrifice as "pagan" (to use Greenberg's term), this passage may seem at first to pose no problem: a Moabite king engages there in precisely the sort of rite that, according to prophets like Jeremiah and Ezekiel, typifies idolatry and all that is repugnant to the traditions of Israel. It should not go unnoticed, however, that the terminology of Mesha's sacrifice of his first-born son is almost identical to the language of YHWH's initial command to Abraham in Genesis 22 and to that of Jephthah's vow.[33] At the very least, this argues for more continuity between Israel and its neighbors to the east in the ninth century than the crude dichotomy of Israelite and "pagan" would suggest. More serious is the great "wrath" (*qeṣep*) that falls on Israel in v 27, for there the implication is clear: Mesha's sacrifice worked. By immolating his first-born son and heir apparent, the king of Moab was able to turn the tide of battle and force the Israelites to retreat. Rationalistic commentators conjure up a panic in the camp of the Israelites as the latter learn of this horrid act.[34] But the term *qeṣep* indicates a force external to the people involved. More likely, therefore, is the supposition that the author saw Mesha's sacrifice of his first-born son as having a profound effect upon the deity to whom it was offered, in this case presumably the Moabite national deity Chemosh (whose name is, nonetheless, conspicuously absent from the text).[35] At the least, 2 Kgs 3:26–27 suggests that Israel in the mid-ninth century was not so divorced from the theology of child sacrifice as the great prophets who were to preach two and a half centuries later wanted them to be. At the most, it suggests the full acceptability of this act even to the Israelite author of this narrative.

In their different ways, each of the three texts that we have been examining—the binding of Isaac, the vow of Jephthah, and Mesha's sacrifice—sheds light on the issue of just how we are to take that disturbing last clause in Exod 22:28: "You shall give Me the first-born among your sons." Earlier, I argued that the absence of textual and archaeological evidence for a general practice of child sacrifice in ancient Israel does not require us to interpret "give Me" there as indicating some other form of donation than sacrifice.[36] In the Hebrew Bible, as elsewhere in the cultural world in which it was composed, law often articulates a theological and moral ideal; it does not always stipulate a practice that all can reasonably be expected to undertake. The theology underlying Exod 22:28b is that first-born sons, like the male first-born of animals and the first fruits of the soil, belong to YHWH; they are not the father's, to do with as he sees fit.[37] The clause leaves unclear *whether* YHWH will exercise his proprietary claim on the first son and *how* the father is to honor the claim, should YHWH choose to do so. The aqedah suggests that YHWH might exercise his claim through an oracle, demanding of the father that he make of his son a burnt offering, that is, a sacrifice in which the son is, with the exception of the skin, totally consumed in the fire. The end of the aqedah suggests that God may relent and choose to forgo his option on the son, allowing a sheep to take the place of the human victim. But there is, as I have been at pains to point out, nothing in Genesis 22 to support the idea that God could not command the sacrifice of the son or that an animal is always to be substituted. Were the latter condition to obtain, the Israelite hearer or reader could rest content that God would never test him as he tested Abraham. But this implies that Abraham's piety was not to be taken as paradigmatic—a most unlikely interpretation.

The story of Jephthah and his daughter suggests, though with less clarity than the aqedah, another way a father might donate his first-born to YHWH: through fulfillment of a vow uttered in extremis. If, with the Talmudic rabbis, we deem Jephthah's vow altogether reckless, then we should not see YHWH as here exercising a claim upon the hero's only child: the whole sorry mess is the father's doing. Whereas the rabbis, however, saw Jephthah's vow as invalid, the Bible seems not to fault him for honoring it once it was uttered. In fact, both he and his daughter are portrayed as devoutly upholding YHWH's law that "if a man makes a vow to the LORD . . . he must carry out all that has crossed his lips" (Num 30:3). "I have uttered a vow to the LORD and I cannot retract," Jephthah, grief-stricken, tells his doomed daughter. "Father," she poignantly replies, "you have uttered a vow to the LORD: do to me as you have vowed, seeing that the LORD has vindicated you against your enemies, the Ammonites" (Judg 11:35–36). This last comment suggests that God may have been exercising his claim upon the first-born in this tale after all. For Jephthah's vow was always conditional upon victory (vv 30–31), and YHWH, in granting the victory, doomed whatever would come out of Jephthah's house to meet him as he returned from battle. The key question is this: is YHWH also behind his daughter's being the first to greet her triumphant father? If not, if this is only a tragic coincidence, then the sacrifice, though evidently totally acceptable to YHWH, was not at his initiative. But if Jephthah's daughter's being the first to meet her father is providential, then it is precisely through this vow that YHWH exercises his claim upon Jephthah's first-born child. In sum, YHWH is indirectly implicated in Jephthah's sacrifice through the sacral norm that vows must be executed at whatever cost and through his awarding Jephthah his victory over Ammon. Whether YHWH is *directly* involved depends upon whether we reckon the role the daughter plays to a hideous coincidence or to the hidden and terrifying hand of providence.

In the case of Mesha, we see a father sacrificing his first-born son, but without any of the strange twists that the stories of Abraham and Jephthah take. It is conceivable that Mesha performed his grisly deed in fulfillment of a vow similar to Jephthah's, with Israel taking the place of Ammon as the enemy whom the deity is begged to consign to defeat. If so, then, as in the case of Jephthah, the vow worked. But whether the sacrifice of Mesha's unnamed son is votive or not, the theology of warfare in the biblical world indicates that at least indirectly, the deity must be seen as lying behind the event. For it was he rather than any earthly figure who determined the outcome of battle, so that when Mesha's sortie failed, he knew that he was not standing in the deity's favor. Given the extremity of the situation, only an extreme act of devotion could turn the tide, and none surpasses a royal father's immolation of "his first-born son, who was to succeed him as king" (2 Kgs 3:27). The failure of the sortie of v 26 was, in Mesha's eyes, the deity's way of telling him that he was at last exercising his claim on the first-born. The sudden Israelite retreat in v 27 is proof that Mesha's theological interpretation of the situation was not in error.

"You shall give Me the first-born among your sons" (Exod 22:28b). Most fathers did not have to carry out this hideous demand. But some did. Abraham knew it was his turn when he heard God in his own voice, ordering the immolation of Isaac. Jephthah knew when it was his only child who met him at his home on that day of triumph turned to tragedy. Mesha knew when all earthly strategy failed to break Israel's siege and only the supreme sacrifice could reverse the dire situation.

Chapter Two

YHWH versus Molech

The precise relationship of this practice of the sacrifice of the first-born son to the cult of Molech remains in need of clarification. That the two cannot be simply equated is to be inferred from the nature of the respective victims. The biblical denunciations of the rites at the Tophet speak of people "burn[ing] their sons and daughters in fire" (for instance, Jer 7:31) and make no reference to order of birth, whereas the law of the first-born involves only the eldest male.[1] Furthermore, if, as tradition long maintained, Molech is the name of a god worshiped through child sacrifice, then it is clear that giving even the first-born son to him would be mutually exclusive of the donation of the same victim to YHWH. Lest the two practices be too sharply disengaged, however, the obvious point should be restated: both involve child sacrifice, and both seem to have had some frequency in ancient Israel. To portray these two ancient Israelite rites of child sacrifice as utterly out of relation strains the imagination and misses the key point that they share other important features.

The ancient view that Molech was a god—Milton's "horrid king besmear'd with blood / Of human sacrifice, and parents' tears"[2]—was dealt a severe jolt in 1935, when Otto Eissfeldt utilized Punic inscriptions to argue that the term is actually the name of a type of sacrifice, so that to "give" (*nātan*) or to "hand over" (*heʿĕbîr*) a child to Molech means to donate him or her for immolation. If so, then it is actually YHWH himself rather than a rival deity who receives the fiery donation.[3] Mosca's dissertation is an able defense and refinement of Eissfeldt's controversial interpretation. In recent years, however, the older position has also been reaffirmed,[4] and, though the dispute seems unlikely to end soon, a view that Molech was originally a deity seems to me to account for the evidence better. In biblical Hebrew, one does not "give" or "hand over" an offering to a sacrifice, but to a god, and when Lev 20:5 forbids Israel to "whore after"[5] Molech, this, too, is the language of apostasy to another god, not the language of improper worship of YHWH.[6] That Eissfeldt's interpretation of Molech did not emerge until 1935 underscores a simple truth: whatever the case elsewhere, in the Hebrew Bible it is more natural to see in Molech the proper name of a god than the name of a cultic practice. And as a number of scholars have recently noted, the cognate *Malik* does appear as the name of an underworld deity in some extra-biblical texts.[7] Though the evidence for this deity is not overwhelming and though *mlk* still seems to denote a type of sacrifice in Punic, the best conclusion is that the biblical Molech was a chthonic deity honored through the sacrifice of little boys and girls.

In 1971 an archaeologist excavating at Pozo Moro, a town in southeastern Spain, found the remains of a stone tower that he dates to 500–490 B.C.E.[8] On the tower is a relief that is, in one scholar's words, "as close as we are ever apt to come to a photograph of the ancient cult [of child sacrifice] in action."[9] This is Charles Kennedy's description of the scene:

> The relief shows a banquet prepared for a two-headed monster with a body of a human. He sits to the left of the scene on a throne with a fringed cushion or covering for the seat. The two heads of the monster are set one above the other, with large eyes, mouths open and tongues extending out and downwards. In its upraised right hand is a bowl. Over the rim of the bowl can be seen the head and feet of a small person with its head turned to look at the upper head of the monster. The monster's left hand holds the left hind leg of a pig which is lying on its back on the table in front of the throne. Behind the table stands a male figure wearing a long fringed tunic or robe. He raises a small bowl in a gesture of offering. The right-hand panel is broken, but enough remains to show a third figure facing the monster across the table. This figure appears to be standing also, its upraised right hand holding a sword with a curved blade. The head of the figure, only partially preserved, is shaped like that of a horse or bull. Whether this is supposed to be an actual head or a mask cannot be determined. The left hand of the figure reaches forward to touch the head of a second small person in a bowl atop a low altar located alongside the banquet table.[10]

The archaeologists seem fairly agreed that the cultural ambience of the Pozo Moro tower is closely related to that of the Punic, that is, neo-Phoenician, colonies located just across the Mediterranean straits in North Africa. The motherland of these colonies, situated on the Mediterranean coast due north of biblical Israel, was the home of the Phoenician states with which the kingdoms of Israel and Judah had been in nearly continuous interaction. The interaction was not only commercial but also political and religious: Ahab, king of Israel, for example, married Jezebel, daughter of the king of the Phoenician city-state Tyre. Although Jezebel is notorious for having introduced idolatry into her husband's realm (1 Kgs 16:31–33), we should not assume that the YHWHists who have left us the Hebrew Bible were unanimous in believing that Phoenician influence on Israelite religious life was always for the worse. The Book of Kings reports that at Solomon's request, Hiram, king of Tyre, an ally of Solomon's father, David, provided the lumber for the great temple of YHWH in Jerusalem and that Hiram's masons worked alongside Solomon's to shape the huge blocks used in its foundation (1 Kgs 5:15–32). The rediscovery in modern times of the Phoenician language shows it to be probably the nearest thing there was to biblical Hebrew and, along with these commercial, political, and religious interactions, provides evidence for the close affinity of Israelite and Phoenician culture. To be sure, the biblical denunciation of Jezebel should warn us against any facile assumption that the two cultures were interchangeable. But in any investigation of child sacrifice and its theological implications in ancient Israel, it would be equally simplistic to disregard the largest body of data about the grisly practice, and those data come from the Phoenician colonies of North Africa. It is to them we must turn to understand the nature and extent of the cult of Molech, of which the ancient sculptors of Pozo Moro have probably left us the glyptic equivalent of a photograph.

Of those Canaanite outposts in North Africa, the most famous and most extensive was the great city of Carthage. Founded in the eighth century B.C.E. by Phoenician seamen and named for their term for "new city," Carthage became independent of the motherland about 600 B.C.E. and emerged as a major power in the central and western Mediterranean world in the third and second centuries B.C.E. Destroyed by the Romans in 146 B.C.E., Carthage later recovered some of its eminence and served as a major city in the Roman Empire. But its decline coincided with that of the empire itself, and at the end of the seventh century C.E., it was destroyed by Arabs.

The remains of Carthage amply demonstrate the importance of child sacrifice to its religion and culture and thus indirectly speak to the same institution on the Canaanite motherland. The archaeologists Lawrence E. Stager and Samuel R. Wolff have excavated an area in Carthage that is so full of urns containing the charred remains of children that they term it the "Carthaginian Tophet."[11] This area occupies a minimum of 54,000–64,000 square feet (that is, between 1 1/4 and 1 1/2 acres). On the basis of the density of these urns in the excavated area, Stager and Wolff estimate "that as many as 20,000 urns may have been deposited there between 400 and 200 B.C.,"[12] "averag[ing] out at 100 urn deposits per year or slightly fewer than one every three days."[13]

Against this, some argue that these mute remains suggest that the children in these urns died of natural causes and that the urns testify to Carthaginian funerary practices rather than to a cult of child sacrifice. But Stager and Wolff correctly counter that the actual contents of the urns tell a different and more horrific story. For in them they found usually not one but two children, one a newborn and the other of two to four years of age. "It seems unlikely," Stager and Wolff write, "that disease or some other disaster would have affected only the two youngest children . . . . from the same family in such a regular fashion." Moreover, in the same area that they call the Tophet, Stager and Wolff also found urns containing the charred bones of animals. "Should we conclude," they ask, "that the Tophet was also a 'pet cemetery' with cremated lambs and kids?" Instead, they opt for what is surely the more likely reconstruction, "that the burned animals were intended as substitute sacrifices for children."[14]

This substitution of a lamb or a kid for a child has a familiar ring after our discussion of YHWH's claim upon the first-born son in the Hebrew Bible. There the substitution of an animal for a boy did come to be possible and even normative, and it is this transition from human to animal sacrifice that many scholars have—incorrectly, in my view—seen behind the aqedah. It is hard not to associate the lambs and kids in the urns of the Carthaginian Tophet with the ram that Abraham sacrifices in place of Isaac (Gen 22:13), with the sheep that the Israelite father seems to be instructed to substitute for his first-born son in Exodus (34:20), and with the paschal lamb whose death spares the first-born son in each Israelite family on the night of Passover (Exodus 12–13). But at least in Carthage, the substitution of the animal for the child was not a *later* stage in the evolution of the religion. There it seems to have been the case that at any period, the lamb or the kid *could* take the place of the child, but that at no period was the parent *obligated* to make the substitution. This strikes me as essentially the situation in Genesis 22, where Abraham is *allowed* to sacrifice the ram instead of Isaac, but never *commanded* to do so. Child sacrifice is so abhorrent to modern sensibilities that we can only applaud the father who would substitute an animal. But as late as Talmudic times, Jewish scholars could hold a very different view, imagining Abraham disappointed at the revocation of the command to sacrifice his beloved son and begging God to see each part of the ram's anatomy as if it were the corresponding part of Isaac's:

Rabbi Yudan said in the name of Rabbi Benaiah: He prayed: "Master of the universe, regard the blood of this ram as if it were the blood of my son Isaac, the sacrificial portions of this ram as if they were the sacrificial portions of my son Isaac."

Rabbi Phinehas said in the name of Rabbi Benaiah: He prayed: "Master of the universe, regard it as though I had sacrificed my son Isaac first and only afterwards sacrificed this ram." (*Gen. Rab.* 56:9)

Similarly, we can imagine that the Carthaginian father, though he had the option to substitute an animal, would have proceeded with the sacrifice of his children, not out of hatred for them, but from the opposite motivation, the desire to present the god with the most precious possible offering.[15] And so, we should not be surprised that Stager and Wolff found that the substitution of the animal for the child *declined* over the periods in which they studied the Carthaginian Tophet. In the seventh century B.C.E., one out of every three urns contained animal remains; by the fourth century B.C.E., only one out of ten.[16] "Precisely in the fourth and third centuries B.C." they conclude, "when Carthage had attained the height of urbanity, child sacrifice flourished as never before."[17] What this shows is that, at least for Carthage, an evolutionary view of the relationship of human to animal sacrifice will not do. The latter did not *replace* the former. It only *substituted* for it. It was through the lamb or the kid that the devout father's willingness to sacrifice his very children was realized. And increasingly over the centuries, it was realized through the children themselves. The evolutionary view misses the crucial point: deprive the sacrifice of the *child* of all preciousness in the eyes of the deity, and the sacrifice of the *animal* becomes pointless.

Another of Stager and Wolff's arguments against the funerary interpretation of the urns unearthed at Carthage is the nature of the inscriptions found on stelae there, more than a few of which deal with vows to gods made by the offerors. The key term is *mlk 'mr*, about which much controversy has long swirled. The most probable translation is "the offering of a sheep."[18] The practice of occasionally substituting a sheep for the child continued in the Punic world well into the common era. Some of the most explicit evidence for it comes from about the year 200 C.E., in Latin stelae from the village of Ngaous in Algeria.[19] The best preserved of these reads as follows:

Prosperity and salvation! To the holy lord Saturn a great nocturnal sacrifice—breath for breath, life for life, for the salvation of Concessa—on account of a vision and a vow Felix and Diodora have offered a sacrifice *molchomor* with willing hearts, a lamb as substitute.[20]

Algerian stele

Though certainty will necessarily elude us, it would seem that Felix and Diodora were the parents of young Concessa. "For the salvation of Concessa" (*concessae salute*) suggests that the daughter had become ill. Presumably, the parents, crediting the god Saturn with her recovery, wished to present him with an equivalent of the child who, had she died, would have become his.[21] The equivalent is the animal: *agnum pro vikario*, in the non-standard Latin of these stelae, "a lamb as a substitute." "On account of a vision and a vow" (*ex viso et voto*) indicates that the sacrifice was not owing to a spontaneous out-pouring of gratitude on the part of the overjoyed parents but to arrangements made when Concessa's life was still in doubt. The pledge of an animal that would substitute for her fully—"breath for breath, life for life"—appears to have induced the god identified with the Roman Saturn to relent.

So much for the vow. The "vision" is more obscure. It is possible that it refers to a theophany in which the god announced the acceptability to him of the exchange, or at least the recovery of the stricken youngster. In this connection it is curious that words for vision predominate in the narrative of the aqedah. Abraham sees (*wayyar'*) the site of the sacrifice from afar (Gen 22:4); he announces to Isaac that "God will see (*yir'eh*) to the sheep for His burnt offering" (v 8) and, indeed, later sees (*wayyar'*) the ram caught in the thicket, so that he "named that Adonai-Yireh, whence the present saying, 'On the mount of the LORD there is vision (*yērā'eh*)" (v 14). Some of the Talmudic rabbis glossed the enigmatic "land of Moriah" in which Abraham is commanded to offer up Isaac (v 2) also by reference to the root for vision (*r'h*):

> Said Rabbi Simeon ben Yochai: To the place that corresponds (*rā'ûy*) to the supernal Temple. Said Rabbi Yudan: To the place that will be shown (*mor'eh*) to you. (*Gen. Rab.* 55:7)

Though these etymologies are not scientific, they may well reflect the understanding of Moriah in Genesis 22 itself. If so, the very name of the land in which Abraham offers his sacrifice reflects the theme of vision that runs throughout the wrenching little narrative that is the aqedah.

The association of a theophany with a cultic act is ubiquitous in the Hebrew Bible. Abraham builds an altar at Shechem, dedicated "to the LORD who appeared to him" there, promising to grant the land of Canaan to his offspring (Gen 12:7–8). Balaam ben Beor reverses the order: he builds seven altars and sacrifices a bull and a ram on each in the hope of provoking a theophany, a hope soon realized (Num 23:1–4). In the case of Jacob at Bethel, a theophany leads first to his consecration of a sacred pillar and then to a vow:

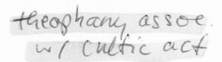
theophany assoc. w/ cultic act

"²⁰If God remains with me, if He protects me on this journey that I am making, and gives me bread to eat and clothing to wear, ²¹and if I return safe to my father's house—the LORD shall be my God. ²²And this stone, which I have set up as a pillar, shall be God's abode; and of all that You give me, I will set aside a tithe for You." (Gen 28:20–22)

It is reasonable to suspect that behind *ex viso et voto* in Ngaous Stela II lies a similar set of events, a theophany and oracle followed by Felix and Diodora, a vow of a lamb in place of Concessa.

Though 1300 years separate Jephthah from Felix and Diodora, his sacrifice, like Abraham's, also has some points in common with theirs. Both offerings result from a vow, and both are presented in gratitude for safety or salvation (*salute; běšālôm* in Judg 11:31; cf. Gen 28:21). But whereas the North African couple offer a sheep in place of their daughter, Jephthah offers his daughter in place of the animal that he thought would greet him upon his return in safety from battle with Ammon. His celebration turns to tragedy; their tragedy turns to celebration. The memorial to his experience is an annual ritual in which maidens chant dirges for his doomed daughter. The memorial to Felix and Diodora's experience is a stela honoring the deity who they thought had rescued their daughter from doom.

Of the three biblical narratives of child sacrifice that we have examined— the stories of Abraham, Jephthah, and Mesha—it is the last that is most distant from the stelae of Ngaous. Mesha offers his son, not an animal, as a substitute. Earlier, I speculated that his sacrifice may have been pursuant to a vow like Jephthah's or Felix and Diodora's: if only the deity would break the deadly siege on Kir-hareseth, the king would offer what was most beloved to him, "his first-born son, who was to succeed him as king" (2 Kgs 3:27). Like Jephthah, and unlike Abraham, Felix, and Diodora, Mesha seems to have lacked the possibility of offering a sheep as a substitute. In his case, the *son* was the substitute, for his death purchased life for his father—"breath for breath," as the Ngaous stela puts it, "life for life." Whereas Abraham offers the ram "in place of (*taḥat*) his son" (Gen 22:13), and Felix and Diodora sacrifice a lamb as a substitute" (*agnum pro vikario*), Mesha offers his first-born son who would rule in his stead (*taḥtāyw*, 2 Kgs 3:27). In place of the father dies the son.

Chapter Three
The Sacrifice of the Son as the Imitation of God

A contemporary of Felix and Diodora and fellow North African, the church father Tertullian held, as one might expect, quite a different view of the sacrifice of children to Saturn:

> In Africa infants used to be sacrificed to Saturn, and quite openly, down to the proconsulate of Tiberius, who took the priests themselves and on the very trees of their temple, under whose shadow their crimes had been committed, hung them alive like votive offerings on crosses; and the soldiers of my own country are witnesses to it, who served that proconsul in that very task. Yes, and to this day that holy crime persists in secret. Christians are not the only people who defy you; no crime is ever wholly rooted out; nor does any of your gods change his ways. Saturn did not spare his own children; so, where other people's were concerned, he naturally persisted in not sparing them; and their own parents offered them to him, were glad to respond, and fondled their children that they might not be sacrificed in tears. And between murder and sacrifice by parents—oh! the difference is great![1]

As his sarcastic conclusion shows, Tertullian regarded child sacrifice—still going on in his time, though "in secret"—as no different from plain murder. Such is the judgment one would expect of an early Christian. More intriguing, however, is the hint that Tertullian offers as to the mythological background of the practice: "Saturn did not spare his own children; so, where other people's were concerned, he naturally persisted in not sparing them." It is not simply that in an extreme situation, the pagans of North Africa take correspondingly extreme action to propitiate their angry god. Rather, their sacrifice of their children is performed in *imitatio dei*, in mimicry of Saturn's deeds with respect to his own offspring. Now one might think that a Christian eager to point out the horrors of pagan religions would flinch from focusing upon the pagan belief in a divine father willing to allow, or even to decree, the death of his own progeny;

the analogy with the God who "so loved the world that he gave his only Son" (John 3:16) might defeat the Christian's polemical goals. Not so in the case of Tertullian. He seems to have thought the myth of Saturn and the gospel of Jesus Christ so distinct that the analogy in question never occurred to him. Presumably, he thought that whereas the divine father of Jesus was willing to "give"[2] his son because of his great love for the world, Saturn's sacrifice was simply an instance of cruelty, a failure to "spare" his own children and, *a fortiori*, those of his worshipers. But the stelae of Ngaous suggest that the opposition was not diametric, for Saturn, too, could have mercy, healing a stricken child and accepting a lamb in place of his votaries' own offspring. And those North African parents, who, by Tertullian's own account, "were glad to respond, and fondled their children that they might not be sacrificed in tears"—were they any more heartless than the Jewish and Christian parents of the same period who would rather see their children die than break faith with their God, in the Christian case, a God thought to have given up his only begotten son out of love for the world? And was their theology crueler than that of Jews and Christians who to this day venerate the memory of Abraham because of his unquestioning willingness to immolate Isaac at God's behest?

A less polemical view of Phoenician mythology or theology appears in the work of another doctor of the church, Eusebius of Caesarea, who flourished early in the fourth century C.E. The less polemical character of Eusebius' material is owing not to him, but to his source, the "Phoenician Theology" of Sakkunyaton, a Phoenician priest whose work was preserved in fragments by Philo of Byblos, whose writings, in turn, Eusebius used in his *Praeparatio Evangelica*. Here is Eusebius' quotation of Philo of Byblos' remarks on Saturn's sacrifice:

reported by Philo of Byblos

> It was a custom of the ancients in great crises of danger for the rulers of a city or nation, in order to avert the common ruin, to give up the most beloved of their children for sacrifice as a ransom to the avenging daemons; and those who were thus given up were sacrificed with mystic rites. Kronos then, whom the Phoenicians call Elus, who was king in the country and subsequently, after his decease, was deified as the star Saturn, had by a nymph of the country named Anobret an only begotten son, whom they on this account called Iedoud, the only begotten being still so called among the Phoenicians; and when very great dangers from war had beset the country, he arrayed his son in royal apparel, and prepared an altar, and sacrificed him.[3]

Saturn → Kronos → El → YHWH

Behind the Roman Saturn, then, lies the Greek Kronos, and behind him the Phoenician El, a name familiar from the Hebrew Bible as well, where, as we shall see, it can appear as a synonym of YHWH as the name of the God of Israel. The sacrifice of children "in great crises of danger" recalls nothing we have seen so well as King Mesha's offering "his first-born son, who was to succeed him as king" in hopes of relieving the siege of Kir-Hareseth (2 Kgs 3:27). That El, according to Philo of Byblos, "arrayed his son in royal apparel" suggests that the clause "who was to succeed him as king" is essential to the point of Mesha's sacrifice. Cristiano Grottanelli argues that sacrifices like these are "to be interpreted as a substitution for the sacrifice or suicide of the king": "Through [his first-born son], the king supplicates the angry gods and pays a great price to ransom his people; but through him the king also ransoms himself, as he covers his child with the insignia of his own rank and person."[4] This variety of child sacrifice is to be associated with the ancient notion that in certain circumstances, the king himself must be offered: the son is here but a substitute for the father, just as the lamb will become a substitute for the son and, in the Christian case, the confessed son of God will become a sub-stitute for the paschal lamb (for example, 1 Cor 5:7).[5] The connections of child sacrifice with this archaic royal theology may help explain a feature of the Carthaginian tophet that Stager and Wolff found "surprising"—"that child sacrifice at Carthage was largely an upper-class custom, at least until the third century B.C."[6]

The text of Sakkunyaton cited above reports "Iedoud" as the name of the child El sacrificed, but another manuscript tradition reads, instead, "Ieoud." This is most likely a transcription of the Phoenician equivalent of the biblical Hebrew word *yāḥîd*. Though this biblical term, in its masculine and feminine   *YAHID*
forms, occurs only twelve times, it is suggestively prominent in stories of   *3 'ח'*
child sacrifices. The aqedah terms Isaac Abraham's *yāḥîd* on no fewer than three occasions (Gen 22:2, 12, 16) and Jephthah's daughter is the *yěḥîdâ* of her father (Judg 11:34). Amos delivers an oracle in which God threatens to make the earth "mourn as for an only child" (*kě'ēbel yāḥîd*), (Amos 8:10), and Jere-miah, employing the same phrase (which he may well have gotten from Amos) issues this macabre summons:

My poor people,
Put on sackcloth,
And strew dust on yourselves!
Mourn as for an only child (*'ēbel yāḥîd*);
Wail bitterly,

For suddenly the destroyer
Is coming upon us. (Jer 6:26)

The bitter wailing (*mispad tamrûrîm*) that is Jeremiah's synonym for *'ēbel yāḥîd* recalls another oracle of Jeremiah's, in fact, the only other attestation of *tamrûrîm* in the book:[7]

Thus said the LORD:
A cry is heard in Ramah—
Wailing, bitter weeping (*běkî tamrûrîm*)—
Rachel weeping for her children.
She refuses to be comforted
For her children, who are gone. (Jer 31:15)

Rachel's children are, of course, Joseph and Benjamin (Gen 46:19). "Who are gone" (*'ênennû*) is doubtless an allusion to the ostensible loss of Joseph. "The boy is gone (*'ênennû*)! Now what am I do to?" cries Reuben, when he returns to the pit in hopes of rescuing Joseph, the beloved son of their father, Jacob (Gen 37:30; see also vv 3–4). And when the surviving sons, with the exception of the youngest, Benjamin, appear before the Egyptian prime minister (who is really Joseph) to buy food, they use the same freighted term: "the youngest . . . is now with our father, and one is no more" (*wěhā'eḥād 'ênennû*, Gen 42:13). Later, using the same term, they report the conversation to their father (Gen 42:32), in hopes that he will, as the prime minister demanded, let Benjamin go with them to Egypt so that Simeon, held as a hostage, may be freed. But Jacob, still grief-stricken for Joseph, retorts: "It is always me that you bereave: Joseph is no more (*'ênennû*) and Simeon is no more (*'ênennû*) and now you would take away Benjamin" (Gen 42:36). The cry that is heard in Ramah is Rachel's mourning for an only child (*'ēbel yāḥîd*), bewailing, like her husband Jacob, the loss of Joseph, who is no more, and, again like Jacob (Gen 37:35), refusing to be comforted until the beloved son, the "one" son (*yāḥîd/'eḥād*), somehow returns from the dead.

If her other son, Benjamin, is also to be counted as a son who is no more in that lament, then we may have an indication of the meaning of the other name given for the son whom El sacrifices according to the old Phoenician myth: Iedoud. This is undoubtedly the equivalent of the rare Hebrew word, *yādîd*, meaning "beloved," "precious," and the like. The only individual to whom this term is applied in the Bible is Benjamin, described in Deut 33:12 as "beloved of the LORD" (*yědîd* YHWH). This epithet is probably to be related to Benjamin's status as the son of his father's old age, like Isaac (Gen 21:2) and like Joseph himself before his ostensible death (37:3), that is, his darling, the only surviving son of his preferred wife, Rachel. Indeed, in each verse in which we hear that one of these children by Rachel is the son of Jacob's old age, we also hear that Jacob loved him, and in Joseph's case we are told explicitly that Jacob loved him more than his brothers (Gen 37:3; 44:20). Though the term for "love" in these verses is from the root *'hb*, not *ydd*, it is reasonable to speculate that the status of Benjamin as "beloved of the LORD" (*yĕdîd* YHWH) may be connected to his special place in the affections of his earthly father, Jacob, as well. The mythological echoes in the Joseph story are more important still: no small measure of the suspense of the tale turns on whether Jacob, to alleviate the great crisis caused by the famine or, as Philo of Byblos puts it, "to avert the common ruin," is prepared "to give up the most beloved of [his] children," here named not Iedoud, as in Philo of Byblos, but Benjamin, elsewhere known as the "beloved of the LORD"—*yĕdîd* YHWH (Deut 33:12). The family of Jacob survives, the people of Israel endures, only because he, like his grandfather Abraham, proved willing to surrender the only son of his preferred wife. But for the father's willingness to sacrifice the beloved son, the people would have perished.

Though Benjamin is alone in having "beloved of the LORD" as an epithet, essentially the same expression does appear in one name formation in the Hebrew Bible:

> [24] David consoled his wife Bathsheba; he went to her and lay with her. She bore a son and she named him Solomon. But YHWH loved him, [25] and He sent a message through the prophet Nathan; and he was named Jedidiah (*yĕdîdyāh*) at the instance of the LORD (2 Sam 12:24–25).[8]

It is possible that the name Jedidiah and the statement that "YHWH loved" Solomon are related to each other but not to the theme of our investigation. It is curious, however, that at birth Solomon was not only the sole surviving son of David through his favored wife, Bathsheba, but also the replacement for the nameless offspring of their adulterous union, who had died soon after birth. Some scholars have associated these circumstances with his name, interpreting *šĕlōmōh* as "his replacement" (cf. the verb *šillēm*, "to make whole, replace").[9] Solomon would, in that case, be the replacement for the dead brother. I suggest that we can go further: the other name, the one God gives, may also be an allusion to the tragic circumstances of the death of Bathsheba's first-born son. For, as we have seen, one of the names of El's only begotten son is Yadid, and it is his death at the hands of the divine king who is his father that brought relief as ruin menaced. In David's case, it was the death of his first-born son through Bathsheba that brought relief, at least for a time, from the calamity that YHWH decreed in response to David's adultery with

Bathsheba and murder of her husband Uriah. Like Isaac and Joseph, that son was the first-born of his father's preferred wife. "Shall I give my first-born for my transgression / The fruit of my body for my sins?" a confused assembly asked Micah (Mic 6:7). Though some scholars have doubted that it would ever have been deemed appropriate to give the first-born son as a sin-offering, David inadvertently—indeed, against his will—did just that, paying for the murder and adultery with the first fruit of his beloved Bathsheba's womb:

> [13] David said to Nathan, "I stand guilty before the LORD!" And Nathan replied to David, "The LORD has remitted your sin; you shall not die. [14] However, since you have spurned the LORD by this deed, even the child about to be born to you shall die." (2 Sam 12:13–14)

The likelihood is that the narrator sees each of Solomon's two names as a reflection of the catastrophic circumstances that led up to his conception. Both as Solomon and as Jedidiah, he is the replacement for the doomed son, whose death helps to expiate David's sin and thus to continue his kingship. The second child is the beloved son *redivivus*.

From the remark of Philo of Byblos that "the only begotten [is] still so called among the Phoenicians," one would expect Ieoud as the name of the sacrificed son, reflecting *yāḥîd*, rather than Iedoud, reflecting *yādîd*, since it is *yāḥîd*, that means "only" or "sole" and thus is more likely to underlie the Greek *monogenēs*, "only begotten." It is interesting, however, that even *yāḥîd* was occasionally rendered into Greek with words indicating love.[10] Thus, when God commands Abraham "Take your son, your only son (*yĕḥîdĕkā*), whom you love" (Gen 22:2),[11] the Septuagint, the ancient Jewish translation of the Torah into Greek, employs the awkward locution "your beloved son, whom you love" (*ton huion sou ton agapēton hon ēgapēsas*). Similarly, one recension of the Septuagint renders *yĕḥîdâ* in Judg 11:34, where it describes Jephthah's daughter, as "his only begotten and beloved" (*monogenēs autō agapētē*).[12] And *'ēbel yāḥîd* in Amos 8:10 and Jer 6:26 appears as *penthos agapētou*, "mourning for the beloved one." It is conceivable that some of these translations reflect a confusion of *yāḥîd* and *yādîd* in the underlying text, but, on the whole, it seems more likely that they testify to the tradition that understands *yāḥîd* as a term for the beloved one, and, in the case of Abraham and Jephthah, for the beloved offspring whom the devout father is obliged to sacrifice and immolate. When, in the synoptic gospels, a heavenly voice declares, just after Jesus' baptism, "You are my beloved son, (*huios mou ho agapētos*); with you I am well pleased" (Mark 1:11 and parallels), a reference to that other beloved son, Isaac, is surely to be understood.[13] And a Jewish audience, versed in the Torah and perhaps even in the Septuagint as well, would have recognized the dark side of the heavenly announcement: that the destiny of the son so loved and so favored included a symbolic death at the hands of his loving father.[14] The theme of the life-giving death of the only begotten and beloved son at the hands of his divine father is nowhere so succinctly put as in the fourth gospel:

> For God so loved (*ēgapēsen*) the world that he gave *(edōken)* his only (*monogenē*) Son, so that everyone who believes in him may not perish but have eternal life. (John 3:16)[15]

"Gave" (*edōken*) reflects the usual language of child sacrifice in the Hebrew Bible, beginning where we began our own discussion, with Exod 22:28b— "You shall give (*titten*) Me the first-born among your sons"—and continuing throughout the tradition of the Hebrew Bible, including Ezekiel, who describes the immolation of the first-born as the presentation of a "gift" (*mattānâ*, Ezek 20:31). And to someone familiar with Phoenician tradition, John 3:16 would recall not only the sacrificial death of Iedoud/Ieoud at the hands of Kronos/El, but perhaps also Philo of Byblos' account of the children "given up (*didomenoi*) . . . with mystic rites."

Chapter Four
El and the Beloved Son

We have seen that Philo of Byblos identifies the deity who sacrificed his only begotten son, *Yādîd* or *Yāḥîd*, with the god El. The recovery of Canaanite religion as it stood just before the emergence of Israel has vastly fleshed out our knowledge of this deity. In the texts discovered at ancient Ugarit, along the Syrian coast, El appears as the father of the gods, the "Creator of Creatures" and "Father of Man," an ageless patriarch who is the "Eternal King," the "Ancient of Days," "the kindly One, El the Compassionate," and a figure of boundless wisdom. We also hear of his hunting, feasting, and, according to the interpretation of many scholars, his prodigious sexual activities as well.[1]

Though we find nothing in the Ugaritic texts of *Yādîd* or *Yāḥîd*,[2] we do see El defined as the father of Baal. Frank Moore Cross points out that this runs counter to the usual identification in this corpus of Dagon as Baal's father and may therefore be only "a fixed oral formula . . . which could be used of any of the sons of El, that is, any god." But Cross also notes that the designation of El as Baal's father fits nicely with Philo of Byblos' listing of one Zeus Belos among Kronos' offspring.[3] In this connection, it is perhaps revealing that in one Ugaritic text, the action begins with the demand of the sea god Yamm that El give over Baal as a slave:

> El, give up the one you are hiding,
> the one the masses are hiding;
> give up Baal and his powers,
> the son of Dagon: I will assume his inheritance.[4]

The patriarch's surrender of Baal is not, however, irreversible. Instead, Baal wins his battle with Yamm (whom he in the end drinks). In another text, however, Baal *dies*, bested by another son of El, the god Mot, whose name means "death." But even this proves reversible, as Baal's sister Anat overcomes Mot and rescues her brother. The sign that the young god has been resurrected is El's dream of renewed fertility:

> In a dream of El the Kind, the Compassionate,
>   in a vision of the Creator of all,
> the heavens rained down oil,
>   the wadis ran with honey.
> El the kind, the Compassionate, was glad:
>   he put his feet on a stool,
>   he opened his mouth and laughed;
>   he raised his voice and shouted:
> "Now I can sit back and relax;
>   my heart inside me can relax;
> for Baal the Conqueror lives,
>   the Prince, the Lord of the Earth, has revived."[5]

Piecing together these texts, we can, with all due caution, speculate that they all reflect a pattern in which El in a moment of crisis, with disaster looming, handed over one of his divine offspring for enslavement or death (the difference is not major, as we shall see).[6] The Ugaritic material does not speak of a child sacrifice in the literal sense, but it does attest to the familiar pattern in which the loss of the son proves to be only temporary: in the end Father El rejoices as his enslaved offspring is freed or his dead son resurrected. If such a pattern is indeed to be detected in Canaanite religion, then it is clearly one with a rich set of reflexes in the Hebrew Bible and the New Testament. One thinks immediately of the story of Joseph, whose father, though knowing of his brothers' enmity towards him, nonetheless sends him to them. The brothers then plot to kill him, but in fact—and perhaps without their knowledge—Joseph is sold into slavery. (Not coincidentally, enslavement and death are also the afflictions of Israel at the hand of the Egyptians in Exodus 1.) Giving Joseph up for dead, his father, Jacob, observes mourning rituals (Genesis 37). But, in reality, Joseph's enslavement is soon over, and the heart-rending report of his death proves premature, as Jacob is at last joyously reunited with the son that he had once mourned (Gen 45:25–28; 46:28–30). Later, I shall have occasion to dwell at length on the relevance of the Joseph novella to the myth of the death and resurrection of the beloved son.[7] Here my point is that it is difficult to deny that it is an analogue in historical prose to the myth of El and Baal (its relationship to the cultic institution of the sacrifice of the first-born son, if it has one, remains murky). And we shall have ample opportunity to see that it is not the only such analogue in the scriptures of Israel and the Church.

reflect

That biblical stories—even stories that tell of the origins of the people of God themselves—should reflect an old Canaanite myth will surprise only those who fail to recognize the continuities of El and YHWH, God of Israel. Whereas Baal becomes, at a certain point, the great rival to YHWH and the target of heated prophetic invective, against El there is no polemic in the Hebrew Bible. Cross points out that "El is rarely if ever used in the Bible as the proper name of a non-Israelite, Canaanite deity in the full consciousness of a distinction between El and YHWH, god of Israel." Instead, "El in biblical tradition is often used simply as an alternate name of YHWH,"[8] as in: "How can I damn whom El has not damned, / How doom when YHWH has not doomed?" (Num 23:8).[9] In fact, Jacob names the altar he builds at Shechem, *'ēl 'ĕlōhê yiśrā'ēl*, that is, "El, God of Israel" (Gen 33:20). Though we need not go so far as Cross, who traces the name YHWH back to a hypothetical title of El,[10] the data compel us to recognize that alongside the Israelite rejection of many features of Canaanite religion, there stood as well many profound continuities. The Ugaritic El of hunt, feast, and sexual exploit is not to be equated with YHWH, the El of Israel. But El as the kind, compassionate, and wise creator and father of gods and humanity lives on in the God of Israel. In the case of the Canaanite El who in a crisis sacrifices his son or hands him over to enslavement or death, the matter is more complex. To say that this El lives on in the God of Israel is to understate the import of the monotheizing and historicizing trends in biblical religion. But to say that he is in radical discontinuity with the biblical Deity is to miss the affinities of this side of El with important features of biblical law and narrative.[11]

profound continuities

affinities

The involvement of the practice of child sacrifice in the Canaanite and Punic regions with the ancient myth of El suggests that the Molech cult and the biblical law of the first-born are not to be so sharply distinguished as most scholars have thought. Mosca, Day, and others are correct to point out that the Molech cult—however one understands the term *mlk* itself—was never limited to males or concerned with the order of birth.[12] But we have now seen that behind the sacrifice of boys and girls in areas of North Africa and elsewhere in the western Mediterranean lies a myth of El, the father-god who offers up his only begotten or beloved son for immolation, or hands a younger god over to the forces of slavery or death. This is a myth with striking resonance in Israelite and early Christian narratives, especially the aqedah, the Joseph story, and the life of Jesus. The precise relationship between the biblical law of the first-born, the Molech cult, and the myth of El remains unclear and may never be clarified on the basis of currently available data.

What is clear, however, is that the law in question is only a part of a much larger biblical theology of the first-born son and his relationship to his father. That theology, in turn, is a matter of more significance to the larger theologies of the people Israel and the Church than has heretofore been recognized.

Chapter Five
The People Israel as the Son of God

Before discussing the wider theological meaning of sonship in the Hebrew Bible, a moment of recapitulation is in order. I began by asking how we are to take the enigmatic clause at the end of Exod 22:28—"You shall give Me the first-born among your sons." Against traditional interpreters and most modern critics, I argued that both the context of the clause itself and the manner of presentation of child sacrifice elsewhere in the Hebrew Bible call for a literal interpretation: the Israelite father is to sacrifice his first-born son to YHWH. That most did not do so need not imply pandemic impiety in early Israel, but only that this law, like others from the same region, stated an ideal that not everyone would be required to realize. About the end of the seventh and beginning of the sixth century B.C.E., some prophets turned their potent rhetorical resources against *all* child sacrifices, not merely those in the service of the obscure Molech, and, as a consequence, the practice became emblematic of idolatry. So, thankfully, has it remained ever since.

I went on to argue, however, that the distance between ancient Israel and its Canaanite cousins on this point was not so great as the heated prophetic critique suggests. In both cultures after a certain point, one could immolate his child to the god but was not obliged to. Instead, one could contribute an animal, usually a sheep. In both cultures, too, animal sacrifice did not, in this situation, *replace* child sacrifice. Rather, the animal *substituted* for the child: the god's claim upon the youngster was realized through the death of the nonhuman stand-in. Greek and Latin accounts of the Phoenician and Punic practice and its accompanying mythology led us from the Roman Saturn to the Greek Kronos and ultimately to the Canaanite El as the god characterized by such worship, and this, in turn, brought us to Ugaritic texts that provided some confirmation. The Ugaritic material suggested a variant myth in which the son whom El hands over in

[margin handwritten note:] Did not replace; rather substituted

a moment of crisis survives nonetheless, to the immense delight of his father. This pattern, I argued, has strong affinities with certain texts in both the Hebrew Bible and the New Testament, which, historicizing the myth to one degree or another, present it as playing itself out in the lives of real people. One of my central claims, therefore, is that without reference to the ancient myths associated with child sacrifice, certain biblical narratives about the origins and character of the people Israel and of the Church cannot be properly understood.

a
central
claim

In rebuttal, it could be argued that what I earlier termed the monotheizing and historicizing trends in the religion of Israel render this reading unlikely. Though El's surrender of Yadid, Yaḥid, or Baal is distantly reflected in narratives like the Joseph story, these biblical examples are fundamentally different, it may be said, from the Canaanite mythological materials to which I likened them. The difference is that the biblical narratives are represented as taking place within historical time, and though the hand of providence is surely meant to be detected behind them (see Gen 50:19–20), the troubled relationships of fathers and sons within them are unrelated to any mythological paradigm and are to be understood only in human, psychological terms. Conversely—the rebuttal would go on to say—the God of Israel is utterly sovereign and in no way enmeshed in familial relationships. If, like the Canaanite El whose name he absorbed, YHWH is eternal and wise, kind and compassionate, unlike his namesake, he has no wife and no children, but exercises his universal dominion in solitary majesty.

What this hypothetical rebuttal misses is, principally, that the Hebrew Bible is not only the story of YHWH but also of Israel his people and of the complicated relationship between them. Central to that relationship is Israel's status not only as YHWH's *son*, but as his *first-born son*. Indeed, this is precisely the point with which YHWH bids Moses to open in his negotiations with Pharaoh:

> [21]And the LORD said to Moses, "When you return to Egypt, see that you perform before Pharaoh all the marvels that I have put within your power. I, however, will stiffen his heart so that he will not let the people go. [22]Then you shall say to Pharaoh, 'Thus says the LORD: Israel is My first-born son. [23]I have said to you, "Let My son go, that he may worship Me", yet you refuse to let him go. Now I will slay your first-born son." (Exod 4:21–23)

In modern times, the tendency is to see the Exodus from Egypt as rooted in God's principled opposition to slavery. In point of fact, however, there is no such opposition in the Hebrew Bible or the New Testament, and the moti-

vation for the Exodus actually lies in the special relationship of Israel to God.[1]
That relationship is of the first-born son to the father; even the language here
is reminiscent of that in the law of Exod 22:28b (cf. *běnî běkōrî* in 4:22 with
běkōr bānêkā there).[2] It is the special status of Israel, son of God, that explains
why the Exodus is not a story of universal liberation at all but only of one
nation's release, the release of the first-born son to rejoin and serve his divine
father. And the cost of that release is the death of all the first-born sons
throughout the realm of God's great rival, the Pharaoh of Egypt. In no small
measure, the story of the Exodus turns on the contrast between the first-born
son whom God enables to survive enslavement and attempted genocide and
the first-born son whom he slays.

Hosea, a prophet of the Northern Kingdom (known in his book as Israel
or Ephraim) in the eighth century B.C.E., develops the image of Israel's divine
sonship at length:

Hosea

[1]I fell in love with Israel
When he was still a child;
And I have called [him] My son
Ever since Egypt.
[2]Thus were they called,
But they went their own way;
They sacrifice to Baalim
And offer to carved images.
[3]I was a guide to Ephraim,
Taking them in My arms;
But they have ignored
My healing care.
[4]I drew them with human ties,
With cords of love;
But I seemed to them as one
Who imposed a yoke on their jaws,
Though I was offering them food.
[5]No!
They return to the land of Egypt,
And Assyria is their king.
Because they refuse to repent,
[6]A sword shall descend upon their towns
And consume their limbs . . .
[8]How can I give you up, O Ephraim?
How surrender you, O Israel?

How can I make you like Admah,
Render you like Zeboiim?
I have had a change of heart,
All my tenderness is stirred. (Hos 11:1–6, 8)[3]

Here again, Israel is the son of God. If v 1 is correctly rendered above, then the divine father fell in love with the boy in Egypt, leading him forth, caring for his health, and drawing him "with cords of love" (v 4). The sins of the son, however, especially the ultimate sin of defection to Baal, should provoke the righteous father to make Ephraim/Israel like Admah and Zeboiim, the sister cities of Sodom and Gomorrah destroyed along with them (Deut 29:22). But once again the father's compassion intervenes, and he proves unable to "give up" or "surrender" his beloved son (Hos 11:8). And once again a father is enabled to avert the death of his beloved son, this time because of the "tenderness" (*niḥûmāy*) that overcomes him after he has called for the sword. The Abrahamic affinities are poignant (Gen 22:10–12).

It is likely that Jeremiah picked up this image of YHWH as father and Israel/Ephraim as son from Hosea, who is known to have influenced him in other ways as well:

[7]For thus said the LORD:
Cry out in joy for Jacob,
Shout at the crossroads of the nations!
Sing aloud in praise, and say:
The LORD has saved His people,—
The remnant of Israel.
[8]I will bring them in from the northland,
Gather them from the ends of the earth—
The blind and the lame among them,
Those with child and those in labor—
In a vast throng they shall return here.
[9]They shall come with weeping,
And with compassion will I guide them.
I will lead them to streams of water,
By a level road where they will not stumble.
For I am ever a Father to Israel,
Ephraim is my first-born. (Jer 31:7–9)

The context seems to be the recovery of the north, the so-called ten lost tribes, that King Josiah of Judah attempted in the early years of Jeremiah's career (2 Kgs 23:15–20; 2 Chr 34:6–7). In the prophet's mind, what has prevented the disappearance of these tribesmen, conquered by Assyria a century earlier, is God's paternal care for his first-born son (cf. Gen 48:8–20). A people who, in the natural course of things, should have vanished now returns in joy and triumph because of the faithfulness of their divine father. Jeremiah's oracles about the recovery of the Israelites of the northland are yet another historical application of the myth of the death and resurrection of the beloved son. God, the father who once gave up Israel/Ephraim to destruction and subjugation at the hands of the Assyrians, now brings him back, gathered from the ends of the earth, to take his proper place in God's own family.

The status of Israel as the first-born son of God is both metaphorical and more than metaphorical. It is metaphorical in that Israel, however delineated, is descended from a line of human fathers and not from the union of a god and a woman. Jacob (whose name becomes Israel) is the son of Isaac. Even his status as the first-born of his human father is due not to nature but to human initiative, specifically his morally dubious acquisition of the rights of primogeniture from his elder brother Esau (Gen 25:27–34). It was Esau whom Isaac favored (literally, "loved," v 28), and Jacob/Israel acquired the prime paternal blessing, in which dominion over his brother is prominently featured (Gen 27:29), only by a ruse (vv 1–27).[4] And he, like Isaac and Abraham before him, having only a human ancestry, with no deity in the lineage, is altogether mortal. The divine sonship that some biblical texts ascribe to him is not biological. It expresses his status as the beloved of God, the eponymous ancestor of the chosen people.

Yet there are dangers in interpreting the statement that Israel is YHWH's first-born son as purely figurative. One is that kinship language in ancient Israel, as in many tribal societies, can express relationships that are other than biological.[5] The vocabulary of paternity and fraternity is common, for instance, in covenant texts. In 2 Kgs 16:7, King Ahaz of Judah proclaims himself the son of Tiglath-Pileser III of Assyria, in hope that his new father will send him military aid. Hiram, king of Tyre, addresses his ally Solomon as "my brother" (1 Kgs 9:13), though the two are not related biologically. To us, these covenantal uses of familial language seem to be straightforward metaphors, but that is only because our culture makes a sharp distinction between biological and other types of relationship and attributes greater reality to the former: "blood is thicker than water." Ancient Israel, following a different convention, could comfortably see a father and a son or two brothers in people who were known to have no blood relationship. To call such usage metaphorical is to presume anachronistically the primacy of biology in Israelite perceptions of kinship. That Israel is the first-born son both of Isaac and of YHWH poses a problem for us, but it posed none, so far as we can tell, for the biblical authors. For them, if one paternity is prior, it is YHWH's, for Jacob/ Israel's dominion over Esau is first announced by an oracle to their mother Rebekah when the twins are yet in utero (Gen 25:22–23), and it is her preference (again, literally, "love") for Jacob rather than Isaac's for Esau (v 28) that mediates God's own designs in the matter. It is not as the son of the hapless Isaac that Israel achieves renown. It is as the first-born son of YHWH, sovereign of the world. To call that sonship a figure of speech is to fail to reckon with the import of the biblical story.

Another danger in interpreting such language metaphorically is that in so doing, we shall miss YHWH's direct involvement in the conception of the fathers of the nation. Ishmael is conceived in the course of nature, from the union of an aged Abraham and Hagar, the young slave of his sixty-five year old wife, Sarah (Gen 16:1–4). But Isaac is born of Sarah herself, the patriarch's true wife, a woman who is not only ninety but barren and past menopause to boot (Gen 17:15–21; 18:9–15). In both versions of the story, the sheer unnaturalness of the annunciation of the promised son provokes a laugh. "Can a child be born to a man a hundred years old," asks Abraham in amazement—or is it disbelief?—"or can Sarah bear a child at ninety?" (Gen 17:17). "Now that I am withered," asks Sarah, "am I to have enjoyment—with my husband so old?" (Gen 18:12). The laughs (*wayyiṣḥāq/wattiṣḥaq*) of Abraham and Sarah are more than mere aetiologies of the name Isaac (*yiṣḥāq*). They also ensure that whenever the second patriarch is mentioned, the miraculous circumstances of his conception will be recalled. This is not a man born of the natural desire of his parents for offspring, but of God's solemn covenantal pledge to make Abraham "the father of a multitude of nations" (Gen 17:3)—a man whose birth was foretold in an angelic annunciation to his astounded parents (Gen 18:9–15). Abraham is his biological father, but it is God who sets aside the laws of biology that have prevented his conception for year upon painful year. And so it is with Jacob/Israel, born of Rebekah, who was barren until God answered her husband's entreaty and she conceived (Gen 25:21), and with Joseph as well, the son of Rachel, another woman barren until "God remembered . . . and opened her womb" (Gen 30:22).

Concentrated in Genesis, the motif of the barren woman is rather rare in the remainder of the Hebrew Bible. Its frequency in the first book of the Pentateuch is owing to its association with the account of the origins of the people of God, that is, Israel, YHWH's first-born son. Though neither Isaac nor Jacob nor Joseph is his father's oldest son, providence allows each to attain the bittersweet status of the first-born.[6] The conception of each son in a barren woman is another refraction of this same heavenly supersession of the hard realities of biology. The ancestor of Israel—and thus also Israel itself—is the first-born son of two fathers, one human and one divine.

It must also be mentioned that several biblical texts term the Israelites individually sons of God as well. In Hosea, the Israelites, having once been given the pejorative moniker "Not-My-People," will, in the era of restoration, be renamed "Sons-of-the-Living-God" (*běnê 'ēl-ḥāy*, Hos 2:1). Similarly, the Deuteronomic code warns Israel:

> ¹You are children [*bānîm*] of the LORD your God. You shall not gash yourselves or shave the front of your heads because of the dead. ²For you are a people consecrated to the LORD your God: the LORD your God chose you from among all other peoples on earth to be His treasured people. (Deut 14:1–2).

Here filiation, consecration, and chosenness—three aspects of one reality— serve as the ground for laws (such as the dietary restrictions that follow) that differentiate Israel from those who are not God's sacred, chosen children. To call Israel's status as the son of God a figure of speech, without qualification, is to miss the thorough-going *practical* difference that this status is intended to make in the lives of the chosen people. That Israel alone is God's son is not only as poetic as prophecy; it is also as prosaic as law.

the practical difference

Chapter Six

The Sacrifice of the First-Born Son:
Eradicated or Transformed?

Even if it is accepted that there was legitimate child sacrifice in early Israel
and that the status of Israel as God's first-born son is a matter of high
import in the Hebrew Bible, it could still be argued that the scenario that I
have sketched pertains to early Israel but not to Israel after Jeremiah and
Ezekiel waged war on child sacrifice about the turn of the sixth century
B.C.E.. For by the end of that century, the institution seems to have
vanished entirely,[1] and yet I have argued for the importance of the myth
associated with it, the myth of the death (and often the resurrection as
well) of the beloved son, not only to materials that are usually dated in the
500s B.C.E. (such as P, the Priestly Source in the Pentateuch) but even to
Christian materials from the late first century C.E. Does this not, my critics
may ask, mean a failure on my part to reckon with the eradication of the
myth and its attendant practices? Am I not underestimating the effect of
the prophetic revolution on the religion of Israel?

The weakness of the question is the assumption that the success of these
prophets in combating child sacrifice was as total as their opposition to the
practice. The opposition was indeed total. Jeremiah denounces *all* burning
of children; he allows for no exception for the first-born son.[2] Ezekiel, as
we have seen, goes further: he subsumes the gift of "the first issue of the
womb" (*kol-peṭer rāḥam*) under "the laws that were not good" that YHWH
gave Israel in the wilderness (Ezek 20:25–26), implying that the gift of the
first-born was no better than the presentation of children to Molech (vv 30–
31). This uncompromising prophetic opposition is almost certainly related
to the position of Deuteronomy, which is usually dated to the end of the
seventh century. For Deuteronomy, in exhorting Israel not to serve YHWH
in the manner in which the Canaanites serve their gods, points out that

those nations "perform for their gods every abhorrent act that the LORD detests; they even offer up their sons and daughters in fire to their gods" (Deut 12:31). The Holiness Code (Leviticus 17–26), usually dated a bit earlier than Deuteronomy, makes essentially the same point, though unlike Deuteronomy, it always names Molech when it condemns the practice (Lev 18:21; 20:2–5).

The case of Deuteronomy is especially revealing because, unlike the Holiness Code, Deuteronomy includes substantial legislation on the disposition of the first-born males of herd and flock:

> [19]You shall consecrate to the LORD your God all male firstlings that are born in your herd and in your flock: you must not work your firstling ox or shear your firstling sheep. [20]You and your household shall eat it annually before the LORD your God in the place that the LORD will choose. [21]But if it has a defect, lameness or blindness, any serious defect, you shall not sacrifice it to the LORD your God. [22]Eat it in your settlements, the unclean among you no less than the clean, just like the gazelle and the deer. [23]Only you must not partake of its blood; you shall pour it out on the ground like water (Deut 15:19–23).[3]

Compared with the laws of the firstling that we examined earlier (Exod 22:28–29 and 34:19–20), Deuteronomy displays a startling omission: it says nothing whatsoever about the first male issue of the human womb. Whereas Exod 22:28b simply states that the first-born son is to be given to YHWH, without explicit specification of the means, and Exod 34:20 requires the redemption of the first-born son, apparently with a sheep (v 19), Deut 15:19–23 accords no special status at all to the oldest manchild. That this is no insignificant datum is further suggested by the treatment in Deuteronomy of the exodus from Egypt, a theme important to this book. Nowhere does Deuteronomy refer to the deaths of the Egyptian first-borns and the deliverance of their Israelite counterparts through the blood of the paschal lamb.[4] In fact, Deuteronomy allows the passover sacrifice to be from the herd as well as from the flock and, apparently, to be boiled rather than roasted—both points in evident contravention of the corresponding law in Exodus (Deut 16:2,7; cf. Exod 12:2–5, 8–9).

The importance of the exodus is a point that Jeremiah and Ezekiel share with Deuteronomy and the Holiness Code. But it has not been noticed that all these documents also share the omission of any reference to the slaying of the Egyptian first-born and the apotropaic effect of the blood of the paschal lamb daubed on the doorposts and lintels of the Israelite houses on the night of the first Passover. What this, in turn, suggests is that the "revolution" in which these sources participated aimed not simply at the *substitution* of animals for the first-born sons, but at the *elimination* of the very idea that God has a special claim upon the first-born son that had to be honored in the cult. The sources that are most outraged at child sacrifice do not allow for the substitution of a sheep for the doomed son. Their theology seems to have no place for the substitutionary etiology of the paschal lamb.

That etiology is known principally from Exodus 12–13, a passage that critical scholars are virtually unanimous in attributing to P, the Priestly Source of the Pentateuch. About the date of P, however, scholars exhibit no unanimity, though most still assign the document to the sixth or fifth century B.C.E. If they are right, and if the substitutionary etiology is ancient, then Exodus 12–13 provides definitive proof of the failure of the sort of reform represented by the Holiness Code, Deuteronomy, Jeremiah, and Ezekiel: even though the practice of sacrificing the first-born son was no longer acceptable, the accompanying myth survived and continued to influence the nature of religious practice. And even if P is earlier than the sources critical of the substitutionary etiology of the paschal lamb, the fact that Exodus 12–13 was preserved, included in the Pentateuch, and taken as normative in some sense in both Judaism and Christianity speaks to the same point: the mythic-ritual complex that I have been calling "child sacrifice" was never *eradicated;* it was only *transformed.*

From the P account of the rite of the paschal lamb, it is all too clear that God's lethal claim upon the first-born son has not been eliminated, but only redirected:

> [21]Moses then summoned all the elders of Israel and said to them, "Go, pick out lambs for your families, and slaughter the passover offering. [22]Take a bunch of hyssop, dip it in the blood that is in the basin, and apply some of the blood that is in the basin to the lintel and to the two doorposts. None of you shall go outside the door of his house until morning. [23]For when the LORD goes through to smite the Egyptians, He will see the blood on the lintel and the two doorposts, and the LORD will pass over the door and not let the Destroyer enter and smite your home." (Exod 12:21–23)

The identity of "the Destroyer" (*mašḥît*) who executes the tenth and climactic plague upon the Egyptians is obscure. Only a few verses earlier, YHWH identifies *himself* as the one who will "strike the land of Egypt" (v 13). It is tempting to see v 13 as demythologizing an earlier conception in which YHWH's control was checked by another being, the mysterious and eerie Destroyer. A more likely scenario, however, commends itself: the Destroyer (*mašḥît*) of v 23 is the same figure as "the angel who was destroying" (*[ham]mal'āk hammašḥît*) the people of Jerusalem as a result of David's census (2 Sam 24:16).[5] It often happens in the Hebrew Bible that the line between God and his angel is so indistinct that the two can be interchanged artlessly (for example, Gen 16:7–13). If this is the case in Exodus 12, then the Destroyer is YHWH in his aspect of slayer of the first-born son. This is not an aspect of the Deity that the biblical tradition is inclined to celebrate, and for obvious reasons. It is, after all, an aspect that recalls Molech and the monster on the Pozo Moro Tower more than the gracious and delivering God of the exodus. And yet the very story of that great act of deliverance, the story of Passover, pays oblique homage to this dark side of the Deity. More than that: it specifies a ritual practice that is to ensure that it is the delivering rather than the destroying aspect of God that triumphs. In the P theology, Passover is not only the story of YHWH's victory over Pharaoh. It is also the story of YHWH's victory over himself, and it stands as a continual reminder of just how narrow that victory was: but for the blood of the lamb, the Israelites would have suffered the same catastrophe as the Egyptians.

NB

Though the rites of the paschal lamb constitute the most familiar transformation of the sacrifice of the first-born son, there were, in fact, others, among which the dedication of the Levites is the most developed:

> [16] For they are formally assigned to Me from among the Israelites: I have taken them for Myself in place of all the first issue of the womb, of all the first-born of the Israelites. [17] For every first-born among the Israelites, man as well as beast, is Mine; I have consecrated them to Myself at the time that I smote every first-born in the land of Egypt. [18] Now I take the Levites instead of every first-born of the Israelites; [19] and from among the Israelites I formally assign the Levites to Aaron and his sons, to perform the service for the Israelites in the Tent of Meeting and to make expiation for the Israelites, so that no plague may afflict the Israelites for coming too near the sanctuary. (Num 8:16–19)

Here, the underlying assumption is the same as in Exod 22:28b: the first-born son is to be "given" to YHWH.[6] The difference is that in Numbers 8, unlike Exodus 22 but like Exodus 12–13, a substitute is provided. This time the substitute is not the paschal lamb, even though the substitution is again grounded in the tenth plague (Num 8:17), but the male Levites, that is, the caste of minor clerics who, according to P, are to minister to the priesthood of the House of Aaron (the *kōhănîm*). More to the point, the consecration of these Levites into the service of God is conceived as a *sacrifice:* Aaron is to "designate the Levites before the LORD as an elevation offering from the Israelites" (v 11; cf. v 13). Their service exempts the first-born sons of the claim upon their very lives that God acquired when he spared them the fate of their Egyptian counterparts. It bears mention that this substitution of the Levite for the first-born son in attending the priesthood continues in a point of rabbinic law, even though, with the loss of the Temple, the practical importance of both the *kōhănîm* and the Levites has diminished drastically. Today, when there is no Levite available to pour water on the hands of the *kōhēn* (hereditary priest) before he pronounces the Aaronic benediction (see Num 6:22–27), a man who is his mother's first-born son carries out the honorific task. And if no first-born son is available, the *kōhēn* pours water on his own hands.

According to the census information in Num 3:39–43, the number of first-born males in the wilderness in the time of Moses totaled 273 more than the number of qualified Levites. The solution to the problem came in the form of monetary ransom:

> [46]And as the redemption price of the 273 Israelite first-born over and above the number of the Levites, [47]take five shekels per head—take this by the sanctuary weight, twenty *gerahs* to the shekel—[48]and give the money to Aaron and his sons as the redemption price for those who are in excess. (Num 3:46–48; see also Num 18:15–18)

Thus, Aaron and his sons were given 1,365 shekels as redemption money for the first-born for whom no Levites were available to serve as substitutes (vv 49–51). Here, again, is evidence for the tenacity of the idea that the first-born son belonged to God and must be redeemed if he is to live. And here, again, is the origin of a Jewish practice that endures to this day, the redemption of the first-born (*pidyôn habbēn*). The son who is the first-born of his mother (provided the father is neither a *kōhēn* or a Levite, nor the mother a daughter of either these two classes of Jews) is presented to the *kōhēn*, who then asks the father whether he wishes to donate the child or to redeem him. The father chooses the latter course and presents the *kōhēn* with the redemption money. The *kōhēn*, holding the money over the boy's head, then recites the formula "this instead of that, this in commutation of that" (*zeh māḥûl ʿal zeh*)".[7]

Today, the redemption of the first-born is obligatory. In Biblical times, by contrast, there does seem to have been a means for donating the boy for actual cultic service. This happened through the curious institution of the Nazirite (*nāzîr*). Nazirites (who could be either male or female) were specially consecrated individuals who were subject to restrictions reminiscent of those of the Aaronite priesthood but whose status was independent of lineage (Num 6:1–21).[8] There seem to have been two forms of Nazirite, those who were consecrated for life and those who were consecrated for only a limited time. It is often said that in the Hebrew Bible only two lifelong Nazirites are known by name, Samson (Judg 13:2–7) and Samuel (1 Sam 1:11), who are joined in the New Testament by John the Baptist (Luke 1:15).[9] There may be another, however, in Joseph, who in the series of tribal blessings in Genesis 49 is given the obscure title *nĕzîr 'eḥāyw* (v 26). This is usually rendered "the elect of his brothers," "the prince among his brothers,"[10] or the like, and may well be only a metaphorical use of the term for Nazirite. But it is surely a remarkable coincidence that Joseph, Samson, Samuel, and John are each the first-born sons of a previously barren mother (Gen 30:2, 22–24; Judg 13:2; 1 Sam 1:2; Luke 1:7). In the case of Samuel, the text is explicit that the boy's mother Hannah *donated* him as a cultic officiant as a result of a vow she made at the old Temple in Shiloh:

> And she made this vow: "O LORD of Hosts, if You will look upon the suffering of Your maidservant and will remember me and not forget Your maidservant, and if You will grant Your maidservant a male child, I will dedicate him to the LORD for all the days of his life; and no razor shall ever touch his head." (1 Sam 1:11)

The term rendered "dedicate" here is the telltale verb "to give" (*nātan*). It recalls not only Exod 22:28b ("You shall give Me the first-born among your sons") but also Num 8:16, in which the Levites are said to be "formally assigned" (*nĕtûnîm nĕtûnîm*) to God in place of the first-born son, and, farther afield, Ngaous Stela III, in which Felix and Diodora announce that they have offered (literally, "given back," *reddiderunt*) a lamb as a substitute for their daughter.[11] Having compared the biblical and the Punic terminology of donation or dedication, James G. Février concludes that in the case of a first-born male who was vowed as a Nazirite, no substitution was necessary. Like a Levite, the child passed directly into the service of YHWH.[12] (Note that in 1 Chr 6:1–13 Samuel is actually given a Levitical genealogy). No claim is here made that the office of lifelong Nazirite was always employed as a means of realizing God's claim upon the first-born, but it does seem on occasion to have functioned in this way and, in so doing, it provides yet another piece of evidence for the continuing vitality of the idea that the first-born son belonged to God. There is no reason to think that the idea lost its vitality after child sacrifice, a practice with which it has strong affinities, met its much-deserved demise.

Excursus: Was Circumcision a Substitution Ritual?

We have now examined four ritual substitutions for the death of the first-born son—paschal lamb, Levitical service, monetary ransom, and Naziritehood. A fifth is suggested in a comment by a Tanna of the early second century C.E., Rabbi Matia ben Heresh:

> Why did the Scripture require the purchase of the paschal lamb to take place four days before its slaughter [Exod 12:3–6]? R. Matia the son of Heresh used to say: Behold it says: "when I passed by you and saw that your time for love had arrived." This means, the time has arrived for the fulfillment of the oath which the Holy One, blessed be He, had sworn unto Abraham to deliver his children. But as yet they had no religious duties to perform by which to merit redemption, as it further says: "your breasts had become firm and your hair had grown, yet you were naked and bare [Ezek 16:6–8]," which means bare of any religious deeds. Therefore, the Holy One, blessed be He, assigned them two duties, the duty of the paschal sacrifice and the duty of circumcision, which they should perform so as to be worthy of redemption. For thus it is said: "When I passed by you and saw you wallowing in your blood, I said to you 'In your blood live!' " [Ezek 16:6]. And again it is said: "You, for your part, have released / Your prisoners from the dry pit, / For the sake of the blood of your covenant" [Zech 9:11]. For this reason Scripture required that the purchase of the paschal lamb take place four days before its slaughter. For one cannot obtain rewards except for deeds. (*Mekilta de Rabbi Ishmael*, Pisha' 5, to Exod 12:6)[13]

What calls forth Rabbi Matia ben Heresh's comment is the Torah's requirement that the paschal lamb be selected on the tenth day of the month, though it is not to be slaughtered until the fourteenth. His solution to the textual oddity is to point to the responsiveness of God to human action, in this case not transgression but good deeds. To affirm the opposite, to attribute Israel's redemption from Egypt *solely* to divine grace, would be to impute arbitrariness to God and thus subtly to undercut the morality of his will and the appropriateness of his actions. But *what* good deeds could Israel have had at the time of the exodus, when the Torah and its hundreds of commandments had not yet been given? The text at hand, Exod 12:3–6, supplies one answer: God redeemed Israel through the blood of the lamb in response to their observance of his instruction to select the appropriate animal four days earlier. A second answer lies in another pre-Sinaitic commandment, circumcision, first enjoined not on Moses, who hears it reiterated on Sinai (Lev 12:3), but on Abraham six generations earlier (Gen 17:9–14). For the task of joining these two commandments, Ezek 16:6 serves as a heaven-sent prooftext, for the word for "blood" therein is formally plural, *dāmayik*, literally, "your bloods," that is, the blood of the lamb and the blood of circumcision. By these two bloods Israel acquired life, meriting deliverance from the House of Bondage.[14]

This emphasis upon the *blood* of circumcision is familiar to anyone versed in rabbinic literature or traditional Jewish practice. Ezek 16:6 is, in fact, still chanted by the *mōhēl* (ritual circumciser) at the ceremony. Circumcision is not, however, the context of that verse, whose addressee is, in any event, female, and blood is absent altogether from the extended account of the revelation of the rite to Abraham in Gen 17:9–14 and from the account of his execution of his new instructions in 17:23–27. But there is one text—among the most obscure and the most disquieting in the Torah—in which blood is indeed a central feature of circumcision:

> [21]And the LORD said to Moses, "When you return to Egypt, see that you perform before Pharaoh all the marvels that I have put within your power. I, however, will stiffen his heart so that he will not let the people go. [22]Then you shall say to Pharaoh, 'Thus says the LORD: Israel is My first-born son. [23]I have said to you, "Let My son go, that he may worship Me," yet you refuse to let him go. Now I will slay your first-born son.' "
>
> [24]At a night encampment on the way, the LORD encountered him and sought to kill him. [25]So Zipporah took a flint and cut off her son's foreskin and touched his legs with it, saying, "You are truly a bridegroom of blood to me!" [26]And when He let him alone, she added, "A bridegroom of blood because of the circumcision." (Exod 4:21–26)

This is not the place to explore the compounded obscurities of vv 24–26 and the variety of interpretations that the passage has understandably spawned over the centuries.[15] What is reasonably clear in it is that the blood of circumcision saves Moses from YHWH's sudden attempt to kill him. Since it seems to be Moses and not his son whom the Deity seeks to kill (though even this is hardly beyond dispute), an analogy with Molech or the child-eating monster depicted on the Pozo Moro Tower is not altogether in order. Nonetheless, some association with the death of the first-born son may be present and seems, in fact, to have occurred to whoever placed vv 24–26 after vv 21–23. For the latter text, which we have already had occasion to examine, identifies Israel as God's first-born son, demands the release of this first-born son so that he may render service to his divine father, and threatens the death of Pharaoh's own first-born son if the release does not take place. What ensures that the Israelite first-born males survive the attack of the Destroyer, we shall learn in Exod 12–13, is *blood*, specifically, the blood of the paschal lamb. In short, the blood of circumcision functions within the larger redacted story of

Moses and Pharaoh as a prototype of the blood of the lamb. It is not the case that the two blood-centered commandments build up a store of good deeds sufficient to invite God's gracious intervention, as Rabbi Matia ben Heresh thought. But that the two texts, Exod 4:24–26 and Exodus 12–13, function remarkably similarly seems clear. And it is made more evident by the placement of the former text after the initial statement of the theme of the first-born son in Exod 4:21–23.

In Exod 4:24–26, it is the blood of the son that saves the father's life: Moses lives because Zipporah has circumcised the boy. Put this way, the incident recalls the story of King Mesha, who survived the Israelite siege because he sacrificed his first-born son and heir apparent (2 Kgs 3:26–27). If circumcision could indeed exhibit something of the character of a substitution ritual for child sacrifice, then it is probably significant that Exod 22:28–29 implies that the first-born son, like the firstlings of herd and flock, is to be given to God on the eighth day of his life.[16] For it is on the eighth day that biblical law requires that circumcision be performed (Gen 17:12; Lev 12:3). Though I know of no indication that circumcision was ever restricted to the first-born son, this circumstantial evidence that the rite may have once functioned as a substitution ritual for child sacrifice, averting the death of the son, should not be ignored. If the evidence has weight, then circumcision must join paschal lamb, Levitical service, monetary ransom, and Naziritehood as a sublimation of child sacrifice in ancient Israelite religious practice. But the obscurity of Exod 4:24–26 and any cultic background that it may have had prevent us in this case from moving beyond conjecture.

Finally, it bears mention that whether or not circumcision had been associated with sacrifice in the Hebrew Bible itself, there is some evidence for exactly this association in rabbinic midrash:

> Rabbi Isaac said: "Man and beast You deliver, O LORD" [Ps 36:7]. The ordinance relating to man and the ordinance relating to beasts are on a par. The ordinance relating to man: "On the eighth day the flesh of his foreskin shall be circumcised" [Lev 12:3]. The ordinance relating to beasts: "and from the eighth day on it shall be acceptable as an offering by fire to the LORD" [Lev 22:27]. (*Lev. Rab.* 27:1)

The homiletical point of Rabbi Isaac's observation is a familiar one in rabbinic literature—to warn against excessive anthropomorphism by stressing God's involvement with animals no less than with human beings. His point would, however, be awkwardly rendered if the only connection between "man and beast" were that something happens to each on the eighth day of life. Rather, it would seem that the connection extends even to the nature of what happens on that fateful occasion, circumcision being itself the way to make the boy an acceptable offering to the LORD. If this is midrash and not plain sense, it is, nonetheless, a midrash that was long waiting to be made.

The survival and elaboration of so many ritual sublimations gives the lie to the charge that the sacrifice of the first-born son was eradicated in Israel. If child sacrifice had been utterly and universally repugnant in ancient Israel, then it would have made no sense to ground these rituals in that very practice. To do so would have been to give them the kiss of death. What these etiologies actually suggest is the opposite, that the impulse to sacrifice the first-born son remained potent long after the literal practice had become odious and fallen into desuetude. The further question can be asked as to whether all the sublimations were of a *ritual* character: were there also *narrative* sublimations of the mythic-ritual complex of the death of the first-born son? Did the same impulse that produced these substitution rituals also contribute to the generation of the several biblical stories of first-born sons and their narrowly averted deaths? It is to these questions that we turn our attention in part II.

Part II
The Beloved Sons in Genesis

My humiliation is my exaltation;
my exaltation is my humiliation. Hillel

The Patriarchs are the archetype; their descendants, the antitype. Traditional

Chapter Seven
First-Born and Late-Born, Fathers and Mothers

That the impulse to sacrifice the first-born son never died in ancient Israel but was only transformed is hardly surprising. For the special status of the oldest boy continued to be a point of great significance in the society and of noteworthy resonance in its law. Deuteronomy is the most insistent:

> [15] If a man has two wives, one loved and the other unloved, and both the loved and the unloved have borne him sons, but the first-born is the son of the unloved one—[16] when he wills his property to his sons, he may not treat as first-born the son of the loved one in disregard of the son of the unloved one who is older. [17] Instead, he must accept the first-born, the son of the unloved one, and allot to him a double portion of all he possesses; since he is the first fruit of his vigor, the birthright is his due. (Deut 21:15–17)

The intention of this law is to prevent the status of a man's wives from impairing the claim of the husband's first-born son as chief heir to his father's estate. That the scenario it envisions was not hypothetical is suggested by narratives in which a father prefers the late-born son of a favored wife over the first-born of an unfavored one. Abraham, for example, accepts—though not without hesitation—the demand of his primary wife Sarah that he expel his first-born son Ishmael, offspring of his secondary wife, Sarah's Egyptian slave Hagar, so that Sarah's son Isaac—Abraham's second—will not have to share the inheritance (Gen 21:9–13). Similarly, Jacob, who, in language strikingly reminiscent of Deut 21:15–17, "loved Rachel more than Leah," who was "unloved" (Gen 29:30–31), in turn "loved [Rachel's son] Joseph best of all his sons" (37:3) and transferred the status of the first-born from his own two oldest sons, Reuben and Simeon, to Joseph's boys, Ephraim and Manasseh (48:5; see 1 Chr 5:1). The examples of Isaac and Joseph suggest that a father's preference for a late-born son over his first-born may, at one stage in the evolution of law and custom, have violated the principle of primogeniture less than seems the case at first glance. For Isaac and Joseph were both the first-born sons not of their fathers but of their mothers, Sarah and Rachel, respectively. That Israelite primogeniture may at some point have involved matrilineal factors is perhaps to be inferred from a few biblical texts that equate "the first-born male" (*bĕkôr*) with "the first issue of the womb" (*peṭer reḥem*), such as the etiology of Levitical consecration in the Book of Numbers:

> [11] The LORD spoke to Moses, saying: [12] I hereby take the Levites from among the Israelites in place of all the first-born (*bĕkôr*), the first issue of the womb (*peṭer reḥem*) among the Israelites; the Levites shall be Mine. [13] For every first-born (*bĕkôr*) is Mine: at the time that I smote every first-born (*bĕkôr*) in the land of Egypt, I consecrated every first-born (*bĕkôr*) in Israel, man and beast, to Myself, to be Mine, the LORD's. (Num 3:11–13; cf. 8:13–18)

The oracle in Ezekiel about God's having given Israel "laws that were not good and rules by which they could not live"[1] reinforces the same inference. For here, when Ezekiel addresses child sacrifice, he speaks only of "every first issue of the womb" (*kol-peṭer rāḥam*) and never of the first-born son (*bĕkôr*)— as if it is maternal primogeniture that identifies the child to be sacrificed (Ezek 20:25–26). It is, to be sure, possible that *peṭer reḥem* in texts like these is not to be taken in so literal a way as to imply reference to the mother rather than the father; it may be simply a synonym for *bĕkôr*, the father's first-born son.[2] But against this speaks Abraham's and Jacob's preference not for any late-born son, of which both had several, but only for the first-born of their mothers. And the expression "every first-born among my sons" (*kol-bĕkôr bānay*) in Exod 13:15 surely implies that the father can have more than one.

A glance at the way the rabbinic tradition handles the ambiguity between "the first issue of the womb," with its maternal orientation, and the "first-born [son]," with its paternal reference, is instructive. For as early as the Mishnah, rabbinic law recognizes the difference and seeks to limit the rights of each category of offspring:

> A Firstborn may sometimes be deemed a firstborn in what concerns inheritance (*bĕkôr lannaḥălâ*) but not in what concerns [the rights of] the priest (*bĕkôr lakkōhēn*): and a Firstborn may sometimes be deemed a Firstborn in what concerns both the inheritance and [the rights of] the priest, and a Firstborn may sometimes be deemed a Firstborn neither in what concerns inheritance nor in what concerns [the rights of] the priest. (*M.Bek.* 8:1)[3]

The technicalities of these three divisions of first-born sons, fascinating in themselves, need not detain us. The point is simply that the *halakhah*, normative rabbinic law, assumes the differentiation of *bĕkôr lannaḥălâ*, the son who may claim the double portion, and the *bĕkôr lakkōhēn*, the son who must be redeemed by payment to the priest of five shekels, the latter being determined by reference to the mother. It bears mention here that according to the *halakhah*, a Jewish father's obligation to redeem his first-born son still extends to the first son of each wife that he may have occasion to take.

Behind this careful rabbinic definition of different categories of first-born lies a long history of legal evolution. The biblical narratives about the divine and the human father's preference for the younger son suggest that in early biblical times, the Israelite father had a wider range of options than did his descendant of Tannaitic times. One hypothetical option would have been to honor both claims, treating the two (or more) oldest boys of their mothers equally. This is surely the option less likely to have been historical, for direct legal or narrative evidence for it is not forthcoming. One can speculate, nonetheless, that this is what Abraham had planned to do, at least according to the Elohistic source (E), before Sarah insisted on Ishmael's expulsion—an insistence that distressed Abraham greatly and called forth God's consoling reassurance that the divine promise to make Abraham a great nation would still devolve upon Ishmael (Gen 21:11–13; cf. 16:9–12 [J] and 17:18–21 [P]). This remains at the level of speculation because we cannot know what precise arrangement of his estate Abraham would have made had Sarah not demanded that "the son of that slave shall not share in the inheritance with my son Isaac" (21:10). An equal division between the two first-born sons is not to be assumed.

The other option is to declare only one "first issue of the womb" to be the "first-born," thus consigning the other(s) to the status of the late-born son(s). This is, in fact, what Abraham accepted, after Sarah's demand and God's consolation. It may also be what Jacob intended when he made Joseph the "ornamented tunic," or, as it is traditionally known in English-speaking lands, the "coat of many colors" (Gen 37:3). The presentation of the special garment may have been an act of investiture, analogous to the special apparel that Aaron and his descendants don in connection with their ordination to the priesthood (Exod 28:40–41) or to the mantle that Elijah threw over Elisha when he designated him his successor (1 Kgs 19:19). If these analogies hold, then the presentation of the ornamented tunic to Joseph was more than a doting father's innocent (if catastrophically insensitive) demonstration of affection; it was, instead, Jacob's designation of his primary beneficiary. If this be the case, then it is readily understandable why Joseph's brothers "hated him so that they could not speak a friendly word to him" (Gen 37:4). With that one act of investiture, Jacob's biological eleventh son became his legal first-born, leapfrogging over Leah's first-born son as well as over those of the two slaves, Bilhah and Zilpah.

The law of Deut 21:15–17 prevents precisely the sort of fratricidal jealousy of which the story of Joseph gives moving evidence. Verse 15 makes clear that there can be only one first-born son (*bĕkōr*), and he is defined in relation to the father, not the mother. The law employs the term *bĕkōr* in each of its three sentences but never mentions *peṭer reḥem*, the "first issue of the womb" familiar from sacrificial law. It stands to reason that the law of the birthright in Deut 21:15–17 was formulated to counter an attested practice—the very practice that nearly cost Joseph his life. Whether the same provisions would have placed Hagar, foreigner and slave, or the slaves Bilhah and Zilpah on the same plane as the "unloved" wife is unclear. That all three of these women became matriarchs only through the ancient equivalent of our own justly controversial practice of surrogate motherhood adds a further wrinkle to a picture already obscure. What is beyond doubt, however, is that the law of the birthright protects the chronological first-born and removes the father's option to show favoritism in disposing of his estate.

The exalted status of the first-born son is further underscored by the provision of Deut 21:17 that the paternal testator must "allot to him a double portion [*pî šnayim*] of all he possesses, since he is the first-fruit of his vigor [*rē'šît 'ōnô*]." As translated here, the law requires that the *bĕkōr* receive twice the portion of his brothers. If there are twelve sons, for example, and therefore twelve portions to be allotted, the eldest son would receive two, and his eleven brothers would then further divide the remaining ten. Disputing this interpretation, some scholars point to the appearance of the same obscure term in Zechariah as evidence for a different construction of the law of the birthright:

> Throughout the land
>   —declares the LORD—
> Two-thirds [*pî-šnayim*] shall perish, shall die,
> And one-third of it shall survive. (Zech 13:8)

If we make the rather large assumption of a unitary meaning of *pî-šnayim*, then the evidence of Zech 13:8 suggests that in our not altogether hypothetical case of the twelve brothers, the first-born would take eight portions, leaving four to be divided among the other heirs.[4] On this construction, the special status of the first-born son is all the more vivid. But on either reading his importance to the father and the continuity of the family is patent.

The rationale for the dominant and indefeasible claim of the father's first-born son is given in Deut 21:17—"since he is the first fruit of his vigor, the birthright is his due." Underlying this rationale is the ubiquitous biblical notion that the first is also the best. The term *rēʾšît* ("first fruit"), however, invokes a darker side of the status of the eldest son as well. For the *rēʾšît* belongs not to the human producer, but to God. As M. Tsevat puts it, "It would be presumptuous for man to enjoy something without first giving God his portion."[5] God's portion must be the first and the best. The Israelite farmer is admonished in two very ancient collections of laws, "The choice first fruits [*rēʾšît bikkûrê*] of your soil you shall bring to the house of the LORD your God" (Exod 23:19; 34:26). In the case of animals, as we have noted at length, the firstling is to be donated to God by sacrifice. "Therefore," the Israelite father is to instruct a son curious about the odd observances of Passover, "I sacrifice to the LORD every first male issue of the womb, but redeem every first-born among my sons" (Exod 13:15). The redemption of the human first-born—the verse assumes there can be more than one to a father—is necessary because the first-born son belongs to YHWH and can be gotten back only through substitution: "Consecrate to Me every first-born; man and beast, the first issue of every womb among the Israelites is Mine" (Exod 13:2). The underlying theology of the redemption of the first-born son is that, even more so than in the case of other human beings, the life of the son in question is his not by right, but by gift. He is alive only by virtue of a legal fiction, one of the several rituals that Israelite religion evolved as a substitute for the literal sacrifice of the son who belongs to God rather than to his mortal father.[6] It is the central thesis of this study that a basic element of the self-understanding of both Jewry and of the Church lies in stories that are the narrative equivalent of these ritual substitutions—narratives, that is, in which the first-born or beloved son undergoes a symbolic death. The symbolic death corresponds to the demand that the *rēʾšît* or the *peṭer reḥem* be sacrificed to God. That the death is only symbolic, that the son, mirabile dictu, returns alive, is the narrative equivalent of the ritual substitutions that prevent the gory offering from being made. Justice is not done to the complicated role of the first-born son if we fail to note both his exalted status and the precariousness of his very life. The beloved son is marked for both exaltation and for humiliation. In his life the two are seldom far apart.

The special status of the first-born son in the Hebrew Bible is inextricably associated with the theology of *chosenness*. The eldest son is his father's choice offspring, and it is his elevated position that the law of Deut 21:15–17 seeks to protect (or establish) by forbidding the father to choose another over him. Indeed, in a society in which close relationships are cast—perhaps even *perceived*—in genealogical terms, it is not surprising that "son" (*bēn*) and "first-born son" (*bĕkôr*) should have come to apply to the chosen person, including

N B

Central

Israel, the chosen people of God.[7] The first-born and the chosen are not, of course, synonymous, but their semantic fields overlap so extensively that an investigation of the one concept will inevitably illumine the other. In the case of the Patriarchal narratives of Genesis, the urgent and constantly repeating issue of which son is chosen cannot be disengaged from the painful question of which shall inherit the status of the first-born, or, to put it differently, which is the beloved son? For in the narratives of Israel's origins, chosenness means having the status of the one upon whose very life God has acquired an absolute claim.

Chapter Eight
The Loved and the Unloved

The law of the birthright in Deut 21:15–17 speaks directly only to a situation in which the father has two wives, each the mother of one son. Its point, as we have seen, is to insure that the offspring of the "unloved" wife, if he is the oldest of the father's sons, does not suffer from his mother's unfortunate status. The impression the law conveys is that order of birth among the father's male offspring must count for everything, and this impression may well correspond to the legislator's intent and the ongoing community's understanding of the statute. On a strict construction, however, the law of the birthright cannot be interpreted to cover another common situation easily productive of fratricidal discord, the case of multiple sons of the same mother. The spirit of Deut 21:15–17 should preclude paternal preference for any but the eldest of only one mother's sons as well, but neither this statute nor any other in the Hebrew Bible explicitly forbids the particular variety of favoritism in which the younger of two full brothers is preferred.

Whereas Abraham is ultimately induced, conjointly by wifely demand and divine promise, to expel his first-born, Ishmael, in favor of his second son, Isaac, and whereas Jacob, in an act of rank favoritism, prefers Joseph, son of his beloved Rachel, over his ten older brothers, the patriarch of the intermediate generation Isaac, poses no challenge to the principle of order of birth. Of his twin sons by his sole wife, Rebekah, "Isaac favored [or, "loved," *wayye'ĕhab*] Esau because he had a taste for game, but"—and here is the rub—"Rebekah favored [or, again, "loved," *'ōhebet*] Jacob," the younger of the twins (Gen 25:28). As the story unfolds, Jacob acquires Esau's birthright twice. First, taking advantage of Esau's weakened, famished condition, he induces him to sell the birthright for a pot of red stew (25:29–34), and then taking similar advantage of his blind, dying father, he impersonates Esau and thus diverts the paternal blessing upon the first-born onto himself (27:1–45). Here we must resist the temptation to hasty moralization. Jacob is such a consummate trickster and Esau so obviously a boor that only the dourest of readers could fail to be entertained by the story of the crafty younger twin's supplantation of his brother. But the pathos of the innocent boor's victimization by his witty and unscrupulous junior casts a pall upon our amusement:

> [34] When Esau heard his father's words, he burst into wild and bitter sobbing and said to his father, "Bless me too, Father!" [35] But he answered, "Your brother came with guile [bĕmirmâ] and took away your blessing." [36] [Esau] said, "Was he, then, named Jacob [ya'ăqōb] that he might supplant me [wayya'qĕbēnî] these two times? First he took away my birthright and now he has taken away my blessing!" And he added, "Have you not reserved a blessing for me?" [37] Isaac answered, saying to Esau, "But I have made him master over you: I have given him all his brothers for servants, and sustained him with grain and wine. What, then, can I still do for you, my son?" [38] And Esau said to his father, "Have you but one blessing, Father? Bless me, too, Father!" And Esau wept aloud. (Gen 27:34–38)

Like Ishmael, also supplanted, Esau does finally receive a blessing but one inferior to that of which Jacob robbed him (vv 39–40; cf. vv 28–29). For whereas Isaac wishes both brothers natural abundance, he blesses Jacob alone with mastery over his brothers and with the key Patriarchal provision, "Cursed be they who curse you / Blessed they who bless you" (v 29; cf. 12:3, to Abraham). The author devotes too much attention to Esau's sorry plight for us to treat Gen 27:1–45 as only an extraordinarily successful example of the familiar genre of the trickster story. That moral concerns are to be brought to bear against Jacob is further suggested by a prophetic oracle that makes the same pun as 27:36:

> [3] Beware, every man of his friend!
> Trust not even a brother!
> For every brother takes advantage ['āqôb ya'qōb]
> Every friend is base in his dealings.
> [4] One man cheats the other,
> They will not speak truth;
> They have trained their tongues to speak falsely;
> They wear themselves out speaking iniquity.
> [5] You dwell in the midst of deceit.
> In their deceit [bĕmirmâ], they refuse to heed Me
>   -declares the LORD. (Jer 9:3–5).

What motivates the allusion in Jer 9:3 to Jacob's supplantation of Esau is not outrage at the violation of the principle of order of birth; about Jeremiah's view of that issue we can form no secure idea. The prophet is concerned only with denouncing those who take advantage through deceit and dishonesty, a group that he thinks are descended from the national eponymous ancestor Jacob/Israel in more senses than only the genealogical. But just here another objection to the moralistic reading of Gen 27:1–45 presents itself. Isaac's preference for the chronological first-born, Esau, may have proleptically conformed to the spirit of Deut 21:15–17, the law of the birthright, but it runs directly counter to the oracle that YHWH provided Rebekah when the matriarch-to-be inquired as to the meaning of the commotion within her uterus:

> Two nations are in your womb,
> Two separate peoples shall issue from your body;
> One people shall be mightier than the other,
> And the older shall serve the younger. (Gen 25:23)

It is, in short, Rebekah's preference for Jacob rather than Isaac's for Esau that *NB* mediates the providential design. And though it is Jacob rather than Rebekah whom Jeremiah regards as the archetype of deceit, it was Rebekah who devised the strategem by which her beloved son, not altogether without reluctance, would at once deceive his father and defraud his older brother (27:5–17). Though Jeremiah's pun leaves no doubt as to the prophet's evaluation of the morality of Jacob's acquisition of the birthright, the narrative in Gen 27:1–45 presents us with the disquieting thought that the ugly deceit at issue realized a higher plan. That the oracle to the pregnant matriarch was not only a prediction but a statement of YHWH's own preferences is further suggested by the opening oracle of the Book of Malachi:

> [2]I have shown you love, said the LORD. But you ask, "How have You shown us love?" After all—declares the LORD—Esau is Jacob's brother; yet I have accepted [or "loved," *wā'ōhab*] Jacob, [3]but I have rejected [or, "hated," *śānê'tî*] Esau. I have made his hills a desolation, his territory a home for beasts of the desert. (Mal 1:2–3)[1]

In sum, we are faced with a much larger problem than that of a mother and a brother who refuse to adhere to the principle of primogeniture, employing loathsome trickery to accomplish their ends. We are faced as well with a Deity who disregards the principle of order of birth no less than they, even preferring the unscrupulous trickster over the uncouth first-born. And as Mal 1:3 makes clear, the preference affects far more than familial relations: it determines the exaltation of Israel, the people descended from Jacob, and the humiliation of Edom, the nation that issued from Esau.

It is conceivable that Malachi's ringing endorsement of Jacob's status as the beloved son derives from a tradition that knows nothing of the story of the double deceit by which Jacob became the third patriarch. More likely, however, is the supposition that Malachi did indeed know of that story—and spoke of Jacob as YHWH's beloved nonetheless. Note the allusion, in another oracle a few verses after the one quoted above, to brothers, sons of the same father, who act deceitfully toward one another:

> Have we not all one Father? Did not one God create us? Why does each of us act with bad faith toward his brother, profaning the covenant of your fathers? (Mal 2:10)[2]

And in chapter 3 is to be heard a variant of the pun on Jacob's name of Genesis 27 and Jeremiah 9:

> [6]For I am the LORD—I have not changed; and you are the children of Jacob [ya'ăqōb]—You have not ceased to be. [7]From the very days of your fathers you have turned away from My laws and have not observed them. Turn back to Me, and I will turn back to you—said the LORD of Hosts. But you ask, "How shall we turn back?" [8]Ought man to defraud [hăyiqba'] God? Yet you are defrauding [qōbě'îm] Me. And you ask, "How have we been defrauding You [qěba'ănûkā]?" In tithe and contribution. [9]You are suffering under a curse, yet you go on defrauding [qōbě'îm] Me—the whole nation of you. (Mal 3:6–9).

The use of the rare verb qāba' four times in Mal 3:8–9—it occurs in only one other verse in the entire Bible (Prov 22:23)—strongly suggests a pun on the name Jacob (ya'ăqōb) in v 6. The root of the verb is comprised of the same three consonants as appear in the root of Jacob's name and in the verb translated as "supplant" in Gen 27:36 and as "take advantage" in Jer 9:3, of which the verb in Mal 3:6–8 is probably but a variant. Informed by the tradition about Jacob's defrauding his brother, Malachi calls upon "the children of Jacob" to return to God and his laws, specifically the laws about sacred donations. The opening oracle of the book makes clear, however, that the return for which the prophet calls will not restore the *status quo ante:* Jacob will still be "loved" and Esau "hated," even after the wrongs deplored in 3:8 have been righted. And in this, Malachi and Genesis, whatever the chronological relationship between them, agree, for the bitter weeping of Esau in Gen 27:34,38 is all the more poignant when one considers that even the reconciliation of the twin brothers years later in no way reverses Jacob's assumption, and Esau's dispossession, of the status of Isaac's first-born son. For when, after Jacob's long exile, the twins next meet, and Jacob in self-effacement and the hope of reconciliation offers Esau a gift that is called a "blessing" (*birkātî*), he never returns the birthright (*běkōrâ*) (Gen 33:10–11; cf. 27:36). Jacob remains the beloved son for life, and the House of Jacob, we are given to understand, shall have that status for all time.

As the first-born and beloved son, Jacob meets humiliation before he comes to know the exaltation associated with his special status. Esau, condemned to serve his brother just as the oracle to their mother predicted (Gen 27:40; 25:23), resolves to even the score: "Let but the mourning period of my father come, and I will kill my brother Jacob." Fearing for her beloved son's life, Rebekah sends Jacob to live with her brother Laban until Esau's fratricidal rage shall subside (27:41–45). And so Jacob, heir to the Abrahamic blessing, finds himself more like his grandfather than he wished. For, just as Abraham is no sooner promised the land of Canaan than he is forced into exile in Egypt (Genesis 12), so is Jacob no sooner blessed with dominance over his brother and heirship to his father than he is forced into exile in Paddan-aram by fear of the vengeance of the very brother he is to dominate. No sooner is the promise made than it is sorely tested; no sooner is exaltation conferred upon the beloved son than his humiliation begins.

In light of the great patriarchal promise to which Jacob has now become heir, his exile to his mother's homeland is a humiliation of the first order. For central to that promise is the assignment of the land of Canaan (Gen 12:7; 26:3). The land that his father, Isaac, was explicitly forbidden to leave (26:2) Jacob is now compelled to flee: his very acquisition of heirship has forced him to break with the testator, his father. Or, to put it differently, the preference of the divine father for Jacob over Esau has deprived the human father of his second and unfavored son and forced that son, the beloved of God, onto a journey that seems anything but a fulfillment of the promise he has exacted by guile. The afflictions of that journey can be interpreted as punishment for his act of fraud, and so they in part are. But they can also be interpreted as a result of the transference of paternity from the human father, whose preference has now been irrevocably denied, to the divine father, whose mysterious plans for the trickster have only begun to unfold. Isaac and Rebekah do not lose Jacob as she feared (27:44), that is, through his death at the hands of a furious Esau. But they do lose him to a lengthy exile, during which, so far as we know, he is incommunicado, and from which he will return to see his father but never again, apparently, his loving mother (35:27–29). Jacob's exile in Paddan-aram substitutes for death at the hands of Esau and follows from his designation by God as the beloved son—a designation that, paradoxically, entails the gift of the land he now flees. The homology of death and exile that is to be detected in the story of Jacob is the inverse of the frequent biblical association of vitality with residence in Canaan. To go into exile is to enter into a diminished vitality and to risk death itself:

> [37] ... You shall not be able to stand your ground before your enemies, [38] but shall perish among the nations; and the land of your enemies shall consume you. (Lev 26:37–38)

The afflictions that Jacob suffers in exile re-present the process of his acquiring the status of the first-born, only in an inverted form: they are the humiliations that are inseparable from his exaltation. In love with the younger sister, Rachel, Jacob learns that deceit can cut both ways, for it is the older daughter Leah whom Laban craftily substitutes on the wedding night. The explanation to a stunned Jacob—"It is not the practice in our place to marry off the younger before the older" (Gen 29:26)—drives home in the most painful way the sanctity of primogeniture, the very principle that Jacob, by deceiving his father Isaac on his deathbed, circumvented. Laban has played Jacob to Jacob, except that the uncle's deceit upholds the very principle that the nephew's violated. To win Rachel, Jacob has worked for seven years, a term suggestive of slavery (as in Exod 21:2–6) and gotten Leah whom he has never wanted; now he must work another seven to receive the bride of his desire whom custom has denied him. He of whom it was predicted that "the older shall serve the younger" (Gen 25:23) now serves an extra term so as to win the younger daughter. He who received the blessing of mastery—"Be master over your brothers, / And let your mother's sons bow to you" (27:29)—now finds himself a servant to his mother's brother. The trickster has been tricked, the younger has been forced to work for the older, the master has been reduced to servitude: exaltation has become humiliation.

It cannot be underscored enough that the man of whom this story is told is the eponymous ancestor of the nation, Jacob/Israel. At its deepest level the Jacob narrative is more than biography: it is the national history and speaks, therefore, of the self-conception of the people Israel and not merely of the pranks of the trickster from whom they are descended. In its most important features, the pattern of Jacob's life will be reproduced in the story of his son Joseph—another younger son beloved of his parent, exalted above his brothers, and condemned to exile and slavery because of their fratricidal jealousy.[3] The immediate link between the two successive stories of exaltation and humiliation is Jacob's doing what the Deuteronomic law of the birthright would come to forbid, "treat[ing] as first-born the son of the loved [wife] in disregard of the son of the unloved one who is older" (Deut 15:16), that is, favoring Rachel's

"the inegalitarian character of the
6d of the chosen people."

The Loved and the Unloved   67

son Joseph. But, as we shall see in chapter 13, this favoritism, no less than Rebekah's, reflects God's own preference and testifies anew to the inegalitarian character of the God of the chosen people.

The striking parallels between the stories of Jacob and Joseph are thus, at the profound level, owing to their common refraction of the foundational story of the people Israel. Like much in Genesis, these two narrative cycles adumbrate the great national epic in which the people of God, "Israel . . . My first-born son" (Exod 4:22), leaves the promised land in extremis, endures enslavement and attempted genocide in Egypt, and yet, because of the mysterious grace of God, marches out triumphantly. The story of the humiliation and exaltation of the beloved son reverberates throughout the Bible because it is the story of the people about whom and to whom it is told. It is the story of Israel the beloved son, the first-born of God.

In the older sources, the YHWHistic (J) and the Elohistic (E), Jacob seems never to have seen his father alive again after his fateful—nay, providential—deception. In the Priestly narrative (P), Jacob returns just as Isaac, about to die when he left, finally passes on:

> [27]And Jacob came to his father Isaac at Mamre, at Kiriath-arba—now Hebron—where Abraham and Isaac had sojourned. [28]Isaac was a hundred and eighty years old [29]when he breathed his last and died. Isaac was gathered to his kin in ripe old age; and he was buried by his sons Esau and Jacob. (Gen 35:27–29)[4]

The reunion is narrated in the spare, matter-of-fact style that characterizes the Priestly source. Its lack of emotion, especially relative to the parallel reunion of Jacob and Joseph (Gen 46:28–30 [J]), however, is surely owing to more than the stylistic proclivities of the respective documentary sources. For the son with whom Isaac is reunited is not, as was Joseph, "the child of his old age" whom he most loved (37:3), but rather the son whom Rebekah (and God) preferred over his own favorite, Esau. But the Priestly notice of the death of Isaac is moving, nonetheless, for it shows that the divine preference, though never reversed, need not destroy the family after all. Jacob and Esau have finally been reconciled—an astonishing turn when one considers the circumstances of their estrangement. In the moment of their first encounter after so many years, Jacob, bearer of a reiterated promise that Esau would serve him (25:23; 27:29, 37), pointedly and repeatedly refers to himself as Esau's "servant" and to Esau as his own "master" (33:5, 8, 13, 14, 15). Indeed, as we have occasion to note, when he offers his brother a "present"—tribute with which to secure favor—he terms it his "blessing" (birkātî, v 11), as if offering to make restitution for the cause of the estrangement. Esau, for his part, is no longer the crude and vengeful man Jacob escaped. He is now a person of consummate graciousness. "I have enough, my brother," he tells Jacob; "let what you have remain yours" (v 9)[5]. Without ever giving up the birthright he assumed by deception, Jacob forgoes the hegemony it entails. Without reinstatement as the first-born, Esau forgoes the vengeance that nearly destroyed the family. The act of choosing, God and Rebekah's special preference for Jacob over Esau, has not proven fatal after all; at long last all involved seem able to accept it. The son beloved of God, the son threatened with fratricide and condemned to exile and harsh servitude, has not been lost. If he has undergone a symbolic death, as I believe he has in these narratives, the death is only symbolic, and from it he returns a better man, ready to assume the Patriarchal role with which he was blessed just before his flight for his life to Paddan-aram. God's exaltation of Jacob over Esau nearly destroys the chosen family; it condemns Jacob, Rebekah, and probably Isaac as well to untold misery. Yet the family survives, and when we last see Isaac, he is once more with his two sons, who are not fighting now but cooperating—in the burial of their father. The day when Esau dreamt of killing his brother during the mourning period for their father (27:41) is long forgotten. The twins who struggled with each other even in their mother's womb are now, like their father, at peace.

Chapter Nine
Favor and Fratricide

The story of Jacob and Esau testifies to a stage in the history of Israelite law and theology in which the status of the first-born son was a matter of great importance but less fixity. The importance is seen in the way in which God's greater love for Jacob is realized—through Jacob's assumption of the status of Isaac's *bĕkôr*. To say that YHWH favored and chose the younger son over the older is too simple. Rather, he reversed the order of the two and assigned the one he favored the status of the first-born. That such a reversal could take place at all, violating, as it does, the spirit (though not the letter) of Deut 21:15–17, shows that this was not yet a fixed status, but one that the father could still assign. Another way of saying this is that in Gen 27:1–45, two important items in Israelite culture collide, *bĕkōrâ* and *bĕrākâ*, the birthright and the blessing (see v 36), and the one that yields is the *bĕkōrâ*, the status of the first-born son, which Isaac now unwittingly but irreversibly transfers to the younger of the two brothers. From now on, the descendants of Esau, the Edomites, will be seen as collateral members of the family of Abraham. The trunk of the chosen family continues through Jacob and his descendants, the Israelites, or, as they came later to be called, the Jews.

That the God of Israel tends to favor the late-born over the first-born sons is a point of venerable antiquity among Christian theologians. In those circles, the observation reflects the anxiety of the self-designated "new Israel," the Church, relative to the "old Israel" it claims to supersede, that is, the Jewish people. In the Epistle to the Galatians, one of the earlier documents in what was to become the New Testament, the apostle Paul was already claiming the status of Isaac for the community of the gospel and assigning the status of Ishmael to the community of the Torah (Gal 4:21–5:1; cf. Rom 9:6–9).[1] And in what is probably his last letter, the Epistle to the Romans, he points out that God's love for Jacob and hatred for Esau in Mal 1:2–3 shows that God's favor is unrelated to the character of the recipient, a matter, that is, of grace as opposed to works, which is for Paul another way of saying gospel and not Torah (Rom 9:10–13). That the apostle to the gentiles came to think that the grace of the choosing God still attached itself in some measure to Israel according to the flesh (vv 4–5) qualifies but does not nullify the astonishing reversal of the positions of Jew and gentile that he helped bring about. Without such precedents as the partial dispossession of Ishmael by Isaac and of Esau by Jacob in the Hebrew Bible—the only Bible he knew—Paul and the Church's partial dispossession of the Jews could hardly have been conceived. Christian supersessionism is much indebted to the narrative dynamics of the Jewish foundational story and, ironically, cannot be grasped apart from the story it claims to supersede.

Divine favoritism toward late-born sons is attested too many times in the Hebrew Bible to be a mere coincidence. The list of non-first-borns who attain special eminence reads like a roster of the great names of early Israel: Isaac, Jacob, Levi, Judah, Joseph, Ephraim, Moses, Eleazar, Ithamar, Gideon, David, Solomon. It is surely noteworthy that both the priestly and the royal dynasties of the southern kingdom trace their lineage through late-born sons— Eleazar, Ithamar, and ultimately Levi for the priesthood; Solomon, David, and ultimately Judah for the royalty. But just here is to be detected the critical difference between the principle as it appears in the Hebrew Bible and as it appears in Pauline and much later Christian theology. For in the Hebrew Bible, in the main, the substitution of a younger for an older son results in a shift in the lines of descent, away from Reuben, Jacob's first-born, for example, and onto Judah and Joseph, or away from Manasseh, Joseph's first-born, and onto Ephraim, ancestor of the tribe that becomes the more important, away from Esau and onto Jacob, or, ultimately for the Patriarchal line, away from Ishmael and onto Isaac. The point is not to replace birth with faith, and the natural family with a sodality of pneumatics, as in Paul's proto-gnostic theology. In point of fact, most of these substitutions are *genealogical* through and through: their function is to justify the privileged bloodlines. But the justification usually proceeds by reference to a deliberate and surprising act of choosing on God's part. In this way are upheld both the preeminence of the chosen bloodline and the freedom and authority of God.

To some, these unpredictable acts of choosing will be best described as grace and celebrated as proof of the generosity of God. This is the dominant view within both Judaism and Christianity, though Christianity has generally been more comfortable than Judaism with the utter unpredictability of the choices, that is, with the irrelevance of human worthiness to the intention of God. To others, these unpredictable acts of choosing will be best described as arbitrariness and condemned as unworthy of a God of justice. This view, though rejected by the dominant trends in the Jewish and the Christian traditions, is to be detected behind some biblical narratives. That the justice of the God who chooses is broached at all in the Hebrew Bible is eloquent testimony to the challenge that the theology under discussion posed, the challenge of accepting chosenness as a category of ultimate theological meaning.

The difficulty of accepting the God who makes these mysterious choices appears early in the Bible, in fact as early as the time of the world's first two brothers:

¹Now the man knew his wife Eve, and she conceived and bore Cain [*qayin*] saying, "I have gained [*qānîtî*] a male child with the help of the LORD." ²She then bore his brother Abel. Abel became a keeper of sheep, and Cain became a tiller of the soil. ³In the course of time, Cain brought an offering to the LORD from the fruit of the soil; ⁴and Abel, for his part, brought the choicest of the firstlings of his flock along with their fat. The LORD looked with favor on Abel and his offering, ⁵but He did not look with favor on Cain and his offering. Cain was much distressed and his face fell. ⁶And the LORD said to Cain,

"Why are you distressed,
And why is your face fallen?
⁷Surely, if you do right,
There is uplift.
But if you do not do right
Sin couches at the door;
Its urge is toward you,
Yet you can be its master."

⁸Cain said to his brother Abel, "Come, let us go into the field," and when they were in the field, Cain set upon his brother Abel and killed him. (Gen 4:1–8)²

The cause of YHWH's rejection of Cain's offering has put commentators into a quandary for millennia. Why should the first sacrifice ever brought have been deemed unacceptable? An ancient rabbinic interpretation that comes to us without its author's name finds the answer in the variant ways that Cain's and Abel's offerings are phrased. Cain's "fruit of the soil" (v 3) is here glossed as "refuse," and a parable is made of "a bad sharecropper [on a royal estate] who eats the first fruits and honors the king with the last fruits" (*Gen. Rab.* 22:5). The terminology of Abel's offering—"the choicest of the firstlings of his flock along with the fat" (v 4)—offers some support for this explanation of the variant receptions of the two sacrifices. The commentator Abraham ibn Ezra (d. 1167) points out that the absence of similar terminology in the account of Cain's sacrifice creates a presumption that the older brother failed to bring the first fruits.[3] This, in turn, indicates an inferior measure of devotion. As a contemporary commentator puts it, "Cain's purpose was noble, but his act was not ungrudging and openhearted."[4]

The chief deficiency of this line of interpretation is that it rests on but two words in the Hebrew, "the choicest of the firstlings" and "along with their fat" (v 3). If the point were to moralize about the relative degrees of devotion of the two brothers, the text could have dwelt on this, for the Hebrew Bible is not inhibited about pointing out the violation that results in a calamity and even using the calamity as an object lesson for future generations.[5] Indeed, given the biblical propensity for finding the basis of later practices in episodes involving early figures,[6] the story of Cain and Abel ought to have proven a heaven-sent etiology for the sacrifice of the first fruits and the first-born of the flock. Yet such was not to be the case. And if we are to rationalize the rejection of Cain's offering and the acceptance of Abel's by reference to a word or two in the text and on the basis of an argument from silence, we could just as easily rationalize the reverse result, for whereas Cain brought his sacrifice "to the LORD" (v 3), Abel, on this sort of microscopic over-reading, did not. I have the suspicion that if Cain's sacrifice had been accepted but Abel's rejected, commentators into our own time would be telling us that Cain acted out of religious devotion, but Abel out of mere imitation of his older brother, and on the basis of the same text (4:1–4a) that is now often said to testify to Abel's moral superiority to the hapless Cain. The truth is that the sentence structure of vv 3–4a stresses not the substance of the two offerings, but the fact that the two brothers each brought something. The words rendered "and Abel, for his part, brought" (wĕhebel hēbîʾ gam-hûʾ) could more accurately, if less fluently, be rendered, "and Abel brought—even he" or "and Abel brought—he also." What the sentence in vv 3–4a underscores is Abel's following Cain's precedent, and not the variation in the respective sacrifices, as the moralizing interpretation would suggest.

Some modern scholars have proposed a different rationale for the success of Abel's offering and the failure of Cain's. They build their case upon the contrast between the occupations of the two brothers that the text is at pains to point out in v 2b: "Abel became a keeper of sheep, and Cain became a tiller of the soil." In this verse, the order of the names has been reversed; the younger son has taken priority, perhaps in an ominous foreshadowing of most of the rest of the Book of Genesis, as Isaac, Jacob, Joseph, and Ephraim move to the fore in place of Ishmael, Esau, Reuben, and Manasseh, respectively.

In the case of the primordial brothers, the preference for the younger is said to be founded upon an ancient Israelite identification with pastoral nomadism at the expense of cereal agriculture.[7] Abel the shepherd is thus more acceptable to YHWH than Cain the farmer, and this is manifest in the divine response to the two offerings, which are, in turn, characteristic of the two occupations.

The major problem with this theory is that the antipathy of shepherds and farmers on which it is based is more in the minds of the modern scholars who adhere to it than in the text of Genesis 4 or the culture of biblical Israel. The notice about the occupations of Abel and Cain in v 2 is not necessarily connected to the story of their sacrifices. The early chapters of Genesis exhibit many such notices, without any indication that some professions are preferred or that these notices provide the key to interpreting any larger narratives. Later in the same chapter, for example, Cain will be identified as the builder of the first city (v 17), and his descendant Jabal will be called "the ancestor of those who dwell in tents and amidst herds" (shades of Abel!), while Jabal's brother Jubal will be identified as "the ancestor of all who play the lyre and the pipe," and their half brother Tubal-cain will be said to have "forged all implements of copper and iron" (vv 20–22). And if the Hebrew Bible truly manifests an antipathy to agriculture, it is passing strange that it conceives the primordial paradise as a garden that the first man is bidden to till and to tend (2:15). It is no less strange that so many blessings throughout the Hebrew Bible should involve abundance of crop and not just fertility of flock.[8] In fact, it has increasingly been recognized by scholars of ancient Near Eastern societies that the dichotomy of pastoral nomad and agriculturalist is simplistic to the point of inaccuracy. Research conducted over the past three decades has shown that the putative nomads of the Romantic imagination are, in fact, in a constant symbiotic relationship with permanent settlements and rarely at odds with them. This sort of arrangement, which M. B. Rowton dubbed "enclosed nomadism," results "in a 'dimorphic' socio-political system . . . in which the basic dichotomy was not between nomadic and sedentary peoples, but rather between the 'autonomous tribal chiefdom,' composed of both pastoralists and villages, and the sovereign state dominated by powerful urban centers."[9] In light of this phenomenon of dimorphism, it is scarcely a source of wonderment that Genesis 4 depicts Cain and Abel as living together and participating in a common religious ceremony. It *is* a source of wonderment, however, that some scholars should see their occupations as the source of God's differentiated response to their offerings.

Denying that YHWH was thought to favor pastoralists over agriculturalists does not necessarily entail denying that animal sacrifices were deemed more precious than vegetable offerings. Such does indeed seem to be the case.

"the origin of inequality"

Leviticus 5, for example, specifies that, under conditions that need not detain us here, a person is obligated to bring a female from the flock as a sin offering. If he cannot afford a sheep or goat, then he may substitute two turtledoves or two pigeons—obviously a less impressive offering. Finally, if he lacks the means even to acquire the two birds, then he may bring a tenth of an ephah of flour (vv 6–13). Given these rankings, it is beyond doubt that Abel and not Cain brought the choicer sacrifice. What this does not answer, however, is the question at point: why does YHWH look with favor on Abel's offering but not Cain's? For if this God is not by nature the author of mysterious choices, then he could just as easily have accepted *both* sacrifices, just as in theory Abraham could have willed his estate equally to both Ishmael and Isaac, and Isaac could have blessed Jacob and Esau with benedictions of equal worth. Indeed, given the presence in ancient Israelite worship of *both* animal and vegetable offering, this acceptance of the sacrifice of each primordial brother is just what we should expect—even if one offering elicited more favor than the other. What actually happens is quite different: Cain's sacrifice is rejected altogether, and Abel loses his life precisely because he is the son in whom God found favor. Abel's exaltation at the altar brings about his humiliation in the field.

The misguided quest for the sin of Cain that supposedly prevented the acceptance of his offering deflects attention from the true focus of the story as narrated: the inability of Cain to suffer the exaltation of the younger brother at his own expense. Claus Westermann's observation is illuminating:

> The point of departure is equality; both have the means of subsistence in the division of labor. Both recognize the giver in their gifts and therefore both are linked with the power which is the source of blessing. Now inequality enters in; it has its origin in the regard of God. Blessing or its absence depends on the regard of God. It is a misunderstanding in the real meaning to look for the reason for the inequality of God's regard. The narrator wants to say that in the last analysis there is something inexplicable in the origin of this inequality.[10]

The burden of God's warning to Cain in Gen 4:6–7 is this: the resentment that this inequality provokes need not prove fatal; sin, crouching beast-like at the door, need not overwhelm; the brother whose offering has not been regarded can still live in dignity—if only he masters the urge to even the score, that is, to pursue equality where God has acted according to the opposite principle, with divine inequality. The warning locates the source of the crime in the criminal himself: it is not God's favoring Abel that will bring about the murder, but rather Cain's inability to accept a God who authors these mysterious and inequitable acts of choosing. What Cain cannot bear is a world in which distributive justice is not the highest principle and not every inequity is an iniquity.   NB

The closest biblical analogy to Cain's rage is the reaction of another older brother who, this time also not without justice, feels himself wronged—the reaction of Esau to Jacob's usurpation of both the blessing and the birthright: "Let but the mourning period for my father come, and I will kill my brother Jacob" (Gen 27:41). What prevents the murder of Jacob and paves the way for the unexpected reconciliation two decades later is the presence of mind of their mother, Rebekah, who sends her—and God's—beloved son away before Esau's fratricidal resentment can attain its goal. But Eve, alas, is no Rebekah, and once Abel, the favored son, is slain, it is Cain who is sent away, forbidden to till the soil that absorbed his brother's innocent blood and condemned to be "a ceaseless wanderer on earth" (4:11–12). In this, he foreshadows still another older brother dispossessed by providence itself, Ishmael, whose compensatory blessing will make him "a wild ass of a man; / His hand against everyone" (16:12) and who later "dwelt in the wilderness and became a bowman" (21:20).[11] Unlike Esau and Ishmael, however, Cain receives no compensatory blessing. The hard reality of God's regard for his brother's offering and not for his is in no way mitigated: it must simply be accepted. But Cain does learn that the arbitrariness of God has its positive side, that it can be realized as grace and not only as caprice. For whereas his condemnation to wander could easily have led to his death (4:14)—as the justice of "life for life" requires (Exod 21:23; Lev 24:17–18; Deut 19:21)—God promises him that "if anyone kills Cain, sevenfold vengeance shall be taken on him" (Gen 4:15). This, too, is a kind of divine inequality: the symmetry of "life for life" yields to the gracious asymmetry of exile as the penalty for murder. Cain, the primordial first-born who is not the beloved son, will, like the beloved sons Jacob and Joseph, endure an exile that substitutes for death, and he, too, survives, despite the atrocity he has committed. Like them, he survives by the grace of God—ironically, the very principle that evoked his murderous impulse in the first place.

Abel, for his part, seems at first glance to break decisively with the paradigm of the beloved son. Though at the altar he is favored above his older brother, he is not the first-born of his mother, as are Isaac and Joseph, but, like Jacob and Ephraim, the second of two boys. Unlike Jacob, however, and perhaps Ephraim as well (Gen 48:17–20), Abel never secures for himself the status of the first-born son that nature has denied him. His is not a story of the beloved son who, by God's love and his mother's, overcomes the limitations imposed by nature. Nor is his the story of the beloved son whose death is averted by the intervention of an angel and the sudden, providential appearance of a ram caught by its horns in a thicket (22:11–13). Abel's, rather, is the only story in Genesis that we have considered to which the term "tragic" seems fitting—the story of the son favored by God whose exaltation lasts but a moment and whose humiliation is the ultimate and unending one of death without descendants. For exaltation above his brother, which he never sought, he pays with his life, and this exaltation, unlike that of Isaac, Jacob, Joseph, and Ephraim, privileges no bloodline even if it does testify, like theirs, to the freedom and authority of God. To an extent that exceeds the others, the story of the first beloved son of Genesis shows the horrific price that the favor of God entails.

That Abel should have died a tragic death, a death neither avenged nor reversed, stuck in the craw of the ongoing Jewish and Christian traditions. How could the God of justice have failed to counteract an injustice of such magnitude? And how could the God of redemption have left Abel's worthy and beatified life unredeemed from the cold-blooded murder that brought it to its ignominious end? It is in light of the insult to the faith of Israel that Abel's death represents that we must understand the late traditions that give the victim of the first murder an especially exalted station in the upper realm. In the Testament of Abraham, for example, the Patriarch, translated to heaven, witnesses this scene there:

> [4]And between the two gates there stood a terrifying throne with the appearance of terrifying crystal, flashing like fire. [5]And upon it sat a wondrous man, bright as the sun, like unto a son of God. [6]Before him stood a table like crystal, all of gold and byssus. [7]On the table lay a book whose thickness was six cubits, while its breadth was ten cubits. [8]On its right and on its left stood two angels holding papyrus and ink and pen. [9]In front of the table sat a light-bearing angel, holding a balance in his hand . . .

> [15]And Abraham asked the Commander-in-chief Michael, "What are these things which we see?" And the Commander-in-chief said, "These things which you see, pious Abraham, are judgment and recompense."

> [1]And Abraham said, "My lord Commander-in-chief, who is this all-wondrous judge? . . . " [2]The Commander-in-chief said, "Do you see, all-pious Abraham, the frightful man who is seated on the throne? This is the son of Adam, the first-formed, who is called Abel, whom Cain the wicked killed. [3]And he sits here to judge the entire creation, examining both right-

eous and sinners. For God said, 'I do not judge you, but every man is judged by man.' " (Testament of Abraham A 12:4–9, 15; 13:1–3)[12]

Here, in this Jewish text of late Hellenistic or Roman times, the humiliation with which Abel's life seems to end in Genesis 4 is reversed: the innocent victim has been exalted into the position of judge over all creation. In a scene more suggestive of the New Testament than coincidence allows,[13] the martyred Abel, "like unto a son of God," now dispenses justice in his divine father's universal kingdom.

A somewhat similar connection between Abel's treatment at the hand of Cain and his preciousness in the sight of God was later drawn in rabbinic midrash:

> Rabbi Yehudah son of Rabbi Simon said in the name of Rabbi Yosé son of Rabbi Nehorai: The Holy One (blessed be he) always exacts vengeance for the persecuted from those who persecute them. You can know that this is the case from Abel, who was persecuted by Cain and the Holy One (blessed be he) chose Abel, as it is said, "The Lord paid heed to Abel and his offering" [Gen 4:4] (*Lev. Rab.* 27:5).

Rabbi Yosé's observation assumes a midrash in which God's preference for Abel does not precede Cain's mistreatment of him, as in the biblical text, but follows it: it is not out of jealousy of the younger brother's favor that Cain persecutes Abel, at least initially. The favor, rather, is a *consequence* of the persecution: Abel's chosenness depends upon his antecedent suffering. The chosenness has become the manifestation of divine justice, reversing the relative status of persecutor and victim. The perspicacious reader will not have missed, however, that even in this midrashic retelling, the sign of Abel's chosenness—God's paying heed to his sacrifice—is at the same time the occasion for Cain's most extreme persecution of his innocent sibling, the murder that is the climax of the story of the primal brothers. For this, too, God exacts vengeance, by exiling Cain. But this does not detract from the intimate association—drawn in different ways by Genesis, the Testament of Abraham, and rabbinic midrash—between Abel's status as the preferred son and his violent death.

The idea that the death of Abel was not a tragedy, that is, an event utterly unredeemed, was not an innovation of the post-biblical Judaism in which the Testament of Abraham and Rabbi Yosé's midrash are to be situated. For Genesis itself evinces an anxiety lest the human family take its descent solely from the primal murderer Cain:

Adam knew his wife again, and she bore a son and named him Seth [šēt],
meaning "God has provided [šāt] me with another offspring in place of
Abel, for Cain slew him." (Gen 4:25)[14]

In Eve's mind, the birth of Seth is a providential compensation for the loss
of Abel: the new boy's very name testifies that its bearer is God's substitute
for the lost son. To us, to be sure, the birth of a third son hardly seems to
reverse the murder of the second at the hands of the first. But this is owing
to the immense cultural divide that separates us from ancient Israel. The
arrival of Seth is a salvific event for Adam and Eve not least because it promises
them the support in old age that became impossible when Abel died and Cain
was sentenced to become "a ceaseless wanderer on earth." Having lived
through the gruesome fate that Rebekah only dreaded—that because of the
older brother's fratricidal jealousy, she would "lose . . . both [sons] in one day"
(27:45)—Eve is understandably theological in her reaction to the birth of a
third son. That Seth is a different individual from Abel and his birth therefore
not in every sense a reversal of the latter's murder is likely to be a point of
more moment to us than to an ancient Israelite. For the culture that produced
the Hebrew Bible was not so individualistic as to hold that the loss of one
person can be made good only through the return of that same individual.
Thus, for example, when "the LORD blessed the latter years of Job's life more
than the former," he gave him seven sons and three daughters—the same
number that he had at the beginning of the tale, before he lost them all and
his property as well. The *greater* blessing lies in his being given at the end
twice the livestock as he had at first (Job 42:12–13; 1:2–3). Clearly, we are to
understand that Job has been restored and then some, though the latter children are not the former ones resurrected, who are, in fact, lost forever. Similarly, though Seth is not Abel, he does, it seems to me, stand "in place of"
(*taḥat*) the dead son in a more profound sense than is comprehended merely
in his being the younger brother of Cain in a family of two male offspring.
Within the limits of ancient Israelite culture before it had developed the idea
of resurrection, Seth is Abel redivivus, the slain son restored to his parents.
His birth is proof that the loss of the son favored by God's inscrutable grace
is not final. The death of the beloved son, even when it is not averted, can
still be reversed.

The notice of the birth of Seth is soon followed by a long and detailed
genealogy in the style that scholars have long associated with the Priestly
source (P) of the Pentateuch (Genesis 5). The difference between this genealogy of the line of Seth and the preceding genealogy of the Cainites (4:17–
26) is patent. Here, for example, it is not Eve but Adam who names the boy

(5:3), in conformity with P's view as opposed to that of the YHWHist (J), in whose narratives it is the mother who tends to do the naming.[15] It is likely, however, that the two genealogies are not independent but, instead, derive from a common tradition. For, even though the first traces the line of Cain and the second the line of Seth, the two share certain names, those of Enoch (4:17–18; 5:18–19) and Lamech (4:19–24; 5:25–31), both names unattested elsewhere in the Hebrew Bible. It is also worthy of notice that two names of the same infrequency from the first list sound suspiciously like names that appear in the second—Mehujael (4:18) and Mahalalel (5:12–13), Methusael (4:18) and Methuselah (5:21–22, 25–27). At least in the case of the identical names, Enoch and Lamech, it seems exceedingly improbable that we are to believe that there were thought to be *two* primeval figures with each of these names. More likely, we have in the J and the P genealogies under discussion two variant but related accounts of the earliest generations of the human race. That the second of them, the P genealogy in Genesis 5, is the later depends on more than the universal consensus among biblical critics as to the relative chronologies of J and P. Note that J's Lamech boasts, using good biblical parallelism, "If Cain is avenged sevenfold, / Then Lamech seventy-sevenfold" (4:24), and P's Lamech lives to the unusual age of 777 years (5:31). The likelihood is that the lifespan of P's Lamech, son of Methusaleh, is derived midrashically from the speech of J's Lamech, son of Methusael. Carrying this logic one step further, we can reasonably conclude that P identified the two figures, or, to be more precise, intended his genealogy to *replace* J's, not to stand beside it, as it now does in the redacted Pentateuch. P, in other words, tried to supplant the Cainite with a Sethite genealogy.

The regularity of P's genealogy in Genesis 5—who begot whom, at what age, how long he lived afterward, and at what age he died—is interrupted by speech in only one verse. It is surely revealing that the speaker is also the only figure to speak in J's genealogy, Lamech:

> [28]When Lamech had lived 182 years, he begot a son. [29]And he named him Noah [*nōaḥ*], saying, "This one will provide us relief [*yĕnaḥămēnû*] from our work and from the toil ['*iṣṣĕbôn*] of our hands, out of the very soil [*hā'ădāmâ*] which the Lord placed under a curse." (Gen 5:28–29)

This folk-etymology of Noah's name harks back rather obviously to the words of YHWH to Adam after the grievous episode of the forbidden fruit:

> [17]Cursed be the ground [*hā'ădāmâ*] because of you;
> By toil ['*iṣṣābôn*] you shall eat of it
> All the days of your life.

[18]Thorns and thistles shall it sprout for you.
But your food shall be the grasses of the field;
[19]By the sweat of your brow
Shall you get bread to eat,
Until you return to the ground—
Far from it you were taken.
For dust you are,
And to dust you shall return. (Gen 3:17–19)

The notion that Noah provided compensation for the disobedience of Adam is probably based on the identification of Noah as the first viticulturalist and the first wine-maker (9:20–21): wine, so Lamech is represented to have thought, will provide relief from the labors of agriculture. In expressing Lamech's wish, P refers to a text that is not his own, for the curse of the ground is nearly universally recognized by critical scholars to be part of the YHWHistic creation story. Given the obvious and multiple affinities of 5:28–29 with 3:17–19, it is reasonable to suspect that the speech of Lamech in the P genealogy is actually a YHWHistic fragment that P has incorporated.[16] If this be so, then we have additional evidence that P's genealogy of the antediluvians is intended to supplant J's: P has transformed Noah's Cainite father into a Sethite. And the effect of this, indeed, the effect of the whole of Genesis 5, is to replace Cain with Seth as the second father of the human race. For if only Noah, his wife, his three sons and their wives survived the great deluge, and if Noah was a Sethite, then it is from Seth and not Cain that all humanity derives. If, as seems likely, there was once a J genealogy in which the Lamech who begot Noah was a Cainite, that genealogy has been lost, except for the speech of Lamech at the birth of Noah, and we now see the human race continued only through the lineage of Adam's third son, Seth, the descendants of his first son Cain presumably having perished in the flood.

Earlier, I had occasion to remark that the people Israel and its royal and priestly dynasties took their derivation not from first-born but from late-born sons. The people are descended not from Ishmael and Esau, but from Isaac and Jacob. The Judean royal family is derived from Jacob's fourth son, Judah, and from David and Solomon, neither of whom was his father's first-born. The hereditary priesthood is derived from Levi, Jacob's third son, and its Aaronite clan from Ithamar and Eleazar, and not their elder brothers, Nadab and Abihu. Now we see that the same principle pertains not only within the chosen family, but within universal humanity as well: humankind is descended not from Cain but from Seth, not from Adam and Eve's first son but from their third. And if Seth is to be seen as Abel redivivus, then I must amend my earlier remark that Abel died the most tragic of deaths, death without descendants, for through Seth the line of the dead brother does indeed come into existence.[17] In that case, Abel's humiliation in the field is not final and irreversible, for upon it follows his assumption of the exalted status of ancestor of all that live. God's favor at the altar leads to more than fratricide: it leads also to the survival of the human family through Cain's younger brother.

Chapter Ten

"Let me not look on as the child dies"

²There were ten generations from Adam to Noah, in order to make known how patient God is. For all those generations had been provoking him—until he brought upon them the waters of the flood.

³There were ten generations from Noah to Abraham, in order to make known how patient God is. For all those generations had been provoking him—until our father Abraham came and received the reward they all should have earned. (*'Abot* 5:2–3)

With this observation, the Mishnah discerns a decisive aspect of the interplay of genealogy and theology in the Priestly (P) account of the early history of the human race. The line of the primordial couple, Adam and Eve, continuing through their third son Seth, the stand-in for the slain Abel, culminates, in the tenth generation, in the figure of Noah, the man who alleviates the pain that the first father and mother inflicted upon their descendants (Genesis 5). Only the family of Noah survives the great flood, and from Noah to Abraham ten generations are rapidly and colorlessly reported, with none of the intervening figures ever addressed by God (11:10–27): "this is the line of Shem" (v 10), and the Shemites occupy center stage, marginalizing the descendants of the other two sons of Noah, Japheth, and Ham. Just as in the ten generations from Adam to Noah the sparse, factual style gives way only at the end, with Lamech's expression of hope as he names his son Noah (5:29), so in the ten generations from Noah to Abram (his name is not changed to Abraham until Genesis 17), the monotony of the genealogical data gives way only with the figure of Terah, father of Abram:

²⁶When Terah had lived 70 years, he begot Abram, Nahor, and Haran. ²⁷Now this is the line of Terah: Terah begot Abram, Nahor, and Haran; and Haran begot Lot. ²⁸Haran died in the lifetime of his father Terah, in his native land, Ur of the Chaldeans. ²⁹Abram and Nahor took to themselves wives, the name of Abram's wife being Sarai and that

of Nahor's wife Milcah, the daughter of Haran, the father of Milcah and Iscah. [30]Now Sarai was barren, she had no child.

[31]Terah took his son Abram, his grandson Lot the son of Haran, and his daughter-in-law Sarai, the wife of his son Abram, and they set out together from Ur of the Chaldeans, for the land of Canaan; but when they had come as far as Haran, they settled there. [32]The days of Terah came to 205 years; and Terah died in Haran. (Gen 11:26–32)

"Now Sarai was barren, she had no child." With this, the first reference to infertility in the Bible, P seems to be telling us that the Shemite lineage in which he is interested will continue through Nahor or his nephew Lot, but not through the hapless Abram, whose wife was barren. And when Terah uproots his family, mysteriously leaving Ur for Canaan, taking along Abram and Lot but not Nahor, the implication is that it is the grandson rather than the son through whom the special lineage will continue. Nature and circumstance seem to have conspired to designate Lot as the rightful heir to whatever blessing may lie at the end of the great trek from Mesopotamia to Canaan. That it is through the line of Haran, Lot's father and Terah's third son, that the special family is to continue is curiously reminiscent of the situation some twenty generations earlier, when, according to P, it was through Adam and Eve's third son Seth that the human race descended, and not through Cain or Abel. Indeed, P initially presents Abram in ways reminiscent of Cain and Abel—as a branch that does not survive, as the inscrutable process of selection focuses instead on a different lineage of the family of Terah. Nahor, left behind at Ur, and Abram, married to a barren woman, seem to resemble Japheth and Ham as well, the two sons who are passed over, as the mysterious specialness attaches itself, instead, to the other brother, Terah's son Haran and Noah's son Shem, respectively. That Haran is already dead and his line continued through Lot has some affinity with the situation in the primal family, when the line that leads from Adam to Noah goes through Seth, who is introduced as Abel redivivus, the stand-in for the favored son slain by the brother whom divine grace had passed over (4:25). In each case, it is, as it were, through the son who has died that the lineage will survive—or so it seems at the end of Genesis 11.

Against this conspiracy of nature and circumstance to favor Lot, God's first address to Abram seems an astonishing bolt out of the blue:

[1]The LORD said to Abram, "Go forth from your native land and from your father's house to the land that I will show you.

[2]I will make of you a great nation,
and I will bless you;
I will make your name great,
and you shall be a blessing.
[3]I will bless those who bless you
and curse him that curses you;
And all the families of the earth
Shall bless themselves by you." (Gen 12:1–3)

For Abram to be made into "a great nation" is, in the course of nature, impossible, at least if he is to remain in faithful monogamy with Sarai (her name will be changed to Sarah also only in Genesis 17). For the man cursed with a sterile wife to "be a blessing"—indeed, a universal byword of blessing— is equally preposterous. Yet "Abram went forth as the LORD had commanded him" (v 4), breaking with family and homeland to start—against all odds—a new family in a new and as yet undesignated land. When he arrives in Canaan, YHWH appears to him and, apparently as a reward for following the initial command, adds a third element to the promises of nation and blessing: "I will assign this land to your offspring" (v 7). "It cannot fail to strike one," Michael Fishbane observes, "that these three blessings are, in fact, a typological reversal of the primordial curses in Eden: directed against the earth, human genera- tivity and, human labour [3:16–19]."[1] Abram, the tenth generation from Noah, who, in turn, is tenth in descent from Adam, is, no less and, in fact, more than Noah himself, the realization of the hoped-for reversal of the curses on Adam. The man without a country will inherit a whole land; the man with a barren wife will have plenteous offspring; and the man who has cut himself off from kith and kin will be pronounced blessed by all the families of the earth.

The absurdity of the promise to Abram is underscored by its immediate derailment. No sooner does Abram enter the land and build an altar to the God whose command he has obeyed than he is forced by famine to descend into Egypt and, what is worse, to surrender his wife to the Pharaoh, lest he be put to death (Gen 12:10–15). The man to whom a land is promised is in exile; the man who is to beget a nation is without a wife; and the man whom God has promised that he will curse whoever curses him now takes extreme measures out of fear for his very life. And yet, just as our conviction seems confirmed that Abram has staked his life on an unrealizable, nay, absurd promise, we hear that "because of [Sarai], it went well with Abram," and he acquired a massive estate (v 16)—evidence that the blessing, however diverted, has not been cancelled. The irony of v 16 should not be missed: the patriarch-to-be found his barren wife, in this one situation, a boon and not a curse. The verse raises the possibility—if it really *is* a possibility—that Sarai's infertility will not prove fatal to the blessing of Abram also in the larger situation in which the couple find themselves. But how this will be is suggestively unclear. Will Sarai's infertility be circumvented? Or will it be overcome? The notice, ascribed to P in an otherwise YHWHistic narrative, that "Abram was seventy-five years old when he left Haran" and took Lot with him (vv 4b–5) casts yet another shadow on the blessing. For it suggests that Sarai may be not only childless but past the child-bearing years and that Abram's promised patriarchy may have to come about through adoption, either of the orphaned Lot or of some other individual among "the persons that they had acquired in Haran" and taken with them to Canaan (v 5). Or are there among these unspecified persons potential wives whose fertility will compensate for Sarai's barrenness and thus realize the promise that is made, in its initial statement (12:2–3), to Abram alone, and not to the couple together? If this be the case, then it is not Abram but Sarai who will endure the fate of Cain and Abel, having turned out to be the branch that does not develop, as the family of Abram survives and the promise comes true because of another woman.

This dizzying sequence of hopes and frustrations, blessings and curses, fulfillments and setbacks serves to underscore the magnitude of Abram's faith and obedience. His hopes are hopes against the backdrop of frustration; a seventy-five year old man is still childless. His blessings are blessings despite the curses; he has already lost the promised land, his wife, and almost his life. His fulfillments are fulfillments alongside the most painful of setbacks; having lost temporarily—or is it permanently?—land and wife, he yet amasses an enormous estate as a stranger in a strange land. The continual reiteration of the impediments heightens our awareness of Abram's seemingly irrational faith in the promise. The reports of the realizations of the promise suggest that faith of this magnitude may not be irrational after all. Were the impediments non-existent or nugatory, Abram would be remembered not as a man of faith and obedience, but as one with a fine instinct for rational calculation. It is between the poles of impediment and realization that the faith of Abram is situated. It affirms, trustingly and courageously, that the promise will be realized—not out of blindness to the enormity of the impediments, but with them in full view, as they surely are in this first part of the story of Abram.

Genesis 12 ends as it began, with a scene of Abram and Sarai departing for the promised land:

> [17] But the LORD afflicted Pharaoh and his household with mighty plagues on account of Sarai, the wife of Abram. [18] Pharaoh sent for Abram and

said, "What is this you have done to me! Why did you not tell me that she was your wife? [19]Why did you say, 'She is my sister,' so that I took her as my wife? Now, here is your wife; take her and begone!" [20]And Pharaoh put men in charge of him, and they sent him off with his wife and all that he possessed. (Gen 12:17–20)

As Fishbane points out, the language here is too suggestive of Israel's Exodus from Egypt in the next book of the Bible to allow for coincidence.[2] YHWH afflicts Pharaoh with plagues (cf. v 17 and Exod 11:1) until he sends Abram out (v 20; cf. Exod 5:1; 14:5) with the fortune he has amassed in Egypt (v 16; cf. Exod 12:35–36), a fortune that includes not only cattle but silver and gold as well (Gen 12:16; 13:2; cf. Exod 12:32, 35–36). And so in Genesis 12 we have in the life of Abram and Sarai a prefiguration of the Exodus: famine forces the couple into Egypt, where they settle, but with Sarai taken into Pharaoh's palace, as Moses will later be (v 15; Exod 2:10). It is possible that Sarai's diversion from Abram to Pharaoh prefigures the diversion of Israel, the first-born of YHWH (Exod 4:22), from his service to that of the Egyptian tyrant. It is much more than merely possible, however, that the fear Abram expresses to Sarai that the Egyptians "will kill me and let you live" (v 12) prefigures Pharaoh's order to the Hebrew midwives: "if it is a boy, kill him; if it is a girl, let her live" (Exod 1:15–16). And surely Fishbane is correct that YHWH's plaguing of Pharaoh and his household and the triumphant departure of Abram and Sarai prefigure the great national story that has given the Book of Exodus its English name.

With the exodus of Abram and Sarai amidst their new wealth, the promises of land and blessing seem once again to be on course to fulfillment. But the striking connections of Genesis 12 to the Book of Exodus only highlight Sarai's continuing affliction of barrenness. For language about Pharaoh's sending Abram off with his fortune after the plagues is connected most specifically in the Exodus story with the tenth plague, the death of the Egyptian first-born sons and the sparing of their Israelite counterparts through the blood of the paschal lamb (Exodus 12–13). A first-born son is precisely that which Abram and Sarai are missing, for the "offspring" to whom God has promised the land of Canaan (Gen 12:7) has yet to be conceived, and, according to P at least, Abram and presumably Sarai are advanced in years. This is particularly ominous in light of the overall tendency of the human lifespan to decrease over the generations of the Shemites. Shem, the patriarch of the line, lives six hundred years, whereas the Nahor who is the eighth generation and Abram's grandfather lives to a much shorter age of one hundred forty-eight (11:10–11, 24–25). Indeed, at seventy-five Abram is older than any of the other nine figures of the Shemite genealogy when they begot their first son, with the single exception of Shem himself, who begot Arpachshad at the enviable age of one hundred (11:10). All of the other figures did their first begetting between twenty-nine and thirty-five years of age, except for Abram's own father Terah, who did so at the ripe age of seventy (v 26), still younger than Abram when he left Haran for Canaan (12:4). Abram leaves Egypt as he came, childless. The God who was to spare the Israelites' first-born sons has yet to make good on his promise to make of Abram "a great nation" that will possess the land to which he, like the people Israel, returns after a painful and humiliating sojourn in Egypt. *That* clause of the promise remains unfulfilled and is, to all appearances and rational calculations, increasingly unlikely ever to be fulfilled.

The final separation of Abram from Lot takes place in the next chapter, Genesis 13. When Lot, whom Abram allows the first choice of land, elects the Jordan plain, oblivious to the approaching destruction of Sodom and Gomorrah, it seems that providence is once again actively arranging the fulfillment of the astonishing promise that set Abram on his way. "Abram remained in the land of Canaan, while Lot settled in the cities of the Plain, pitching his tents near Sodom" (v 12): now it is Abram who is in the promised land, and Lot who—by his own choice and perhaps the hidden hand of God—is outside it. That the nephew would not have a valid claim upon his childless uncle's allotment is vouchsafed in revelation:

> [14]And the LORD said to Abram, after Lot had parted from him, "Raise your eyes and look out from where you are, to the north and south, to the east and west, [15]for I give all the land that you see to you and your offspring forever. [16]I will make your offspring as the dust of the earth, so that if one can count the dust of the earth, then your offspring too can be counted. [17]Up, walk about the land, through its length and its breadth, for I give it to you." (Gen 13:14–17)

It has been observed that Abram's trek through the land in v 17 derives from an ancient legal institution by which title to real estate was conveyed by just such a walk as Abram here undertakes.[3] It is unlikely that what is mandated is only "a tour of inspection," as E. A. Speiser terms it,[4] for the walk culminates in the land grant with which the verse closes. The beneficiary is Abram himself (as was not the case in the first such text in the story, 12:7) and the as yet unconceived and, in the course of nature, inconceivable offspring, who, we are now told, will be innumerable (13:15–16). The promise of land and the promise of offspring being inseparable, the dramatic conveyance of the land renders the absence of an heir all the more poignant. Promised that he will be the father of "a great nation" as numerous as the dust of the earth (12:2; 13:16), Abram is still the father of nobody. And time is running out.

In Genesis 15, Abram finally voices the worry that has been on our minds from the time the great promise is first made to the childless man with the barren wife. Promised a great reward, Abram replies:

> ²"O Lord GOD, what can You give me, seeing that I shall die childless, and the one in charge of my household is Dammesek Eliezer!" ³Abram said further, "Since You have granted me no offspring, my steward will be my heir." ⁴The word of the LORD came to him in reply, "That one shall not be your heir; none but your very own issue shall be your heir." ⁵He took him outside and said, "Look toward heaven and count the stars, if you are able to count them." And He added, "So shall your offspring be." ⁶And because he put his trust in the LORD, He reckoned it to his merit. (Gen 15:2–6)

The mysterious and otherwise unmentioned Eliezer goes the way of Lot, as YHWH solemnly seals the great promise with a covenant, and in the midst of the covenant-making ceremony, announces to Abram in a trance that his offspring "shall be strangers in a land not theirs . . . enslaved and oppressed four hundred years," but, after YHWH "execute[s] judgment on the nation they shall serve," they shall return to Canaan "with great wealth" (vv 13–16). This curious oracle is not only the first mention in the Bible of the Exodus event. It is also an exquisitely artful interlacing of the story of Abram with that of his Israelite descendants. For their descent into the unspecified "land not theirs" recalls nothing so much as Abram and Sarai's descent into Egypt three chapters earlier. Their oppression and enslavement might suggest, as we have seen, Sarai's incorporation into the house of Pharaoh in order to save her husband's life (12:11–15), and their return "with great wealth" not only predicts the circumstances of the Exodus but also recapitulates Abram's own departure from Egypt (12:16; 13:1–2). In the oracle amidst the covenant-making ceremony (15:13–16), in sum, YHWH provides Abram with the interpretation of his own life. Abram has not only been living in anticipation of his unconceived and inconceivable progeny; he has also been proleptically living their life in his. In the prophecy that interrupts the covenant-making ceremony, Abram's experience is shown to have been itself akin to a prophetic sign-act. It is a biographical pre-enactment of the providential design for the whole people Israel.

To the reader familiar with the outlines of the larger Pentateuchal story, YHWH's pledge to "execute judgment on the nation they shall serve" (15:14) again adumbrates, this time more directly than before (12:17–20), YHWH's climactic judgment on Egypt, the death of the first-born sons and the deliverance of their Israelite counterparts through the blood of the Passover lamb. And here again, Abram's lack of a son assumes especial poignancy. For this is one item in the story of the nation that is, so far, unexampled in the biography of its Patriarch-designate, who remains childless and his wife barren, despite the solemn promise, by this point reiterated severalfold, that he shall father a great nation. It seems out of the question that the climax of the plague narratives, the gracious sparing of the first-born son and the substitution of the sheep, can ever be the climax of the story of Abram. That the promise of progeny has now been solemnized as a stipulation of covenant only underscores the absurdity of Abram's situation and renders more urgent a resolution of the anomaly. A way has to be found past the barrenness of Sarai highlighted in the introduction of Abram into the story of Genesis (11:30) and a sticking point thereafter. Otherwise, the man reckoned meritorious "because he put his trust in the LORD" (15:6) will have been proven only a pious fool.

Imagine Abram's relief when it is Sarai who suggests a way to circumvent the enduring curse of her own sterility:

> [2]And Sarai said to Abram, "Look, the LORD has kept me from bearing. Consort with my maid; perhaps I shall have a son through her." And Abram heeded Sarai's request. [3]So Sarai, Abram's wife, took her maid, Hagar the Egyptian—after Abram had dwelt in the land of Canaan ten years—and gave her to her husband Abram as concubine. (Gen 16:2–3)

What Sarai suggests and Abram accepts is a variety of surrogate motherhood. It is through Hagar's womb that Sarai will at long last "have a son" (*'ibbāneh*), or, as the double entendre can just as well be translated, "be built up": on the obscure legal mechanism presupposed here hangs Sarai's sole hope to become the matriarch of the House of Abram that YHWH has covenanted to establish. The narrator's technique in these two verses reinforces the paradox that it is the barren wife who is responsible for the birth of the Patriarch-designate's long-awaited son. Sarai alone speaks here; Abram only "heeded her request," or, more literally, "listened to her voice." In reporting that Sarai "took" (*wattiqqaḥ*) Hagar and "gave" (*wattittēn*) her to Abram, the narrator employs the language of marriage,[5] and more to the point, to the reader familiar with the law of the slave in Exod 21:2–6, he suggests the situation in which a master, having provided a wife for his slave, lays claim to the offspring of the union he has arranged. This is, obviously, not the precise legal background of Gen 16:2–3, but the analogy does lift up the pathos in Hagar's actions. The mistress provides a fertile slave woman not to a male slave, but to her own husband, and not to produce more field hands, but to conceive the child on whom the couple's life has been staked, in a wager that the mistress' own barrenness has so far rendered most unlikely.

How we are to assess Sarai's attempt to circumvent her sterility is shrouded in ambiguity. To her credit it can be argued that the promise to Abram of progeny has never specified the mother; the matriarch of the great nation as numerous as the dust of the earth or the stars of the heavens has never been designated. On this reading, Sarai's arranged marriage of Abram and Hagar is an act of altruism; as in Gen 12:10–20, Sarai is here willing to make a certain sacrifice so that God's promises to her long-suffering husband can come true. The analogy with that incident does, however, suggest that Sarai is acting out of something other than pure self-sacrifice. For in Gen 12:10–20, the alternative to accepting Abram's suggestion that she pretend to be his sister and thus likely find herself in some Egyptian's harem is to admit her real relationship with Abram, thus dooming him to death and herself to life in some Egyptian's harem after all. Similarly, in Gen 16:2–3 she is hardly stepping aside selflessly. Instead, she is taking the only course available for her to "have a son" and thus attain the glorious status of matriarch of the House of Abram. It is a course that entails the intense humiliation of acknowledging that it is her own deficiency that accounts for Abram's childlessness and the derailment of God's promise to him of progeny. But Sarai's humiliation is in the service of her exaltation; it is the means by which she becomes the mother of progeny as numerous as the dust of the earth and the stars of the heavens.

Sarai's suggestion and Abram's acceptance of it in Gen 16:2 might, however, also be attributed to a lack of faith. As a rational calculation, the notion is absurd that the woman with whom Abram has been in monogamous union so many years—ten in the land of Canaan alone (v 3)—could ever conceive a child. But it is no more absurd than the notion that he should break his ties with kith and kin and emigrate to an unnamed land; no more absurd than the notion that God would plague Pharaoh until he restored Abram's "sister" to him; and no more absurd than the notion that God could convey the title to all of Canaan to one man. Abram's faith has always been, as we have seen, a trust that the extravagant promises of God will be fulfilled in spite of the obvious and enduring impediments to them. It is arguable that his decision to leave the promised land during the famine (12:10) showed a lack of faith comparable to the one with which he might be charged for accepting Sarai's suggestion that they resort to surrogate motherhood. Perhaps he should have stayed in the promised land, as God would later command Isaac to do in a similar situation (26:1–5). But Isaac's temptation to depart Canaan for Egypt came *after* the conveyance of title, as the narrative line of the redacted Pentateuch would have it, whereas Abram's decision *preceded* it; in 12:7, YHWH had assigned the land to Abram's offspring only, not yet to him (cf. 13:15), and his departure could not be conceived as abandonment of inalienable property. In the instance of Sarai's suggestion of surrogate motherhood, the case that Abram exhibits a lack of faith is stronger, for here the action is not a temporary expediency, like the sojourn in Egypt, but a permanent solution to the outstanding impediment to the fulfillment of God's promise. Should he not have trusted in YHWH once again? Should he not have followed the point of Moses' advice to Israel when they were stricken with terror with the sea in front and Pharaoh's cavalry behind them: "The LORD will battle for you; you hold your peace!" (Exod 14:14)? And if his acceptance of Sarai's suggestion is not owing to a loss of faith, why has he not resorted to surrogate motherhood earlier, or taken a second wife? If the answer is his sensitivity to Sarai, then why has he been valuing this over his role in the providential drama? Is this sensitivity not also a manifestation of a lack of commitment to the God who set him on his journey?

Another argument that the union of Abram and Hagar is to be seen as an act of faithlessness rests on an astute intertextual observation made by Joel Rosenberg. Rosenberg notes an intriguing similarity between the verse in which Sarai gives her handmaiden to Abram and the verse in which Eve gives the forbidden fruit to Adam:

So Sarai, Abram's wife, took [*wattiqqah*] her maid, Hagar the Egyptian—after Abram had dwelt in the land of Canaan ten years—and gave [*wattittēn*] her to her husband [*'îšāh*] Abram as concubine. (Gen 16:3)

When the woman saw that the tree was good for eating and a delight to the eyes, and that the tree was desirable as a source of wisdom, she took [*wattiqqah*] of its fruit and ate. She also gave [*wattittēn*] some to her husband [*lĕ'îšāh*], and he ate. (Gen 3:6)

"Other reverberations," writes Rosenberg, "suggest themselves, as well": "Abram heeded Sarai's request" (16:2), if rendered more literally ("Abram listened to Sarai's voice"), recalls YHWH's rationale for cursing Adam, "Because you did as your wife said" (3:17), or, literally, "Because you listened to your wife's voice." And when the conception of Ishmael is, in a sense, partially reversed with the expulsion of the boy and his mother in Genesis 21, God's instruction to an aggrieved Abraham echoes both these verses: "whatever Sarah tells you, do as she says" (v 12), or, literally, "listen to her voice," once again.[6] The problem is not men's obeying their wives, but men and women's acting against God's wishes. One can go further than Rosenberg and note that the expulsion of Ishmael from the promised land into the Negeb desert, where he becomes a bowman (v 20), has interesting affinities with the expulsion from Eden of Cain, who becomes "a ceaseless wanderer on earth" (4:11–16). From the ethnological perspective, these affinities of Ishmael and Cain undoubtedly reflect the similarities of the nations whose characters are projected onto the eponymous ancestors, the Ishmaelites and the Kenites (or Cainites). Note that in Judg 1:16 the Kenites "settled among the people in the Negeb of Arad" (cf. 1 Sam 27:10), that is, not far from where Hagar and Ishmael's ordeal of Genesis 21 takes place. From the literary and theological perspectives, however, one must note again that Cain and Ishmael both fall within the category of the older boy whose younger brother—Abel and Seth for Cain, Isaac for Ishmael—is favored by God over him. Given these subtle but suggestive intertextual connections to Genesis 3–4, it becomes harder to view Sarai's suggestion in 16:2 and Abram's acceptance of it as anything but ominous.

In defense of Abram and Sarai against the charge of faithlessness, however, it must be noted not only that the matriarch of the promised progeny has never been indicated, but also that the Hebrew Bible does not generally support an equation of faith with passivity. Even on the shore of the Sea of Reeds, Israel is not only enjoined to hold their peace, but also, in the very next verse, "to go forward" (Exod 14:15)—not to wait quietistically for YHWH to rescue them, but to act boldly in the face of an impossible situation. The Hebrew Bible must be said, on balance, to endorse the traditional Jewish dictum, "one is not to rely on miracles" (compare, for example, b. Pes. 64b), and, this being the case, Sarai and Abram were in no sense faithless to the promise of progeny when, after more than ten years of unsuccessful attempts to conceive a child, they resorted to surrogate motherhood. If we view their decision in Gen 16:2–3 in this light, then the couple must be seen as willingly playing their role in the divine-human synergy through which the astonishing providential design will be realized. The arranged union of Abram and Hagar is yet another deed of faithful response to the promise that set Abram, Sarai, and their entire household on their strange journey. That providence would actually solve the problem of Sarai's barrenness by overcoming it through a miracle rather than circumventing it through surrogate motherhood (17:15–21; 18:9–15) was not to be known at the point in the story narrated in Genesis 16.

Immediately after Hagar conceives the long-awaited child, friction between the wife and the surrogate mother, well known also in our own time, surfaces (16:4–6). The difference is that the cause of this friction is not the question of the relative rights of the two mothers, but rather the humiliation that Sarai experiences when Hagar conceives so promptly.[7] "I am lowered in her esteem," she complains to Abram (v 5). The legal fiction by which Sarai is at long last to "have a son" remains, when all is said and done, only a legal fiction: it cannot overcome the continuing curse of her barrenness. Abram dares not argue with his wife: "Abram said to Sarai, 'Your maid is in your hands. Deal with her as you think right.' Then Sarai treated her harshly, and she ran away from her" (Gen 16:6). With Hagar's flight into the wilderness, Abram and Sarai seem to have lost the chance for an heir that the slave's pregnancy represents. No sooner does a fulfillment to the promise loom on the horizon than another set of impediments, Sarai's humiliation and consequent jealousy and Abram's puzzling nonchalance, threatens to overwhelm it. If Hagar's unborn child is a boy, as turns out to be the case, then Genesis 16 represents the first explicit instance of the motif that is the subject of our inquiry, the averted loss of the promised son. For an angel finds the pregnant slave woman by a spring in the wilderness and gives her a bittersweet message:

⁹And the angel of the LORD said to her, "Go back to your mistress, and submit to her harsh treatment." ¹⁰And the angel of the LORD said to her,

"I will greatly increase your offspring,
And they shall be too numerous to count." (Gen 16:9–10)

The command to "submit to [Sarai's] harsh treatment" is shocking. It is the most pointed counter-example to the misleading overgeneralization, popularized by liberation theologians, that the biblical God is on the side of the impoverished and the oppressed, exercising, as a matter of consistent principle, a "preferential option for the poor."⁸ In Genesis 16, Hagar confronts the twin immoveable realities of her slavery and her surrogate motherhood. Each testifies to her status as an object to be possessed by others for their purposes, and God removes neither source of suffering from this oppressed woman. His interest, rather, is in the promise to Abram, and it is his desire to fulfill this through Hagar's child that constitutes the sweet side of the bittersweet message delivered by the angel of the LORD by the spring in the wilderness. The promise to grant Hagar offspring too numerous to count in v 9 is an obvious allusion to the promise of progeny that is now the principal concern in the story of Abram. The point is unmistakable: Hagar does have a positive role in the providential drama centered on Abram, and her offspring will indeed fall within the bounds of the promise to the Patriarch, Sarai's wishes notwithstanding. But Hagar's conceiving plays an even more crucial part within the larger symbolic structure of the Book of Genesis. Consider that the expression "I will greatly increase" (*harbâ 'arbeh*) occurs in only two other places in the entire Hebrew Bible. One of them is God's curse on Eve:

And to the woman He said,
"I will make most severe [*harbâ 'arbeh*]
Your pangs in childbearing;
In pain shall you bear children.
Yet your urge shall be for your husband,
And he shall rule over you." (Gen 3:16)

The reappearance of this rare expression in Gen 16:10 suggests a further ramification of Fishbane's observation that the promise to Abram reverses the curse on Adam. If Abram is, like Noah, the counterpoint to Adam, then Hagar is the counterpoint to Eve, and the multiplication of the slave's offspring is the gracious promise of God that is the antithesis to the pain of childbirth decreed in Eden. The only other occurrence of *harbâ 'arbeh* is in Gen 22:17, when the angel of the LORD, having countermanded the order to sacrifice Isaac as a burnt offering, promises to "make [Abraham's] descendants as numerous as the stars of the heavens and the sands on the seashore." As we shall see, the connections between Genesis 16 and Genesis 22 extend well beyond this suggestive point of diction. In different ways, both chapters play out the drama of the near-loss and miraculous restoration of the hoped-for son.

As in Genesis 22 (vv 11–18), so in Genesis 16 the angel of the LORD supplements one positive oracle (16:10) with another:

¹¹The angel of the LORD said to her further,
"Behold you are with child
And shall bear a son;
You shall call him Ishmael [*yišmāʿēʾl*],
For the LORD has paid heed [*šāmaʿ*]
to your suffering [*ʿonyēk*].
¹²He shall be a wild ass of a man;
His hand against everyone,
And everyone's hand against him;
He shall dwell alongside of all his kinsmen."
(Gen 16:11–12)

In this second promissory oracle to Hagar, something not altogether dissimilar to the "preferential option for the poor" can be detected after all. Whereas Sarai had "treated her harshly" (*wattěʿanneħā*, v 6) and the angel had, using the same root, directed her to "submit to her harsh treatment" (*wěhitʿannî taħat yādêħā*, v 9), he now announces not only the birth of the long hoped-for son, but also YHWH's attention to her "suffering" (*ʿonyēk*, v 11). God does indeed hear the cry in pain of the suffering slave, but his gracious response comes not in the form liberation theology would lead us to expect—emancipation of the slave and thoroughgoing social reform, if not quasi-Marxist revolution—but as a set of assurances that the larger Abramic promise shall devolve, to one degree or another, upon her unborn child. The fierce independence of the Ishmaelites will vindicate the humiliating thralldom of their matriarch's life.[9]

The triple occurrence of the root *'nh,* within a few verses in Genesis 16 (vv 6, 9, 11), all with meanings of oppression, recalls the only place where the root has heretofore appeared, Gen 15:13. There Abram is told that his "offspring shall be strangers in a land not theirs, and they shall be enslaved and oppressed (*wĕʿinnû*) four hundred years." The oppression that follows in chapter 16 is not of Abram's descendants by the unspecified foreigners of this oracle, however, but of Hagar by her mistress, Abram's primary wife. The reader aware of the larger Pentateuchal narrative will recognize in Genesis 16 a remarkable inversion of the story of the Exodus: the mother of *Israel* is abusing an *Egyptian* slave, and the God who reveals himself to the runaway bondswoman in the desert gives her there not a charter of freedom, but an order to return to the mistress of her oppression. The oracular assertion to Hagar that "the LORD has paid heed [*šāmaʿ*] to your oppression [*ʿonyēk*]" in v 11 is also redolent with suggestions of the exodus of Sarai's descendants from Hagar's homeland. Consider as an illustration this excerpt from the affirmation that the Israelite farmer is to make as he presents his first fruits to the priest:

> [6]"The Egyptians dealt harshly with us and oppressed us [*wayʿannûnû*]; they imposed heavy labor upon us. [7]We cried to the LORD, the God of our fathers, and the LORD heard [*wayyišmaʿ*] our plea and saw our plight [*ʿonyēnû*], our misery, and our oppression." (Deut 26:6–7)

The troubling disparity between God's response to the oppression of Hagar, on the one hand, and of the Israelites, on the other, will appear to be an inconsistency only to those who ascribe the Exodus to the "preferential option for the poor." In fact, however, the Book of Exodus, again in language reminiscent of the episode of Hagar, gives a different rationale for God's removal of Israel from bondage in Egypt:

> [23] . . . The Israelites were groaning under the bondage and cried out; and their cry for help from the bondage rose up to God. [24]God heard [*wayyišmaʿ*] their moaning, and God remembered His covenant with Abraham and Isaac and Jacob. [25]God looked [*wayyar'*] upon the Israelites, and God took notice of them. (Exod 2:23b–25)

What motivates the Exodus is not God's identification with the oppressed, who surely were thought to include far more people than the descendants of Abraham, Isaac, and Jacob, nor is it his passion for justice. Rather, it is the covenant with the Patriarchs, a central feature of which, it will be recalled, was the grant of the land of Canaan. God's remembering that covenant in Exodus 2 results in his revelation to the great emancipator Moses in the next chapter: "I will take you out of the misery [ʿŏnî] of Egypt to the land [of Canaan]" (3:17). YHWH's revelation to Moses, who, fleeing injustice, has escaped to the desert, stands in marked contrast to his unfeeling order to Hagar in very similar circumstances: "Go back to your mistress, and submit [hitʿannî] to her harsh treatment" (Gen 16:9).

Within the larger providential drama of the Pentateuch, however, Sarai's abuse of her Egyptian bondswoman does not go unvindicated. In Genesis 37, Sarai's great-grandchildren, the brothers of Joseph, who are the eponymous ancestors of the tribes of Israel, feel toward their favored little brother much the way Sarai felt toward Hagar when the latter conceived a child when she could not. Once again, searing feelings of being slighted result in irrational and nearly homicidal actions, as the brothers resolve to kill Joseph, or at least to sell him into slavery. In one of the accounts that have been woven together in Genesis 37, those who buy Joseph from his jealous siblings are none other than the Ishmaelites, that is, the descendants of the child whose conception led to the abuse of Hagar and nearly ripped apart the household of Abram. And the land to which the Ishmaelites take Sarai's great-grandson is none other than their own matriarch's homeland, Egypt (v 25, 28b). But it is not just Joseph who reenacts the bitter experience of Hagar. As he later puts it to his brothers, "God sent me ahead of you" (45:5): the whole of Israel will learn what Hagar knew as the defining reality of her life—exile, destitution, and, when "[a] new king arose over Egypt who did not know Joseph" (Exod 1:8)—slavery. The exaltation of the chosen brother—Isaac over Ishmael, Joseph over the tribes—has its costs: it entails the chosen's experience of the bitter reality of the unchosen's life. Such is the humiliation that attends the exaltation of the beloved son.

The notion that the vindication of Hagar is visited upon Joseph may also underlie the curious phrasing of the first part of the blessing on Joseph in Genesis 49:

²²Joseph is a wild ass,
A wild ass by a spring [ʿāyin]
—Wild colts on a hillside [šûr].

²³Archers bitterly assailed him;
They shot at him and harried him.
²⁴Yet his bow stayed taut,
And his arms were made firm
By the hands of the Mighty One of Jacob—
There, the Shepherd, the Rock of Israel. (Gen 49:22–24)

Of this obscure and problematic oracle, Nahum M. Sarna observes:

> Hebrew *'ayin, shur* may well be wordplay concealing a reference to the
> Ishmaelites who sold Joseph to Egypt, as related in Genesis 37:25, 28.
> "The spring (*'ayin*) on the road to Shur" plays an important role in the
> birth narrative about Ishmael (16:7), who is also described as "a wild ass"
> (16:12). Further, the following two verses here refer to hostile archers, and
> Ishmael was indeed "a bowman" (21:20). It is also worth noting that both
> *'ayin* and *shur* are terms of "seeing," and Hagar, mother of Ishmael, referred
> to the "God of Seeing," who reassured her at "the Well of the Living One
> Who sees me" (16:13ff.).¹⁰

"The Patriarchs are the type; their descendants, the antitype." This holds
true not only for the venerable ancestors Abram and Sarai, but also and
equally, for Sarai's miserable handmaiden, the Egyptian Hagar. She serves
to foreshadow the fate of Israel in Egypt, to which her descendants deliver
Sarai's great-grandson Joseph as the first of the Israelites to know slavery in
the Ishmaelite matriarch's homeland. That God paid heed to her suffering is
memorialized in her son's name, *yišmā'ē'l,* "God listens." But Hagar's ad-
umbration of the fate of Israel is, in the last analysis, by way of inversion.
For, whereas God listens to the plea and sees the plight of those who fall heir
to the covenant with Abraham in Egypt and liberates them, he does not liberate
Hagar or assign her descendants a land of their own. Though Ishmael, falling
within the *promise* to his father, will be "a great nation" and "a wild ass of a
man," he falls, nonetheless, just outside the *covenant* of Abraham and shall
not inherit the promised land.

The disinheritance of Ishmael is one of those themes that appear in interesting variations in two of the three documentary threads that source critics
detect in Genesis, P (17:15–21) and E (21:9–21). The P account displays
impressive affinities with the preceding story of the pregnant slave's abortive
flight:

> ¹⁵And God said to Abraham, "As for your wife Sarai, you shall not call
> her Sarai, but her name shall be Sarah ["princess"]. ¹⁶I will bless her;
> indeed, I will give you a son by her. I will bless her so that she shall give

rise to nations; rulers of peoples shall issue from her. [17]Abraham threw himself on his face and laughed [*wayyiṣḥāq*], as he said to himself, "Can a child be born to a man a hundred years old, or can Sarah bear a child at ninety?" [18]And Abraham said to God, "O that Ishmael might live by Your favor!" [19]God said, "Nevertheless, Sarah your wife shall bear you a son, and you shall name him Isaac [*yiṣḥāq*]; and I will maintain My covenant with him as an everlasting covenant for his offspring to come. [20]As for Ishmael [*yišmā'ē'l*], I have heeded you [*šěma'tîkā*]. I hereby bless him. I will make him fertile and exceedingly numerous. He shall be the father of twelve chieftains, and I will make him a great nation. [21]But My covenant I will maintain with Isaac, whom Sarah shall bear to you at this season next year." (Gen 17:15–21)

As in Genesis 16, so here we find an etymology of Ishmael's name that derives from his parent's cry to God on his behalf (v 20; cf. 16:11). In chapter 17, the etymology is, of course, retroactive, a wordplay on his name rather than an etymology stricto sensu. The same is true of the parallel in 21:17. In each case, the name is explained by reference to God's heeding the wishes of the parent and blessing the child with future progeny. "I will make him fertile and exceedingly numerous" (17:20) is close to a paraphrase of the angel's first oracle to Hagar in her distress: "I will greatly increase your offspring, / And they shall be too numerous to count" (Gen 16:10). If, as we have seen, the angel's words served to announce that the unborn child did indeed fall within the promise to Abram, the P text makes this indubitable: "I will make him a great nation" (*ûněṭattîw lěgôy gādôl*, 17:20) echoes the original promise, "I will make of you a great nation" (*wě'e'esěkā lěgôy gādôl*, 12:2). Ishmael is not, however, the one through whom the everlasting covenant just announced will be carried forth (17:19, 21). In pointing this out, P corrects the impression that the reader may have gotten from Genesis 15 and 16, in which J has God first assuring Abram that his heir shall be his own as yet unconceived child (15:4) and then solemnly pledging so in a covenant (v 16), only to follow this with an account of the conception of Ishmael (16:4). In Genesis 17, P reformulates the Abramic covenant of Genesis 15 so as to exclude Ishmael explicitly, though without otherwise disinheriting him from the promise. His inclusion in the latter is only owing to God's heeding Abraham's intercessory supplication: "O that Ishmael might live by Your favor!" (17:18). Without Abraham's intervention, the providential design would presumably have had no role for Hagar and Abraham's son. P resolves the ambiguity surrounding Ishmael's conception through surrogate motherhood by including him in the *promise* (at Abraham's behest) but excluding him from the *covenant*.

In explaining Abraham's supplication on behalf of Ishmael (17:18), the eleventh-century commentator Rashi holds that the Patriarch was only humbly pointing out that he was undeserving of the extraordinary blessing of a son by Sarah: "I am not worthy to receive such a reward!" Hezekiah ben Manoah (*Chizquni*), of the thirteenth century, offers a less pious interpretation: As can be seen by his question, "Can a child be born to a man a hundred years old?" Abraham appeared incredulous of the glad tidings of Isaac's future conception and expressed his satisfaction with the son already born. Moshe ben Nachman (Nachmanides), also of the thirteenth century, on the other hand, holds that "Abraham feared that Ishmael would die" now that it was announced that Isaac and not he would be his promised heir. Each of these interpretations has its strengths, and it may well be that electing one at the expense of the others would only impoverish a richly and perhaps intentionally ambiguous verse. As we shall soon have occasion to see, however, Moshe ben Nachman's interpretation raises an issue critical to the Elohistic parallel in Gen 21:9–21— the issue of Ishmael's death and how it is to be averted. E, with his well-known interest in angels,[11] will have the death of Abraham's first-born son averted by angelic intervention. "Come, lift up the boy and hold him by the hand," the angel of God will instruct Hagar from heaven, "for I will make a great nation of him" (*kî-lĕgôy gādôl 'ăśîmennû*, 21:18). P, with an aversion to angels and a much more thorough-going monotheism, shows Ishmael's pre-mature death averted by Abraham's own intervention (17:20). The theme of the narrow averting of the death of the first-born son is, as we shall see, vastly more dramatic in E, but, in a muted way that is consistent with Priestly style and theology, it is also to be detected in Genesis 17.

The YHWHist (J), in contrast, never deals with the conflict of the two first-born sons, Ishmael and Isaac. Instead, he simply narrates the divine annunciation of Isaac's birth (Gen 18:9–15) as if Ishmael's disqualification were already a matter of record. This may be because J once had his own narrative more directly parallel to the Priestly and Elohistic texts about Ishmael, a narrative lost, perhaps, when those texts were spliced in. Or it may be that J thought he had disposed of Ishmael in Genesis 16, when Hagar was given the promise of progeny without mention of land or covenant. In favor of the latter argument it can be noted that 16:11 presents the J account of the naming of Ishmael that, mutatis mutandis, corresponds in P to 17:20 and in E to 21:17 ("God has heeded [*wayyišmaʿ 'ĕlōhîm*] the cry of the boy where he is!"). In any event, within the Pentateuch as it now stands, the YHWHistic account of the annunciation of Isaac's birth to Abraham and Sarah repeats, with interesting variations, the Priestly announcement that the longstanding obstacle of Sarah's barrenness will be not circumvented, but overcome—a proposition that is, in the course of nature, ridiculous and prompts a laugh from Sarah (18:12), just as, in P, it prompts a laugh from Abraham (17:17). And, once again, it is this laugh that we are to understand as the source of Isaac's name. In J, the name Ishmael derives from YHWH's paying heed to Hagar's suffering, but in P, it emerges, or is at least reconfirmed, when God heeds Abraham's prayer for his son's survival. Similarly, in J, Isaac gets his name from Sarah's laughing at the message of YHWH, whereas in P he receives the same name because of Abraham's laughing when God announces that the aged Sarah shall have a son. For Ishmael God intervenes, but for Isaac he overcomes nature itself. Ishmael is the natural son, born of ambiguous human machinations to circumvent a natural curse. Isaac is the promised son, born of an undeniable supernatural plan to overcome the curse of nature in order to realize the blessing God has promised to visit upon Abraham and his descendants through his beloved son.

The plan, so long thwarted, comes at last to fruition in Genesis 21, when "the LORD took note of Sarah as He had promised, and the LORD did for Sarah as He had spoken," enabling her to conceive and bear Isaac (vv 1–2). On the words "as He had promised," the commentator Ovadiah Seforno, an Italian rabbi of the late fifteenth century, remarks that the promise at issue had come in 17:16 with the words "I will bless her." Now, Seforno observes, God has "removed from her the curse of Eve with regard to the conception, birth, and rearing of a child": "I will make most severe / Your pangs in childbearing" (3:16). That a childbirth should be a blessing is indeed a reversal of the postlapsarian order of things and suggests that Fishbane's observation about the promise to Abraham in Genesis 12 needs to be expanded so as to include Sarah as well.[12] It is not simply Abraham's "generativity" that is blessed; were that the case, the matter could have come to rest with the birth of Ishmael, a state of affairs that Abraham, according to Rashi's understanding of 17:18, was quite satisfied to accept. But now, in 21:1–2, we see the miraculous fulfillment of the promises of 17:15–21 and 18:9–15, as an aged Sarah, barren all her life and past menopause to boot, conceives and gives birth to the son promised by the very God who had cursed Eve with the pains of labor.

As at the annunciation of Isaac's impending conception in Genesis 17, so here after his birth in Genesis 21, the nettlesome question of Ishmael's future comes to the fore:

[9] Sarah saw the son whom Hagar the Egyptian had borne to Abraham playing. [10] She said to Abraham, "Cast out that slave-woman and her son, for the son of that slave shall not share in the inheritance with my son Isaac." [11] The matter distressed Abraham greatly, for it concerned a son of

his. [12] But God said to Abraham, "Do not be distressed over the boy or your slave; whatever Sarah tells you, do as she says, for it is through Isaac that offspring shall be continued for you. [13] As for the son of the slave-woman, I will make a nation of him, too, for he is your seed." (Gen 21:9–13)

And as at the conception of Ishmael in Genesis 16, so here it is Sarah's jealousy that motivates the expulsion of Hagar and her son. The precise nature of the "playing" (*mĕṣaḥēq*, v 9) that calls forth the matriarch's jealousy is unclear, though the term is obviously yet another turn on Isaac's name (*yiṣḥāq*). The likelihood is that the passage in question is a variant of some sort to 16:4–6, in which Hagar's pregnancy motivates Sarah's complaint, "I am lowered in her esteem." If this is the case, then 21:9 refers not to the innocent play of children, but to Ishmael's mockery, presumably of Sarah herself. As Seforno comments on this verse, Sarah "thought he was aroused to such ridicule because he heard it from his mother." In this case, however, Sarah appeals to a higher principle than was available to her in Genesis 16, the principle of Isaac's heirship rather than pique at her diminished status. The annoyance is, of course, still in evidence. Note that though Sarah's speech in 21:10 includes two references each to Hagar and Ishmael, she never once deigns to mention their names. They are simply "that slave-woman and her son," "the son of that slave." The issue of inheritance, however, raises larger questions: who is the heir to Abraham, might there be more than one, and, if so, what is the relationship between them?

On the basis of Deut 21:15–17, discussed earlier,[13] it would seem that Ishmael as the first-born son should be entitled to the obscure "double portion" mentioned therein—*if*, that is, his descent from a slave and his conception through the legal fiction of surrogate motherhood are immaterial. A midrash suggests that "from our matriarch Sarah's answer to Abraham—'the son of that slave shall not share in the inheritance with my son Isaac [Gen 21:10]' "— it can be deduced that "Ishmael had said ' . . . I am the first-born, and I shall take the double portion' " (*Gen. Rab.* 53:11). Though this midrash retrojects Deuteronomic law into the Patriarchal narratives anachronistically, it does bring out nicely the irregularity of Sarah's demand. It is, after all, the first-born son whom she is insisting be expelled and disinherited, and Abraham's distress at the proposal (Gen 21:11–12) is readily understandable. This distress is a redeeming touch after his nonchalance in 16:6 (when, of course, the son had not yet been born and only the hapless Hagar was put at risk). The divine directive in 21:12–13 strikes a delicate balance: Abraham is to heed Sarah's wishes, and God will see to it that Ishmael thrives nonetheless and inherits a portion of the original promise that Abraham shall father a nation. As in 17:15–21, Ishmael is read out of the covenant but emphatically included in the promise that is larger than the covenant and preceded it. If Sarah succeeds in her campaign to disinherit Ishmael, Abraham is at least assured that his first-born son will not be undone by the strange workings of an inegalitarian providence.

The terse narrative of Gen 21:9–13 looks, Janus-like, both back to the story of the primal family and forward to the next generation of Patriarchs. God's preference for the second son over the first recalls, of course, the tragic story of Cain and Abel (4:1–16). Less directly, Ishmael's destiny as a denizen of the wilderness and a bowman (21:20–21) brings to mind the punishment visited on Cain: "If you till the soil, it shall no longer yield its strength to you. You shall become a ceaseless wanderer on earth" (4:12). That the divine preference is mediated through the matriarch's mouth foreshadows Rebekah's mediation of God's choice of Jacob over Esau, the first-born son (25:23; 27:1–45). Together the two instances demonstrate the exalted role of the mother in the providential drama. That it is none other than Isaac who is duped by his wife and his second son is an exquisite inversion of the process by which Sarah, to Abraham's distress, had engineered the promotion of Isaac himself over Ishmael years before. And in both cases, that of Ishmael and that of Esau, the dispossessed elder brother is still awarded an enviable destiny, fatherhood of a great nation for Ishmael (17:20; 21:18) and a luxurious abode and occasional independence from servitude for Esau (27:39–40). A Priestly genealogical note ties the homology of Ishmael and Esau together beautifully:

> [8]Esau realized that the Canaanite women displeased his father Isaac. [9]So Esau went to Ishmael and took to wife, in addition to the wives he had, Mahalath the daughter of Ishmael, sister of Nebaioth. (Gen 28:8–9)

Esau's becoming Ishmael's son-in-law doubtless reflects ethnic and political relationships in the lands to the south of Canaan. These same relationships have almost certainly played a role in the construction of a narrative in which Ishmael and Esau resemble each other so much. Apart from the ethnographic dimension, however, the image of Esau's fleeing to Ishmael just after his relative disinheritance at the hands of Jacob makes a powerful literary statement. Now, just outside the land promised to Abraham, these two descendants of his make common cause, ruling their mighty nations yet utterly powerless to deflect the providential course that has decreed that the status of the beloved son shall attach not to themselves, but to their younger brothers.

What is painfully unresolved after Gen 21:13 is how God's promise of a glorious future for Ishmael can be reconciled with the expulsion of the boy and his mother, now also endorsed by God:

> [14] Early next morning Abraham took some bread and a skin of water, and gave them to Hagar. He placed them over her shoulder, together with the child, and sent her away. And she wandered about in the wilderness of Beer-sheba. [15] When the water was gone from the skin, she left the child under one of the bushes, [16] and went and sat down at a distance, a bowshot away; for she thought, "Let me not look on as the child dies." And sitting thus afar, she burst into tears. (Gen 21:14–16)

One can only speculate as to Abraham's feelings as he sends away the mother of his first-born son along with the child at the suggestion of his primary wife—the same wife who had also made the suggestion that led to the conception of the same son a few years earlier (16:2). Perhaps we are to think that Abraham trusts so much in the promise of nationhood through Ishmael (21:13) that he obeys Sarah and God's directive with complete serenity, never doubting that Hagar and Ishmael would reach their unspecified destination. Alternatively, perhaps we are to think that Abraham obeyed in "fear and trembling," as Kierkegaard characterized his stance in the parallel text of Genesis 22, understanding full well the perils of sending a young woman and her tiny son alone into the wilderness with only "some bread and a skin of water," but believing that he would yet enjoy them again because, as Kierkegaard put it, "with God all things are possible."[14] The way in which Abraham sends them away bothers the medieval Jewish commentators. "Many will be surprised at Abraham," commented Abraham ibn Ezra (d. 1167):

> How could he expel his son and send away the son with his mother empty-handed? Where was his generosity? The surprise is at those who are surprised, for Abraham acted exactly as the Lord had commanded him. If he had given money to Hagar against Sarah's wishes, he would not have observed the commandment of the Lord. And in the end, after Sarah's death, he did indeed give gifts to Ishmael's sons [see Gen 25:6].[15]

This, of course, presupposes that the scandalous way in which Abraham sends Hagar and Ishmael off derives from Sarah, though the text never tells us this. It also presupposes that God's instruction to Abraham, "whatever Sarah tells you, do as she says" (21:12), was to be taken with minute literalism, even if the result could reasonably be thought to endanger the lives of the mother and her young child. This is not an implication with which the rabbinic tradition, with its high estimation of the saving of life, can be altogether comfortable. On the words, "God was with the boy" (v 20), Rabbi Aqiva (d.

135 C.E.) comments, "including his donkey drivers, his camel drivers, and the members of his household" (*Gen. Rab.* 53:15). It is unclear from context whether the ancient rabbi thought the reference was to Ishmael's later success or whether he thought Abraham had sent Ishmael away not only with his mother, but with a large staff as well. It is revealing of the problem that 21:14 poses, however, that Seforno cites this midrash as proof that, contra Ibn Ezra, "they lacked nothing except water as they wandered in the desert." Seforno's construal of Aqiva's midrash, and possibly the midrash itself, remove the disturbing implication of the Torah that Abraham is not only giving up his first-born son together with the child's mother, but also sending them to their likely deaths.

Verbal connections between Genesis 21 and the following chapter, which details the near-sacrifice of Isaac, reinforce the disturbing implication. In both episodes Abraham acts "early next morning" (21:14; 22:3); the phrase occurs in only one other verse in the story of Abraham (19:27). His placing (*śām*) the bread and the skin of water on Hagar's shoulder (21:14) suggests his putting (*wayyāśem*) "the wood for the burnt offering . . . on his son Isaac" (22:6). The midrash likens Isaac at that moment to "one who carries his cross on his own shoulder" (*Gen. Rab.* 56:3), and in the case of Hagar and Ishmael, too, the bread and the skin placed on her shoulder symbolize impending death. Whether the boy is also placed there, as the translation given above indicates, is unclear. As the narrative line would have it, Ishmael is at least well into his teens, for he was thirteen when he was circumcised (17:25), and that was before Isaac, now already weaned (21:8), was even conceived. If this be the case, then clearly 21:14 cannot be telling us that Abraham loaded a teenaged boy onto the hapless Hagar's shoulder, along with food and drink for the journey into the wilderness. Thus another commentator, David Qimchi (Provence, 1160–1235) understands the verse to mean, "the bread and water he placed over her shoulder and [placed] the child so that he could walk before her, for he was fifteen years old, and when he grew tired, she could carry him on her shoulder or at her bosom." The latter eventuality would still seem unlikely, but Qimchi's view that Abraham did not put Ishmael on Hagar's shoulder has been defended on grammatical grounds by modern scholars. For it is unclear in the structure of the verse whether "the child" is the object of "gave" (*wayyittēn*) (along with "some bread and a skin of water," understood) or of "placed."[16] If "the child" is the object of "gave," then it may not be out of the question to hear in this verse an intertextual echo of another disquieting verse, "You shall give [*titten*] Me the first-born among your sons" (Exod 22:28b), the subject of our first chapter. What cannot be doubted is that the central issue of Genesis 21 is whether the first-born son of Abraham will survive the ordeal into which he has been placed by a father preeminently obedient to God's command.

In favor of the idea that Abraham did indeed place Ishmael on Hagar's shoulders, one can cite Gen 21:15, in which the mother "left the child under one of the bushes," a most unlikely act if the child was fully fifteen years old, as Qimchi and other traditionalists assume. Verse 18 speaks to the same point, for there, when an angel instructs Hagar to "lift up the boy," we again think of an infant or a toddler, but hardly the teenager that the narrative line requires. The simplest solution is the documentary one: the teenaged Ishmael is a product of P, a later source than the one reporting the episode of his near-death, which is almost universally attributed to E. Once one discounts for the moment the Priestly material that is Genesis 17, all one knows about Ishmael's age is that it is greater by an indeterminable figure than that of Isaac, who has just been weaned. This is true whether we are to envision the first-born son riding on his mother's shoulder or walking on his own. But the image of Ishmael's riding on Hagar's shoulder to an unknown fate is the more powerful. It is, in its own way, as wrenching as the image of Isaac's carrying the wood over which his father plans to immolate him in obedience to God's command (22:6).

That Hagar gives up her infant son for dead may seem strange within the context of the narrative line of Genesis. Her poignant words, "Let me not look on as the child dies" (Gen 21:16), suggest a lack of faith in the promise she received when she fled from Sarah—that Ishmael "shall be a wild ass of a man" and "dwell alongside of all his kinsmen" (16:12), and she, the mother of "offspring . . . too many to count" (v 10). Perhaps we are to imagine her as concluding that Ishmael's inheritance of this part of the promise to Abraham and her own ascent to the status of matriarch had always been conditional upon Ishmael's being Abraham's only son. With the miraculous birth of Isaac, things revert to where they were, Hagar and her son become expendable, and her only hope is to be spared the sight of his death—proof that God's paying heed to her suffering (v 11) was only a temporary expedient lest her cruel mistress continue barren.

Source criticism, however, suggests an alternative way of understanding the relationship of Genesis 21 and 16. Adherents of the Documentary Hypothesis almost universally ascribe chapter 21 to E, but chapter 16 to J. On this line of reasoning, the stories of the expulsion of Hagar and Ishmael were not originally sequential, as they have become in the Torah, but variants of each other, doublets that can perhaps be traced back to a common oral archetype. In each case, Sarah's jealousy prompts Abraham to expel the woman and her child, who flee into the wilderness. There one or the other of them cries out, and an angel appears to report that God has heard the cry, which, in turn, is either the source of Ishmael's name (*yišmā'ʾēl*, "God hears") or a suggestive play on it. In the end, the angel relays an oracle of deliverance that concentrates on the progeny to issue from Hagar and Ishmael. If one reads the narrative this way, then Hagar's acceptance of the imminent death of Ishmael in Genesis 21 is not owing to any loss of faith in the great promises of chapter 16. It is simply the understandable reaction to the miserable straits into which the cruel vicissitudes of her life have thrust her. Only for a moment had she risen above the fate of a slave, and that moment came to a sudden end with the birth of Isaac. This was a birth that brought laughter to Abraham (17:17) and Sarah (18:12; 21:6), but only tears to Hagar (21:16).

Those cruel vicissitudes have now brought Hagar to the point where she has given up her first-born son, her only son, to certain death. The proximate cause of Ishmael's demise is the lack of water in the skin Abraham loaded on her shoulder. "If she had walked straight," observes Samuel ben Meir (Rashbem), a rabbinic commentator in the north of France in the twelfth century, on Gen 21:14, "the skin of water that Abraham had given her would have sufficed until [she reached] the inn." Abraham, in other words, cannot be implicated in the death of his first-born son that now seems inevitable. And yet questions of the sort we asked when Abraham agreed to send Hagar and Ishmael away must be asked again here. Why was Abraham so sure that Hagar would know the way? Was it because he trusted in the assurance of v 13 that "a great nation" shall derive from Ishmael? If so, was Abraham not putting God to the test by giving Hagar only enough water to last until she made her way through the wilderness to her destination? Whatever his intentions, Abraham does seem to have become the key player in the cruel providential drama that, in Hagar's mind, will result in the death of her— and his—first-born son. For if Abraham trusted in the oracle about Ishmael in v 13, we cannot assume that Hagar ever heard it or was told about it (or about the P parallel in 17:20). All she knows is that events have conspired to take away the life of the son who is the only counterpoint to her suffering. If the waterskin is the proximate cause of Ishmael's impending death, the ultimate cause is the divine plan that centers on Abraham. The very plan that brought her son into being will, it seems, also bring about his annihilation.

"Let me not look on as the child dies" (Gen 21:16) corresponds in some ways to Abraham's moving supplication in 17:18, "O that Ishmael might live by Your favor." Genesis 17 (P) does not mention Hagar, and in Genesis 21 (E) Abraham actively participates in the events that bring about the mortal threat to Ishmael. Each text shows only one parent in the agony of facing the prospect of losing the first-born son, an agony each faces alone. Taken together, the two texts show that the dreaded loss of the first-born son is an experience that neither parent can evade. In Genesis 21, however, the loss is averted not by Hagar's wrenching words in v 16, which record only her motivation in moving a bowshot away from the child, but by the cry of the child himself:

[17]God heard [*wayyišmaʿ ʾĕlōhîm*] the cry of the boy, and an angel of God called to Hagar from heaven and said to her, "What troubles you, Hagar? Fear not, for God has heeded [*šāmaʿ ʾĕlōhîm*] the cry of the boy where he is. [18]Come, lift up the boy and hold him by the hand, for I will make a great nation of him." [19]Then God opened her eyes and she saw a well of water. She went and filled the skin with water, and let the boy drink. [20]God was with the boy and he grew up; he dwelt in the wilderness and became a bowman. [21]He lived in the wilderness of Paran; and his mother got a wife for him from the land of Egypt. (Gen 21:17–21)

God "heard" or "heeded" the cry of the child, who is never named in Genesis 21:9–21, though he is at the center of its action and though v 17 twice plays on his name. As we have seen, these two instances are the counterpart to Gen 17:20, in which God assures Abraham that, "As for Ishmael, I have heeded you [*šĕmaʿtîkā*] . . . He shall be the father of twelve chieftains, and I will make him a great nation." In chapter 21, the consequence of God's hearing the boy's cry is the well of water that Hagar sees only after "God opened her eyes" (v 19). This recalls the parallel text in chapter 16, where an angel finds her "by a spring of water in the wilderness" (v 7) and she calls YHWH *ʾēl rŏʾî*, apparently meaning "God of Seeing" (v 13). This, in turn, gives the well located at the spot its name, Beer-lahai-roi, which is probably to be understood as meaning something on the order of "the well of the one who survived the vision" (v 14). But the miraculous appearance of the well in 21:19 also looks forward to the episode of the near-sacrifice of Isaac in chapter 22, in which the sudden and unexpected appearance of a ram caught by its horns in a thicket enables Abraham to offer a sacrifice without losing his son after all (v 13). It is even possible that we are to think of the well as lying under a bush, like the one under which Hagar leaves Ishmael (21:15)[17]—and like the thicket in which the ram has been caught in 22:13. The appearance of the ram, in turn, prompts Abraham to name the spot "Adonai-yireh" ("the LORD will see"; cf. v 8,) "whence," the text informs us, "the present saying, 'On the mount of the LORD there is vision' " (*yērāʾeh*) (v 14). Thus in the two accounts of the near-death of Ishmael and in the story of the near-sacrifice of Isaac alike, we find the themes of miraculous vision. The Latin inscription from North

Africa, in which the parents Felix and Diodora offer "a lamb as a substitute" for their daughter "on account of a vision and a vow [*ex viso et voto*]" again comes to mind.[18] In each case the vision seems to involve the supernatural sparing of the doomed child's life.

There is also an important intertextual connection between the supernatural deliverance of Ishmael in Genesis 21 and another story of a first-born son whose life is spared, the story of Joseph. Hagar and Joseph are the only two figures in Genesis who literally lose their way, Hagar when "she wandered about in the wilderness [*wattēta' bĕmidbar*] of Beer-sheba" (v 14), and Joseph when he was "wandering in the fields [*tōʿeh baśśādeh*]" (37:15) on his way to meet his brothers in Shechem. In each case, the story begins with the father's sending the persons away (*wayšallĕḥehā*, 21:14; *wayyišlāḥēhû*, 37:14) to a situation from which they are lucky—or graced by God—to emerge alive. Abraham, as we have seen, sends out Hagar and Ishmael without consideration of the possible dangers of the journey, including the danger that the slavewoman may become disoriented and run out of water, as, in fact, happens. Jacob sends Joseph to check up on his brothers, pasturing in Shechem, without consideration of the resentment that the elder brothers feel toward their father's beloved son (37:2–11) and the possibility that these feelings might result in the loss of the son, as, in fact, happens for a number of years. But the connection between chapters 21 and 37 goes further, as we have had occasion to see,[19] for the fratricidal resentment of Joseph's older brothers results in his being sold to a caravan of Ishmael's descendants and taken as a slave to Hagar's native land (37:25–28). That "a man came upon [Joseph] wandering in the fields" and was able to direct him to his brothers (vv 15–16) is but the first of many incidents in Joseph's life in which he is mysteriously enabled to bound back from a desperate situation. In this case, it can be reasonably suspected that the "man" who finds Joseph disoriented is an agent of providence, and his convenient ability to direct the young man is but the first of many indications that "the LORD was with Joseph, and he was a successful man" (39:2). The midrash goes further, identifying the "man" with the angel Gabriel, on the basis of the expression "the man Gabriel" in Dan 9:21 (*Tanḥ. wayyēšeb* 2). The equation with Gabriel is too specific, but the notion that "man" (*'īš*) can denote an angel in biblical Hebrew is beyond dispute.[20] Whether this is the usage in Gen 37:15–17 is impossible to determine. Negatively, one can cite the absence of angels elsewhere in the Joseph story. Positively, one can argue from the strange way "the man" appears at precisely the right moment, knows who Joseph's brothers are without being told and where they have gone. If "the man" is angelic, then we have another link with the story of Hagar and Ishmael in Genesis 21 (and chapter 16 as well), for in the story of Hagar disoriented and Ishmael about to die, it is an angel who intervenes to save their lives.

When Hagar finds Ishmael an Egyptian wife (Gen 21:21), the boy's severance from the chosen lineage is complete. In the case of Isaac, by contrast, Abraham arranges for the selection of the wife himself and insists that the maiden be from his Mesopotamian homeland (24:2–9). As things turn out, she is Abraham's great-niece, the daughter, in fact, of a nephew whose birth is recorded just after the fateful binding of Isaac: "Bethuel . . . the father of Rebekah" (22:23; cf. 24:24). In the cases of both Ishmael and Isaac, the story of the near-death of the first-born son is followed by mention of the woman from whom the promised great nation will derive. Where death had been expected, the possibility of new life appears.

Like all sophisticated texts, the story of Ishmael's expulsion in Genesis 21 involves more than one motive and serves more than one purpose. From the literary perspective, it serves to eliminate Isaac's chief competitor, the older brother who, according to the expectations of primogeniture alone, could lay a valid claim to the status of Abraham's chief heir. Only after the elimination of Ishmael can Isaac be called Abraham's "favored" son (*yāḥîd*, literally, "only, unique"; 22:2, 16). Without the complex and suspenseful drama of Ishmael's expulsion, the aqedah, the stunning story of the binding of Isaac in 22:1–19, could not be told in the way it is. It is also the case that the pattern of Ishmael's near-death and supernatural rescue helps set the stage for the intensification of the same pattern in chapter 22, where the stakes are much higher and the consequences reach farther. From the ethno-political perspective, the expulsion of Ishmael must be seen as establishing the descendants of Isaac, that is, the Edomites and the Israelites, as the prime lineage in the family of Abraham, just as the stories of Jacob's devious assumption of Esau's birthright and blessing in 25:27–34 and 27:1–45 serve to establish Jacob/Israel rather than Esau/Edom as Isaac's dominant heir. Those inclined toward political interpretations of literature will be content to explain the narratives in question by reference to the fact that this is *Israelite* literature, that it is *Israel* telling the story. One need only consult the Qur'an, in which it is Ishmael whose name usually follows Abraham's (and precedes Isaac's[21]), to see the difference. That both the House of Israel and the House of Islam have historically called Abraham father is a point that ecumenists and pursuers of peace will rightly stress. But it is not a point that enables us to determine who is Abraham's *beloved son*, an issue of capital importance in the Torah, the Qur'an, and, as we shall see,[22] the New Testament as well.

Hugh C. White has put the stories of the expulsion of Ishmael and the binding of Isaac into a different light, one drawn from the study of folklore

NB

"Archaic rituals of initiation"

viewed anthropologically. Examining numerous stories from ancient Greece that center, first, on the abandonment, exposure, or attempted sacrifice of a boy by his father and, then, on his rescue and ascent to power, White argues that the pattern derives from archaic rituals of initiation. In the case of Gen 21:15–21, he maintains that the text actually "constitutes the symbolic death and resurrection of the boy, and derives from the legend of initiation in which a male child passes into manhood."[23] It fits, he cogently argues, into a genre that includes not only the obvious parallel in Genesis 16, but also the strikingly similar story of the flight of Elijah into the desert near Beer-sheba and his miraculous discovery of food and drink provided by an angel in 1 Kings 19 (esp. vv 3–8). In the case of the stories of Ishmael's expulsion, the key points are the "symbolic death of a child . . . through exposure in the wilderness, and his symbolic resurrection through miraculous nourishment." The pattern derives, White concludes, from a "tribal initiation rite" of the Ishmaelites, who would have transmitted the legend about their eponymous ancestor in a cult center in the northern Negeb, their home.[24] Needless to say, the legend underwent a momentous dislocation when it was picked up by Israelite traders, whose national tradition centered on Sarah and Isaac rather than on Hagar and Ishmael. But the story of Isaac, too, at least in Gen 22:1–19, derives, so White argues, from the initiation rites and the accompanying legends of another set of tribes, the tribes of Isaac.

Although White makes a compelling case for the origin of the Ishmael story in tribal initiation rites, it must be noted that his interpretation is not of the manifest texts of Genesis, but of an underlying and preceding cultic situation, one that he acknowledges to have become obsolete or at least less relevant by the time these literary texts were composed. The texts themselves focus, I have argued, on two points: first, the pain of the parents as they surrender their child, in whom they have invested so much, and, second, the miraculous recovery and restoration of the child whose death had seemed inevitable a moment before. In this, the texts seem to me to have another cultic correlative in addition to the one White reconstructs. This is the series of ritual substitutions discussed earlier,[25] in which the doomed first-born son, marked for sacrifice to YHWH, can yet be restored alive to his parents. The narrative correlatives of these rituals are texts in which God commands that the first-born or beloved son be exposed to a life-threatening situation—in the case of the aqedah, slaughter at the hands of his own father—and yet enables him to survive unharmed. For the purposes of our inquiry, this is the main meaning of the story of Ishmael, the boy who was able to live by God's favor after all.

Chapter Eleven
The Aqedah as Etiology

The story of the near-sacrifice of Isaac in Gen 22:1–19, known in Jewish tradition as the *aqedah* ("binding"), falls into both categories of the transformation of child sacrifice, the ritual and the narrative. At first commanded to make of his beloved son a burnt offering, an obedient Abraham is later instructed not to harm the boy in any way, and in his son's stead, offers a ram that appears just at the right moment, caught in a thicket. The affinity of the aqedah with the story of the first Passover in which the blood of a yearling lamb saves the Israelite first-born from the Destroyer (Exod 12:1–28) is patent. Indeed, Gen 22:1–19 presents the strongest biblical evidence for the proposition that the story of the Passover is, in part, a secondary etiology for an older and more general substitutionary ritual. The Canaanite and Punic evidence discussed earlier further bolsters the proposition.[1]

Its affinities with the paschal lamb lead rather easily—in my judgment, much too easily—to the assumption that the aqedah, too, served as an etiology of the substitution of animal for human sacrifice. That those making the assumption share a proper horror for human sacrifice further discourages them from scrutinizing the analogy more carefully, lest it come to appear that this treasured text, of such eminent centrality to both Judaism and Christianity, actually accepts something that the normative teachings of both those traditions condemn categorically. But it is precisely in a case like this that the brutal honesty of the historical-critical method is required. If we are to subject the interpretation of the aqedah as an etiology of animal sacrifice to the requisite critical scrutiny, we must first distinguish between two types of such etiologies. The first type is an etiology of the *permissibility* in certain circumstances of substituting a sheep for the most important son. Gen 22:1–19 is too much embedded in the specialness of Isaac for us to interpret it as addressing the general subject of

NB!

human sacrifice—a subject that does not seem to have been at issue in the Canaanite or Israelite cultures. At most, one would have to say that the story licenses the ritual substitution of the animal for the "favored" son (*yāḥîd*, vv 2, 12, 16). The question must then be asked, however, under what conditions the license applies. For example, it could be argued that the aqedah allows for such a substitution only when the Deity has signaled his approval—perhaps through an oracle, as in vv 11–12, or through a vision, as was perhaps the case in the Ngaous Stela III (*ex viso*)[2] and may also be the background of the unexpected appearance of the ram in Gen 22:13. Alternatively, it may be that the etiological point of the aqedah, if there is one, is that the substitution of the animal is *always* permissible. Either way, in the more restrictive etiological interpretation, the aqedah does not *forbid* the sacrifice of the favored son or *mandate* the substitution of an animal. It simply enlists the latter in the register of proper cultic practices without implying that it is always to be preferred to the slaying of the beloved son.

Exponents of the notion that the aqedah is an etiology of a particular sacrificial practice rarely, if ever, subscribe to this restrictive interpretation, however. Instead, they subscribe to the second type of etiology and see the story as *opposing* animal to human sacrifice, endorsing the former and anathematizing the latter. Shalom Spiegel, for example, writes, "Quite possibly the primary purpose of the Akedah story may have been only this: to attach to a real pillar of the folk and a revered reputation the new norm—abolish human sacrifice, substitute animals instead."[3] Alberto Green, who acknowledges that "originally child sacrifice had a legitimate place in the cult of YHWH," still sees Gen 22:1–19 as "the product of a religious attitude and period that recoils naturally from associating God with human sacrifice."[4] And even Paul G. Mosca, whose research compels him to the view that child sacrifice in ancient Israel, so long as it was licit, was offered to YHWH and not to any other deity, holds that the "original purpose [of the aqedah] may have been to explain why YHWH no longer—or ever—*demanded* the sacrifice of the first-born son."[5] In none of these very different yet representative scholars' views do we find the idea that the aqedah served to show that the substitution of the animal for the son is *permissible*. All of them retroject the uncompromising denunciations of child sacrifice in the latter prophets onto Gen 22:1–19.

The difficulties with this interpretation of the aqedah, indicated briefly earlier,[6] now require a more sustained exploration. Spiegel's notion that the point of the aqedah may have been "to attach to a real pillar of the folk and a revered reputation the new norm" founders on one observation: none of the several ritual texts that specify substitutions for the sacrifice of the first-born son ever mentions Abraham or alludes, however indirectly, to the aqedah.

Rather, most of these texts attach their norms in one way or another to the story of the first Passover. Exod 34:19–20 is an exception; it, however, presents no etiology at all, only the bare law of the redemption of the first-born son. It is, of course, possible that Israelite literature that has been lost did indeed make the etiological use of the aqedah that Spiegel suggests, but to interpret Gen 22:1–19 by reference to this hypothetical lost corpus relies on unsupported speculation. Similarly, if Green is right that the sensibility behind the text "recoils naturally from associating God with human sacrifice," then it is passing strange that the aqedah begins with that same God's demanding that from which he recoils. Spiegel, Green, and Mosca all interpret the repeal of the demand as a repudiation of the underlying practice, without asking why the God who finally opposes child sacrifice initially commands it. Ezekiel in a similar situation has, as we have seen,[7] an answer to this quandary: God gave Israel "laws that were not good . . . that [He] might render them desolate" (20:25–26). But nothing in Gen 22:1–19 suggests that the command to immolate Isaac in v 2 should be regarded as a law that is other than good. Indeed, the very angelic address that calls off the commanded sacrifice commends Abraham for his willingness to carry it out (v 12; cf. vv 16–18). Imagine Ezekiel commending Israel for their willingness to immolate their children! In Ezek 20:25–26, the repeal of the law is unmistakably a repudiation of it as well. In the aqedah, there is a commendation of the obedient father that is the reverse of the repudiation that so many scholars think they hear in this disquieting story.

Another difficulty arises with the assumption that the aqedah serves as an etiology of animal rather than human sacrifice: the story lacks any etiological notice on the subject. I am thinking of the sort of remark with which the story of Jacob's wrestling match with the divine being at the Jabbok (Gen 32:23–33) ends. Having reported that "the socket of [Jacob's] hip was strained" (v 26), the little narrative concludes with this observation: "This is why the children of Israel to this day do not eat the thigh muscle that is on the socket of the hip, since Jacob's hip socket was wrenched at the thigh muscle" (Gen 32:33). Such notices being in plentiful evidence in the Hebrew Bible, if Gen 22:1–19 really served as an etiology of animal substitution, it is more than a little curious that none appears there. The absence contrasts with the conclusion of the law of the first-born in Exodus 13:1–15b: "Therefore I sacrifice to the LORD every male issue of the womb, but redeem every first-born among my sons."

The cumulative evidence against the ubiquitous idea that the aqedah opposes child sacrifice and substitutes an animal cult is overwhelming: nothing in Gen 22:1–19 suggests that God's command to immolate Isaac was improper,

Abraham is commended and rewarded for obeying it, and the text lacks any formal indicators of an etiological motive regarding the nature of sacrificial offerings. The first two points speak only against the non-restrictive interpretation of the narrative, which maintains that its point is to disallow all human sacrifice. The last one speaks also against the restrictive position, which holds that the aqedah is an etiology of the *permissibility* of substituting an animal for the special son. The likelihood is that Gen 22:1–19 is not an etiology of the substitution in either sense. It may, nonetheless, *reflect* a situation in which the father's substitution of a sheep for the special son can meet with God's favor.

There is another category of etiology in which it can be argued with considerably more reason that the aqedah falls, the etiology of the cult-site. One notes a text like Gen 12:8, in which Abram builds an altar just east of Bethel and "invoke[s] the LORD by name" (cf. 13:3–4). This passage would seem to be an ideal example of the modern critical counterpart to the medieval rabbinic dictum, "the Patriarchs are the type; their descendants, the antitype [*maʿăśēh hāʾābôt sîmān labbānîm*]." It very naturally evokes the common observation that its point is to justify the temple at Bethel that played such an important role in Israelite religion, especially when King Jeroboam I made it one of the official cult-sites of the kingdom of Israel (1 Kgs 12:25–33). The same reasoning can be applied to the parallel passages in which Jacob either anoints a pillar or builds an altar in roughly the same area, naming the site Bethel ("House of God") or El-bethel ("God of Bethel") (Gen 28:10–22; 35:6–7). Indeed, several other passages in the Patriarchal cycles elicit this kind of etiological interpretation, and in none of them do we find a formal, self-conscious indication of the etiological motive: no "this is why" or "therefore I . . . " This tendency to attribute the foundation of the important centers of worship to the Patriarchs has suggested to many scholars that the major etiological function of the story of the binding of Isaac is to account for the establishment of a particular cult-site.[8] The nature of the worship carried out there is not inconsequential to this sort of etiological interpretation, but it is not the paramount point either.

The outstanding question is the identity of the cult-site whose inauguration the aqedah is intended to record. One clue is the site of the action, a unidentified hill in "the land of Moriah" (Gen 22:2). In the entire Hebrew Bible, the only other occurrence of this name appears in 2 Chr 3:1, where "Mount Moriah" is the name of the place where YHWH "had appeared [*nirʾâ*] to [Solomon's] father David" and, of equal relevance to our subject, where Solomon therefore commenced construction on his great Temple in Jerusalem. It is less odd that Moriah is a land in Genesis but a specific mountain in Chronicles if one notes that the sole explicit etiological notice in Gen 22:1–19 centers on a theophany upon a mountain:

> And Abraham named that site Adonai-yireh ["the LORD will see"] whence the present saying, "On the mount of the LORD there is vision [*yērā'eh*]." (Gen 22:14)

That the "mount of the LORD" can be a title of Zion, the mountain atop which sat the great Temple in Jerusalem, is beyond dispute (see, for example, Isa 2:2–4). Though this is the most natural identification of the term, the possibility that some other mountain is intended cannot be eliminated. It is, however, rendered less likely when one considers that of the other two attestations of the expression "on the mount of the LORD," one occurs in an explicitly Jerusalemite context (Isa 30:29; cf. v 19), and the other appears in a psalm whose association with the Jerusalem shrine is commonly accepted (Ps 24:3). That a shrine is built to commemorate a theophany is familiar in the Hebrew Bible. It appears, for example, in those etiologies of the Bethel temple in Gen 28:10–22 and 35:6–7. In the case of Gen 22:1–19 and 2 Chr 3:1, however, the connection is explicit: both passages pun on the verb *rā'â* ("to see") which in its *niphal* stem means "to be seen, to appear." This, in turn, is to be associated with the name of the land and the mountain in it, Moriah (*mōrîyâ*), on which both Gen 22:14 and 2 Chr 3:1 play. That the aqedah serves as the foundation legend for the great Temple of YHWH in Jerusalem is the traditional Jewish answer to our question about the identity of the cult-site at issue in Gen 22:1–19.

For critical scholars, however, the question is more complicated. Ever since Hermann Gunkel published his ground-breaking commentary on Genesis early in the twentieth century, his views on Moriah have dominated critical discussion. According to Gunkel, it is not that "Moriah" in Gen 22:2 reflects an old tradition about Abraham's having inaugurated the worship that culminates, according to 2 Chr 3:1, with Solomon's construction of his Temple on the same mountain. Rather, the reverse is the case: "Moriah" in the story of the aqedah is retrojected from a post-exilic tradition in which the Temple Mount is so designated. The appearance of the name in Chronicles, in other words, has historical priority over the appearance in Genesis. As for the mention of the "mount of the LORD" in Gen 22:14, Gunkel thinks this is secondary and the verse presently represses the wordplay that gave the original site its name.[9] In a more recent discussion, heavily dependent on Gunkel, Rudolf Kilian finds v 14b to be a late expansion by the same hand that added the reference to Moriah in v 2.[10] Originally, he argues, v 14 concluded with the name "Adonai-yireh", which is otherwise unattested and has no connection with the Temple in Jerusalem. Somewhat like Jacob at Bethel, Abraham in Gunkel's (and Kilian's) theory simply provides a new name for an existing cult-site.[11] That the identification of this cult-site with the Temple Mount in Jerusalem is later is further suggested by the appearance in v 14 of the tetragrammaton (YHWH = LORD). This is at odds with the use of the term *'ĕlōhîm* ("God") throughout the episode and has suggested to many scholars that the divine names in v 14 are secondary, along with the tetragrammaton that appears in the expression "an angel of the LORD" in v 11. The parallel to v 11 in v 15 is less of a problem, simply because there is a high degree of consensus among critical scholars that the second angelic address (vv 15–18) is secondary in its entirety.[12]

If the YHWHistic features of Gen 22:1–19 are secondary, then Adonai-yireh ("YHWH will see," v 14) must disguise the original name of the site for which the story serves as a foundation legend. Whether secondary or not, the phrase clearly depends upon Abraham's answer in v 8 to Isaac's question about the sheep to be sacrificed: "God will see [*'ĕlōhîm yir'eh*] to the sheep for His burnt offering, my son." Gunkel draws attention to the similar sounding phrases, "you fear God" (*yĕrē' 'ĕlōhîm*, v 12) and, "his eye fell upon a ram" (*wayyar' wĕhinnēh 'ayil*, v 13). In the latter case, Gunkel suggests that *'ayil*, which in the construct state is pronounced as *'ēl*, homophonous with a name of God (*'ēl*), could be understood as another pun on the name of the cult-site that has been secondarily suppressed to make room for Jerusalem/Moriah. The Hebrew name, he argues, was *yĕrû'ēl* or *yĕrî'ēl* (the difference in the vowel is not significant). This site, located in the Judean wilderness about thirteen miles south of Jerusalem, appears in English Bibles as "Jeruel" (2 Chr 20:16), and it was to Jeruel that Abraham and Isaac trekked for three days, according to Gunkel and the numerous scholars who follow him, including Kilian.[13] Gunkel concludes that Gen 22:1–19 is the etiology of a cult of child sacrifice at Jeruel. One of its etiological functions is to account for the acceptability of a ram in place of the son, but, notes Gunkel, being pre-prophetic, the story subjects the primitive notion of child sacrifice to no polemic. The substitution of Moriah for Jeruel/Jeriel follows, in Gunkel's theory, from the close similarity of the name of the cult-site to "Ariel" (*'ărî'ēl*), one of the names of Jerusalem (see Isa 29:1–8). This led to the misperception that the aqedah took place in Jerusalem, and as Ariel fell out of and Moriah came into common usage, the text as we have it came into being.[14] The process thus conjectured receives some empirical corroboration from Samaritan tradition, which identifies the hill of the aqedah with Gerizim, the sacred mount near Shechem. What appears in the Jewish texts, according to the theory, is simply the Judean equivalent—the Temple Mount in Jerusalem designated by one of its post-exilic names, Moriah.[15] But both Gerizim and Moriah are, in the minds of many, attempts to adapt the story of the binding of Isaac at Jeruel to a later religious situation.

The chief deficiency of the theory that Gen 22:1–19 was, in its original form, an etiology of the worship at Jeruel is the total absence of any indication that this obscure place, mentioned exactly once in all of Scripture, ever served as a cult-site. Indeed, the only evidence for its existence comes not from any early sources but from Chronicles, one of the latest books in the Hebrew Bible. Gunkel brings Jeruel into the discussion only because of the frequent play on the similar sounding roots *rā'â* ("to see") and *yārē'* ("to fear") in Gen 22:1–19, usually in conjunction with *'ĕlōhîm* ("God"). His case would have been stronger, however, if the term for the Deity had been *'ēl*, as in *yĕrû'ēl*, the name of the site in the Judean desert. It is awareness of this that leads Gunkel to bring in v 13, which reports that Abraham's "eye fell upon a ram." The problem is that the form of the word for "ram" here (*'ayil*) is not a homophone of *'ēl* and another word comes between the term for seeing (*wayyar'*) and this word anyway. Gunkel and those who follow him err not in drawing our attention to the wordplay on *rā'â* and *yārē'*, but in resorting to the obscure place-name Jeruel to explain it. As I have noted, the paronomasia in question can just as easily have the name Moriah in view, as has been recognized since rabbinic times. This does not establish the traditional Jewish equation of Moriah with Jerusalem; it does argue that Moriah need not be deemed secondary within Gen 22:1–19.

In place of Jeruel, some scholars have sought to account for the dominant wordplay in the story by reference to the similar sounding name, El-roi, which apparently means something on the order of "God of Seeing." It will be recalled that this is the name by which Hagar refers to YHWH in Gen 16:13, after the appearance in the desert of the angel who announced the birth and great future of Ishmael. The name, obscure in itself, is explained in the text by the even more obscure exclamation, "Have I not gone on seeing after He saw me!" as the new translation by the Jewish Publication Society renders it. It is tempting to emend the exclamation to read, "Have I really seen God and remained alive!" (*hăgam 'ĕlōhîm rā'îtî wā'ehî* in place of *hăgam hălōm rā'îtî 'ahărê rō'î*).[16] The change is small and brings Hagar's surprise into line with the well-known theology that denies that one can survive a theophany. Note, in particular, the similar phrasing of Exod 33:20b, "for man may not see me and live" (*lō'-yir'anî hā'ādām wāḥāy*). Whatever the precise wording and proper translation of Hagar's exclamation, it is the term El-roi that, according to the etiological notice in Gen 16:14, gives the well at which the theophany occurs its name, Beer-lahai-roi, which, as we have seen, means something like "the well of the one who survived the vision." It is in this site or perhaps some other one nearby that shares in the worship of El-roi that some scholars find the location displaced by Moriah in 22:2. Royden Keith Yerkes goes so far as to change "Adonai-Yireh" in v 14a to "El-roi". The second half of the verse he, like Kilian, judges to be a secondary gloss.[17]

El-roi has certain advantages over Jeruel as the original locus of the aqedah. Though it must be argued against Yerkes that no site with that precise name is attested, El-roi does at least appear in Genesis (unlike Jeruel), and in a passage that is, as we shall see, strikingly parallel with Gen 22:1–19. It is also a name that is connected with a place associated with Isaac, who returns from Beer-lahai-roi just as Abraham's servant is coming back from Mesopotamia with his bride-to-be, Rebekah (24:62). The difficulty, however, is not only the absence of El-roi itself as a cult-site or even a place name, but also, once again, the omission of either element of the divine epithet in the story of the aqedah. If, with Yerkes, we change "Adonai-yireh" in 22:14 to "El-roi," we destroy the connection with v 8 and leave the new name oddly unaccounted for in a story almost universally supposed to be etiological.

All these attempts to find a non-Jerusalemite identification for the locus of the binding of Isaac are compelled to do away with Gen 22:14b, with its reference to "the mount of the LORD." Kilian's view that v 14b is a later expansion leaves us with a verse that names the site (v 14a) but never explains the meaning of the name (v 14b). Henning Graf Reventlow is probably right to insist that the two halves of the verse require each other.[18] He is also right in pointing out that it is a strange etiology of a cult-site that never names the place for which it serves as the foundation legend and that shows the founder returning to his point of departure, in this case Beer-sheba.[19] All of this well supports Reventlow's conclusion that the etiological features of Gen 22:1–19 are not the center of gravity of the story. Tracking down these features has been a central preoccupation of critical interpreters of the aqedah in the twentieth century, but the effort has yielded little more than conjectures. The popularity of this form of interpretation is owing in no small measure to the pervasive modern perception, found even among the devout on occasion, that the category of the sacred is a mystification of social and political arrangements. Responsible interpretation, then, is the task of reducing the larger spiritual structures to the institutional arrangements that not only accompany them, but account for them. That such arrangements are real, important, and likely to be missed by religious traditionalists is to be granted. What must not be granted is this quasi-materialist presupposition that correlating the text with its social and political arrangements exhausts the interpreter's task.

We see, in summary, that Gen 22:1–14 is unlikely to be an etiology of the shift from child to animal sacrifice. The most that can be said on this topic is that the story reflects a situation in which the sacrifice of a sheep as a substitute for the favored son can meet with God's approval. If an etiology of a particular cult shrine other than that atop Mount Zion lies behind the story of the aqedah, the identity of the shrine cannot be securely established from the text that has reached us. That text is one that associates Abraham's near-sacrifice of Isaac with the site of the great Temple in Jerusalem.

The question is whether this association is only late, like its first attestation in the Book of Chronicles, or whether Jerusalem was always understood to be the locus of the aqedah. Against the ubiquitous assumption that "Moriah" in Gen 22:2 has been retrojected from 2 Chr 3:1 (or a lost parallel), it must be recalled that in the former text, Moriah is a land, but, in the latter, a specific hill. If the author of "Moriah" in Gen 22:2 got the name from 2 Chr 3:1 or any source like it, it is odd that he then defied the later Jewish identification of Moriah with the Temple Mount and employed it idiosyncratically as the name of the whole region. As the example of "Sinai" shows (e.g., Exod 19:2, 11), the same term can designate a region and the most important mountain within it. But if this is the usage in Gen 22:2, it is not the usage in 2 Chr 3:1.

Gen 22:1–19 includes one occurrence of the root *yr'* ("to fear," v 12) and five of the root *r'h* (vv 4, 8, 13, 14 [twice]), in addition to the similar sounding word "Moriah" (v 2). Every one of the attestations of *rā'â* occurs in the imperfect, that is, with a prefixed *y*. Now these imperfects—*yar'*, *yir'eh*, and *yērā'eh*—like *yĕrē'* in v 12 ("[you] fear God"), can just as easily suggest the Hebrew name of Jerusalem (*yĕrûšālaim*) as that of Jeruel; El-roi they do not suggest in the least. This connection appears also in midrash:

> Abraham called it *yireh:* "And Abraham named that site Adonai-yireh" [Gen 22:14]. Shem had called it Salem, as it is said, "And King Melchizedek of Salem . . . [14:18]." The Holy One (blessed be He) said: If I call it *Yireh*, as did Abraham, Shem, a righteous man, will protest. If I call it Salem, as did Shem, Abraham, a righteous man, will protest. Rather, I hereby name it Jerusalem, according to what both of them called it—"Yireh-Salem": *Yĕrûšālaim*. (*Gen. Rab.* 56:10)

As a scientific etymology of the name of Jerusalem, this midrash is, of course, altogether inadequate. Nor can we endorse the rabbinic assumption that Melchizedek was simply an alternative name for the eponymous ancestor of the Shemite line. The question before us, rather, is whether the midrashic thinking exemplified in this text is likewise exemplified in the passage on which it comments, the story of the binding of Isaac.

Can there be wordplay on only half of the name of Jerusalem? As regards the second half of the name, the answer is an obvious and well-documented positive, as the following three examples illustrate:

And Adoni-bezek said, "Seventy kings, with thumbs and big toes cut off, used to pick up scraps under my table; as I have done, so has God requited [*šillam*] me." They brought him to Jerusalem [*yěrûšālaim*] and he died there. (Judg 1:7)[20]

Then Solomon [*šělōmōh*] awoke; it was a dream! He went to Jerusalem [*yěrûšālaim*] stood before the Ark of the Covenant of the LORD, and sacrificed burnt offerings and presented offerings of well-being [*šělāmîm*]; and he made a banquet for all his courtiers. (1 Kgs 3:15)[21]

He shall banish chariots from Ephraim
And horses from Jerusalem [*mîrûšālaim*];
The warrior's bow shall be banished.
He shall call on the nations to surrender [*šālôm*]
And his rule shall extend from sea to sea
And from ocean to land's end. (Zech 9:10)

But there can be, I submit, also cases in which the first element in the name of the holy city is involved in the same rhetorical practice. The conclusion to Psalm 128 is especially revealing:

[4]So shall the man who fears [*yěrē'*] the LORD be blessed.

[5]May the LORD bless you from Zion;
may you share the prosperity of Jerusalem [*yěrûšālaim*]
[6]and live to see [*ûrě'ēh*] your children's children,
May all be well [*šālôm*] with Israel! (Ps 128: 4–6)

Like the author of Gen 22:1–19, the psalmist plays on both *yārē'* ("to fear") and *rā'â* ("to see"). But, in addition, he involves the name of Jerusalem in the same paronomasia. After presenting the two elements in the name of the city together, the psalmist separates them, re-presenting them in the order in which they occur in the name. The first element is echoed in the imperative of the verb *rā'â*, "to see", the same verb that occurs fully five times in the story of the aqedah, just as it was heralded in *yěrē'* (cf. Gen 22:12); the second element is echoed in the word for peace or well-being, as in Zech 9:10 and many other verses in the Hebrew Bible. That none of these elements is germane to the actual origin of the name of Jerusalem is irrelevant to the matter at hand. The point is the use of assonance and what it reflects about the ancient Israelite understanding of the name of the city. The example of Ps 128:5–6 demonstrates that the first two syllables of "Jerusalem" could be associated with the verb *rā'â*, even in a form that lacks the prefixed *y*. The association is likely to be all the more natural when the prefix appears, as it does in every attestation of the root in Gen 22:1–19, the story of the binding of Isaac on the altar in Moriah. It is worthy of mention that the phrase in v 8 from which the name Adonai-yireh in v 14 is derived (*yir'ehl-lô haśśeh*, "will see to the sheep") also includes at least one of the three consonants of the second element in the name of Jerusalem, the *l*. The sibilant in the phrase (*ś*) is distinct from the sibilant in the name of the city (*š*) in pronunciation, but identical in orthography. As a play on *yĕrûšālaim*, the three words in v 8 are no less convincing than a number of other phrases that are commonly interpreted to involve the name of the city.

The idea that Moriah was always another designation of the Temple Mount in Jerusalem is as rare among critical scholars as it is ubiquitous in Jewish tradition. For example, Martin Noth, the great tradition-historian of ancient Israel, dismisses the identification as "quite improbable" because "the original tradition of Abraham, which, like that of Isaac, was native to the Negeb, did not extend further to the north at all."[22] This, if true, argues only that the story of the aqedah did not form part of "the original tradition." It offers no evidence at all that the shrine was once identified as other than that of Jerusalem. Indeed, if Gen 22:1–19 is later than most of the Abraham and Isaac material, then the likelihood increases that the story involves the Judean cult-site that became important in Israelite tradition only with the Davidic monarchy. The same cult-site almost certainly lies behind the use of the name "Salem" (*šālēm*) in Gen 14:18, a name that otherwise occurs only in Ps 76:3, where it parallels "Zion." The midrashic notion that Jerusalem received the second half of its name in Genesis 14 and the first in Genesis 22, though still unscientific, is thus less far-fetched than at first seems the case. Noth's judgment on the earlier chapter is consistent with his opinion of the identification of Moriah with Jerusalem. Genesis 14, he writes, "hardly stems from flourishing popular narration but is probably a late 'scholarly' composition."[23] The tithe that Abram gives to King Melchizedek of Salem in 14:20 has to do most immediately with deference to Melchizedek's royal privilege rather than with the tithing system of biblical law.[24] It is interesting, nonetheless, that Melchizedek is also "a priest of God Most High" (*'ēl 'elyôn*, v 18), for this makes Abram the first person in the Bible to present a tithe to a priest in Jerusalem. This puts his deference to royal privilege in a different light and suggests that etiological motives are not to be altogether read out of Gen 14:18–20 after all. Similar etiological motives, I submit, are also to be detected in the story of the aqedah, which locates Abraham's great act of obedience on the Temple Mount in Jerusalem.

The claim that the etiological features of Gen 22:1–19 involve the state sanctuary of Judah runs afoul of the critical consensus that the passage is authored by the Elohist (E), a northern source with no reason to endorse Judean traditions. This ascription of the story to E, however, has always had its difficulties, the chief of which being the use of the J name once in vv 11, 15, and 16 and twice in v 14, that is, five times altogether. The response of those who share the consensus, as we have seen, is to exclude all these passages from the original text. The response works better in the case of the second angelic address in vv 15–18 than in that of vv 11 and 14. Indeed, the efforts by adherents of the consensus to excise the YHWHistic features are circular at best and unnecessary once it is recognized that the etiological point of the phrase "God will see to the sheep" in v 8 does not involve the divine name. The classical source-critical assumption that variations between YHWH and *ĕlōhîm* must be explained by the Documentary Hypothesis is, at least in this instance, much to be doubted. Rather than to eliminate the tetragrammaton from vv 11 and 14, it is preferable to retain it at the cost of the classical source-critical presuppositions.

The weakest element in the traditional Jewish equation of Moriah with Jerusalem is the name that Abraham gives the spot in Gen 22:14, "Adonai-yireh." We have already examined the dominant critical thinking on this: the name either applies to a location that cannot be recovered or it disguises the real name, perhaps "Jeruel." Either of these options is plausible, though, as I have argued, the association with Jeruel is exceedingly forced. Often overlooked in the discussion is that for which the name served as an etiology— not the spot, but "the present saying, 'On the mount of the LORD there is vision' " (v 14). Once again, if v 14b is seen as a late gloss, as Kilian wishes,[25] then the point is lost, and we are back to guessing the location to which Adonai-yireh in v 14a refers. But if, with Reventlow,[26] we see v 14 as a unity—the first half giving the name, the second half, its meaning—then we should be less troubled by the absence of any location with the name Adonai-yireh. The narrative tells us that Abraham called it so, but not that it has this name "to this day," in the words of many other etiologies. What survives from Abraham's experience, according to v 14 (if taken as a unity), is not the name of the mountain, but the vision of YHWH that takes place there. The common assumption that the name given must have continued and come into general usage must be questioned. This is true not only for Gen 22:14 but also for other texts in which a name is given that is otherwise unattested.[27]

If the story of the aqedah did serve, in part, as an etiology of the worship atop the Temple Mount in Jerusalem, there may be an additional reason for the failure of the passage to mention directly the location upon whose name it puns repeatedly. Given the centrality of Jerusalem to the history of Israel from the tenth century B.C.E. on, it is striking that the name of the city appears in the Pentateuch not once. This omission sets Jerusalem apart from other important cities, like Shechem, Bethel, Dan, Hebron, and Beer-sheba, each of which is mentioned by name, incidentally, in the Abraham cycle. If "Salem" in Gen 14:18 is another name for Jerusalem, as Ps 76:3 argues, then we are left wondering why the author of this verse chose one of the rarest names for the city over the most frequent. Whatever its explanation, the reticence about naming Jerusalem may account both for "Salem" in chapter 14 and for "Adonai-yireh" in chapter 22. In each instance, the text may be deliberately employing a term that only suggests Jerusalem and does not name it.

The theme of vision in the story of the aqedah, signaled by the fivefold occurrence of the root *r'h* and the etiology in Gen 22:14, is only one of several features that connect the passage with the narrative of the expulsion of Hagar in its two parallel accounts (16:1–14 and 21:9–21). As we have seen, the first of these concludes with an etymology of Beer-lahai-roi based on Hagar's response to her supernatural rescue in the desert (16:13–14). In the case of the second account, the etiological motive centers on Ishmael's becoming a bowman because his mother, giving him up for lost, "sat down at a distance, a bowshot away" (21:16,20). Here, too, however, the theme of vision is prominent: "Then God opened her eyes and she saw a well of water. She went and filled the skin with water, and let the boy drink" (Gen 21:19). What does it mean to say that "God opened her eyes"? Commenting on this verse, Rabbi Ovadia Seforno (fifteenth century) interprets the expression to mean that "he gave her the knowledge to recognize a place of water that was already there, for she was not blind beforehand." The miracle, in other words, was not the creation of a well where none had been before, but only the perfectly timed gift of an ability sufficient to detect it. Seforno's predecessor, David Qimchi, first offers an interpretation along these general lines, adding that the well may have been hidden by one of the bushes mentioned in v 15 or set at a distance, as the words "she went and filled" imply. He then goes on, however, to suggest that God may have created the well at that moment, just as he did for Samson in Judg 15:18–19. The first option, with its image of Hagar's catching sight of the well under the bush at just the right moment, correlates strikingly with the end of the story of the aqedah: "When Abraham looked up, his eye fell upon a ram, caught in the thicket by its horns. So Abraham went and took the ram and offered it up as a burnt offering in place of his son" (Gen 22:13).

Hagar "went and filled," Abraham "went and took," but in each case what the parent sees and goes to appears with such exquisite timing that supernatural intervention must be assumed. For Hagar, the vision of the well verifies the angel's consoling oracle that precedes it: God has heard the boy's cry and resolved to make a great nation of him (Gen 21:17–18). For Abraham, the vision of the ram corroborates the angel's announcement just concluded: the sacrifice need not take place, for God now knows that Abraham's devotion is uncompromising (22:12). In neither instance is it likely that what is unexpectedly seen is supposed to have been created on the spot. In both cases, however, the act of seeing confirms the promise and enlists the parent in an action that symbolizes the son's unexpected deliverance from death. The waterskin that Abraham loaded on Hagar's shoulder had, only a moment before, symbolized their son's death. Now, because of the intervention of the God who had decreed the expulsion in the first place (21:12), it symbolizes his new life. The command to present a burnt offering had, only a moment before, signaled Isaac's impending demise. Now, because of the intervention of the God who had issued the command in the first place (22:2), the actual presentation of the burnt offering—the ram—symbolizes Isaac's gift of new life.

The similarities between the aqedah (Gen 22:1–19) and the two accounts of the expulsion of Hagar (16:4–16 and 21:9–21) are not incidental. They indicate a common structure to the three narratives:[28] in each Abraham is implicated in the near-death of his son, an angel intervenes to reverse the dire situation, and a vision closes the drama. In addition, the angel in each chapter promises a multitude of descendants (16:10; 21:18; 22:15–18). In the case of the aqedah, the promise comes in the angel's *second* speech, whereas in chapter 16, it comes in the *first* (in chapter 21, there is only one angelic address). Though the second speech in the story of the aqedah may be of later origin than the first, the renewal in it of the promise to Abraham of descendants "as numerous as the stars of the heaven and the sands on the seashore" (22:17) fits within the pattern that the two expulsions of Hagar have led us to expect. If 22:15–18 is secondary from the vantage point of compositional history, it is, nonetheless, indispensable to the literary shape and underlying theology of the story. Each of the three stories has its etiological features, but the meaning of none of them *reduces* to its etiological function. Each tells the story of the symbolic death and unexpected new life of the beloved son, a story of far more than mere etiological significance.

Chapter Twelve

Isaac Unbound (OR: CONTRA KIERKEGAARD)
(The Knight of Faith vs Knight of Observance)

Gerhard von Rad sees in the beginning of the story of the *aqedah* a twofold movement. On the one hand, the announcement that "God put Abraham to the test" (Gen 22:1) destroys the tension in the narrative: we know that the following events are only a test, that God does not desire the death of Isaac. On the other hand, this very knowledge, according to von Rad, engenders another tension: how will Abraham conduct himself in this most painful of tests?[1] Through this interpretation, von Rad aligns himself with the school of thought, best exemplified in Kierkegaard's *Fear and Trembling*, that views the aqedah as a test of Abraham's *faith*. The question is not whether God might really command the slaughter of the beloved son, but whether Abraham's faith in the promise of nation and progeny is sufficiently powerful as to allow him even to obey the command to make a burnt offering of Isaac, the one, as von Rad puts it, in whom "every saving thing that God has promised is invested and guaranteed."[2] In subscribing to this view, von Rad, like Kierkegaard a Lutheran, replicates the most basic paradigm movement in the theology of his own tradition, the Pauline paradigm that affirms faith in contradistinction to deeds as the supreme and defining element in spiritual authenticity. Abraham is not rewarded so much for his *act* of slaughtering his beloved son—an act halted only after he has gone so far as to pick up the knife (v 10)—as for his *faith* in the promise that Isaac shall live. The main point about Abraham's preparations for the slaughter is not that he *acts* in obedience to God's commandments, but rather that he demonstrates his *trust* in God's prevenient and gracious word of promise. "God," von Rad writes, "therefore poses before Abraham the question whether he really understands the gift of promise as a pure gift" and not as "a good that may be retained by virtue of any legal title or with the help of a human demand."[3] In and of itself, Abraham's obedience accomplishes nothing. It serves only as a demonstration of his superlative

faith over act

faith, and it is this demonstration of faith that constitutes his passing the great test. Failure to do so would, by the same token, be a sign not so much of disobedience—though it would certainly be that—as of faithlessness, an unwillingness to trust in the "saving thing that God has promised."

The announcement that "God put Abraham to the test" cannot, however, be interpreted as von Rad takes it, as a signal to the reader (though not to Abraham) that the aqedah is only a test. Nothing in the verb used (*nissâ*) implies that the act commanded will not be carried to completion, that Isaac will be only bound and not sacrificed on the altar. Though von Rad wisely objects to the view that the aqedah is intended as an etiology of animal instead of human sacrifice,[4] he is still disinclined to reckon with the point I sought to establish in part I: Israel did not always abominate the sacrifice of the first-born son, and some biblical passages are best taken as an endorsement of the practice. Without uncritical harmonization, there is no reason to exclude Gen 22:1–19 from the roster of such passages. This being the case, Abraham's willingness to heed the frightful command may or may not demonstrate faith in the promise that is invested in Isaac, but it surely and abundantly demonstrates his putting obedience to God ahead of every possible competitor. And if this is so, then if Abraham had failed to heed, he would have exhibited not so much a lack of faith in the promise as a love for Isaac that surpassed even his fear of God. He would, in other words, have elected Isaac his own son over Isaac the beloved son in the larger providential drama, the son whose very existence, from the moment of the angelic annunciation of his impending birth, has run counter to the naturalness of familial life. The aqedah, in short, tests whether Abraham is prepared to surrender his son to the God who gave him. To say, with Kierkegaard and von Rad, that he is prepared so to do because through faith he expects to receive Isaac anew (as indeed happens) is to minimize the frightfulness of what Abraham is commanded to do. It is also, I hope to show, to miss one of the key ambiguities and energizing tensions of the story.

The frightful command itself is preceded by a call: "He said to him, 'Abraham,' and he answered, 'Here I am'" (Gen 22:1b). The pattern will be repeated, with significant variations, in v 7, when Isaac addresses his father, and in v 11, when the angel cancels the original command. "Here I am" is, however, a pallid rendering of the Hebrew *hinnēnî*. Much to be preferred is E. A. Speiser's one-word translation, "Ready." It is all the more to be regretted, therefore, that even Speiser shifts to "Yes" in v 7 and "Here I am" in v 11, thus depriving his readers of a sense of how the Hebrew word functions as a refrain throughout the aqedah.[5] In none of these verses is there an inquiry about the Patriarch's location. What is at stake, instead, is his readiness to act upon a command from God (vv 1, 11) and to face the human consequences (v 7).

The structure of the initial command tells much about the underlying theology of the passage:

And He said, "Take your son, your favored one, the one whom you love, Isaac, and go forth to the land of Moriah, and offer him there as a burnt offering on one of the heights that I will point out to you." (Gen 22:2)[6]

The effect of the four designations of the person to be sacrificed is beautifully brought out in a midrash:

"Your son." He said to him, "I have two sons. *Which* son?" he answered him, "your favored one." He said to him, "Each is the favored one of his own mother." He replied, "the one whom you love." He said, "Is there a limit to the affections?" He answered, "Isaac." And why did He not reveal it to him immediately? In order to make him more beloved to him and to give him a reward for each utterance. This is according to the opinion of Rabbi Yochanan, who said [that in Gen 12:1, "Go forth from your native land, from your kinsmen, and from your father's house to the land that I will show you"] "your native land" means "your province," "your kinsmen" means "your settlement," and "your father's house" means just that. And why did He not reveal it to him immediately? In order to make it more beloved to him and to give him a reward for each utterance and for each step.

Said Rabbi Levi bar Hayta: Twice it is written "Go forth [*lek-lĕkā*, Gen 12:1 and 22:2], and do we not know which was more precious, the first or the second? From the words "go forth to the land of Moriah" (22:2), it must be the case that the second was more precious than the first. (*Gen. Rab.* 55:7)

The beginning of the midrash demonstrates the step effect of the four terms that designate the victim of the slaughter commanded in Gen 22:2. The term "son" is the least powerful: "I have two sons." The word *yāḥîd*, here rendered as "favored one," is more poignant. Given its associations with child sacrifice explored earlier,[8] the term hints at the nature of the "taking" here commanded. It will be a "taking" like that of Exod 12:3, in which the community of Israel is enjoined to "take a lamb to a family, a lamb to a household" for sacrifice on the first Passover. In Genesis 22, however, it is not a lamb that will be sacrificed, at least according to v 2, but Abraham's chosen son. The next term in the series heightens the tension even more. The son sacrificed will be "the one whom you love." To fulfill the frightful command Abraham will have to suppress his paternal affections, placing obedience to God not above ethics, as Kierkegaard would have it, but above his love for Isaac—in some ways a more daunting task. And only last in the series of four terms comes the name of the beloved son who is to be sacrificed by his own father—Isaac. Only when the name has been pronounced, and all ambiguity has been removed— and with it all hope for evasion—only then does the full impact of the command hit home. As the midrash suggests, each of these terms underscores the preciousness of Isaac, the beloved son marked for sacrifice, and yet Abraham does not flinch but goes forth to slaughter the boy whose specialness has never been made so clear as it is at that moment. Had the text "reveal[ed] it to him immediately," as the midrash puts it, naming Isaac first or leaving out the three preceding terms, the literary effect would have been so much the weaker. And the theological point would have been missed: Abraham is ordered not simply to perform an act of radical obedience, not simply to sacrifice his own child, but to slaughter the one person who now occupies the simultaneously exalted and humiliating status of the beloved son. "If Abraham had had a hundred bodies," writes Bachya ben Asher, a Jewish commentator of the fourteenth century, on v 1, "it would have been suitable to give them all up for the sake of Isaac, but this act was not like any other, this trial was not like any other, and nature cannot bear it, nor the imagination conceive it."[9]

Two factors call forth the association in the midrash between the command to Abraham to sacrifice Isaac in Gen 22:2 and the command to commence his great journey in 12:2. First, there is the expression *lek-lĕkā*, "go forth," which is peculiar to these two verses. Second but more important is the step effect of the nouns: "your son, your favored one, the one whom you love" in chapter 22 and "from your native land, from your kinsmen, and from your father's house" in chapter 12. The association having thus been made, we are led to notice an additional common point: in both cases the text refrains from naming the destination. In 22:2, it is simply "one of the heights that I will point out to you"; in 12:1, it is simply "the land that I will show you."[10] That in each instance Abraham begins his trek without knowing where it is to end only enhances our appreciation of his extraordinary obedience to the divine directive. In the case of the aqedah, Abraham's ignorance of the destination is emblematic of the surprise that awaits him on that height in the land of Moriah when the command of 22:2 is countermanded and he, like the community of Israel in Exodus 12, is allowed to substitute a sheep for the beloved son who had been marked for doom.

Two of the four denotations of Isaac in Gen 22:2, the first and the last, reappear in v 3:

So early next morning, Abraham saddled his ass and took with him two of his servants and his son Isaac. He split the wood for the burnt offering, and he set out for the place of which God had told him. (Gen 22:3)

Once again, "Isaac" appears in the climactic position. The preceding term "son" not only echoes the frightful command of the previous verse, but also foreshadows the continual emphasis on the father-son relationship that will appear throughout the report of the events at Moriah. The conclusion of v 3 further underscores the conformity of Abraham's actions to the divine command of v 2. God having commanded him to set out for the height "that I will point out to you" ('ăšer 'ōmar 'ēlêkā), Abraham now goes to the place "of which God had spoken" ('ăšer 'āmar-lô hā'ĕlōhîm). Why he does so remains, and will always remain, unclear. On the basis of the report of the expulsion of Ishmael in the previous chapter, where initially "the matter distressed Abraham greatly" (21:11), we might have reasonably expected some resistance to carrying out the gruesome order to immolate Isaac. Against this expectation, it can be rejoined that the distress in chapter 21 came only in response to Sarah's demand that Hagar and Ishmael be expelled. When God endorsed the demand ("whatever Sarah tells you, do as she says, for it is through Isaac that offspring shall be continued for you," v 12), Abraham acquiesced, and loaded up Hagar for the journey, just as he loads up for the trek to Moriah in 22:3. According to this rejoinder, Abraham is always and ever submissive to God, and since it is God rather than another person who presents him with the gruesome order of v 2, he obeys. Yet, even so, some will wonder why the Patriarch did not question the justice of the order, as he questioned, for example, the justice of YHWH's plan to obliterate Sodom and Gomorrah for their sins:

Far be it from You to do such a thing, to bring death upon the innocent as well as the guilty, so that the innocent and the guilty fare alike. Far be it from You! Shall not the Judge of all the earth deal justly? (Gen 18:25)

The man who spoke these astonishing words now not only agrees to the slaughter of his innocent son but willingly obeys the command to be the very one who offers the sacrifice. Whereas in chapter 18, Abraham passes the test God assigns him (vv 17–19) by speaking up in protest against God's own counsel, in chapter 22 he passes the test by obeying the divine command unquestioningly (vv 12, 15–18). There are, of course, important differences between the two episodes. In Israelite culture, for example, though both were killed, a sacrificial victim was in no way comparable to a guilty person administered capital punishment: not every slaughter was deemed punitive. It must also be noted that in Genesis 18, Abraham questions God's conformity to his own principles, principles reaffirmed even in the divine monologue in which God announces the test (vv 17–19), whereas contrary to what many have thought, there is no reason to suggest that the child sacrifice commanded in chapter 22 contradicts what the society at the time identified as God's own norms. Finally, it should be noted that in the episode of Sodom and Gomorrah, Abraham, ever in a posture of deference and submission, challenges God's *plan*, whereas in the story of the aqedah, the plan remains unknown, and Abraham is left with only a *command*. As always, he obeys his God's wishes.

There is in Jewish tradition the notion that through his prophetic gifts, Abraham knew that he would not have to carry out the command to sacrifice Isaac. For example, on the verse in which Abraham tells the two boys to wait because "we [he and Isaac] will worship and we will return to you" (Gen 22:5), Rashi, the great eleventh-century commentator, remarks, "He prophesied that both of them would return."[11] The knowledge at issue here still involves a not inconsequential measure of faith—faith that the prophetic message is authentic and the God who authors it, reliable. In this, it must be distinguished from empirical knowledge, in which the element of trust is of less importance, if it figures at all. What is tested in Gen 22:1–19 is not Abraham's knowledge, as knowledge is generally understood today, but his devotion to God, the God who now demands the ultimate sacrifice.

Without employing the concept of prophecy, Kierkegaard also endorses the view that Abraham obeyed the command to immolate Isaac with the full expectation that his son would survive:

> But what did Abraham do? He arrived neither too soon nor too late. He mounted the ass, he rode slowly along the way. All that time he believed—he believed that God would not require Isaac of him, whereas he was willing nevertheless to sacrifice him if it was required. He believed by virtue of the absurd; for there could be no question of human calculation, and it was indeed the absurd that God who required it of him should the next instant recall the requirement. He climbed the mountain, even at the instant when the knife glittered he believed . . . that God would not require Isaac. He was indeed astonished at the outcome, but by a double-movement he had reached his first position, and therefore he received Isaac more gladly than the first time. Let us go further. We let Isaac be really sacrificed. Abraham believed. He did not believe that some day he would be blessed in the beyond, but that he would be happy here in the world. God could give him a new Isaac, could recall to life him who had been sacrificed.[12]

Here the profound Pauline-Lutheran wellsprings of Kierkegaard's interpretation assert themselves again. It is not just that Abraham acts according to an inward faith that offers exemption from legal norms; the basis of that faith may even be an expectation of bodily resurrection: if he is slain, Isaac will be recalled to life. The influence of the New Testament could not be more obvious:

> [17]By faith Abraham, when put to the test, offered up Isaac, and he who had received the promises was ready to slay his only son, [18]of whom it was said, "it is through Isaac that offspring shall be continued for you." [Gen 21:12] [19]He reasoned that God was able to raise even from the dead, and he received Isaac back as a symbol. (Heb 11:17–19)[13]

Without those Christian beliefs, it is doubtful that Kierkegaard would have offered an interpretation of the binding of Isaac (or, as Christians tend, revealingly, to call it, the "sacrifice" of Isaac) as based upon faith. As a number of classical Jewish commentators point out,[14] there is another, more pragmatic and less theological explanation of those ominous words, "we will worship and we will return to you": Abraham is worried that if the two boys learn his true intention, they will protest the impending sacrifice or even prevent him from carrying it out. Similarly, it can be argued that he does not want Isaac to know what awaits him on the mountaintop. Will the son share his father's total devotion to God? Or will he lose nerve, resist the sacrifice, and flee for his life? It might also be the case that Abraham cannot bring himself to express the enormity of what he is resolved to do. Perhaps fearing lest the very expression of his intention fracture his resolve and cause him to fail the great test, he resorts to a vague euphemism, "we will worship." Or perhaps the term, which literally means "to bow down," is not a euphemism at all, but conveys Abraham's intention to prostrate himself *in supplication* that the homicidal commandment be rescinded (cf. 2 Sam 14:33). Bachya ben Asher suggests a more chilling interpretation: "Abraham intended to bring [Isaac's] bones back with him, and therefore he said 'we will return to you' in the plural."[15] These alternative construals of Abraham's words and actions would not have come to be, I submit, if Kierkegaard's Christian view of Abraham as a paragon of faith were self-evident, or even reasonably clear. All to the contrary, it is precisely the narrator's technique in telling the tale of the aqedah that keeps us in the dark on the issue of Abraham's subjectivity, the very point about which Kierkegaard claims so much information. It is this narrative austerity that Erich Auerbach highlights in his description of the stylistic characteristics of the passage:

the externalization of only so much of the phenomena as is necessary for the purpose of the narrative, all else left in obscurity; the decisive points of the narrative alone are emphasized, what lies between is non-existent; time and place are undefined and call for interpretation; thoughts and feelings remain unexpressed, are only suggested by the silence and the fragmentary speeches; the whole, permeated with the most unrelieved suspense and directed toward a single goal . . . remains mysterious and "fraught with background."[16]

It is to be wished that the narrator's reticence about Abraham's and Isaac's "thoughts and feelings" would be honored by the theologians who interpret the story of the aqedah: not that interpretation should be forgone, but that it should respect "the silence and fragmentary speeches" characteristic of the narrative and recognize that the ambiguity that these enhance is to be upheld rather than resolved.

The ambiguity comes to its zenith in the middle section of the narrative:

> [6]Abraham took the wood for the burnt offering and put it on his son Isaac. He himself took the firestone and the knife; and the two of them walked together. [7]Then Isaac said to his father Abraham, "Father!" And he answered, "Yes, my son." And he said, "Here are the firestone and the wood; but where is the sheep for the burnt offering?" [8]And Abraham said, "God will see to the sheep for His burnt offering, my son." And the two of them walked together. (Gen 22:6–8)[17]

In connection with the expulsion of Ishmael in 21:14, we have already had occasion to cite the midrashic comment on Abraham's loading the wood for the burnt offering upon Isaac: it is "like one who carries his cross on his own shoulder" (*Gen. Rab.* 56:3). As in the case of Ishmael, so here with Isaac what is loaded on the shoulder symbolizes the impending death of the son, specifically, the waterskin for the older boy, the firewood for the younger. But the aqedah is not merely a reenactment of the near-loss and miraculous deliverance of Ishmael. It is, instead, immensely more suspenseful and immensely more poignant. Ishmael, as we have seen, is a baby in chapter 21, despite the Priestly chronological notice elsewhere that makes him thirteen at Isaac's birth (17:23–27). He thus has no awareness of what looms and no active participation in the events that transpire. In no sense may Ishmael be said to offer his life, nor is his distraught mother asked or prepared to hand it over: "Let me not look on as the child dies" (21:16), Hagar pleads. In the story of the aqedah, by contrast, Isaac is old enough to carry the firewood and does not flinch from so doing, though the animal to be offered has been tellingly omitted from his father's dutiful preparations. And the death of the son is not something that the father seeks to avoid witnessing. He is commanded and thus prepared to slaughter the boy himself and to immolate the body of his beloved son as a gift to the God he serves.

The ambiguity of this middle section of the narrative attaches itself first to Isaac's question, his only words in the entire aqedah: "Father! . . . Here are the firestone and the wood; but where is the sheep for the burnt offering?" (Gen 22:7). The critical information here denied us is the son's age. As is usual when the biblical text exhibits a gap of such significance, the midrash fills it in. On the report in 23:2, that "Abraham came to mourn for Sarah and to bewail her,"[18] Rabbi Yose remarked: "From where did he come? From Mount Moriah, for Sarah died because of that very anguish. Therefore the aqedah appears adjacent to 'Sarah's lifetime' " [Gen 23:1] (*Gen. Rab.* 58:5) The assumption here, one that generates innumerable midrashim, is that the placement of passages in the Torah has been executed with the highest degree of intentionality and self-consciousness. The shift in subject matter between what we know as Genesis 22 and Genesis 23 is less radical than first seems the case. The notice about Sarah's lifespan in the first verse of chapter 23 openly presupposes her death, which therefore must have taken place in connection with the events of the previous chapter. It must, therefore, have been the report of the aqedah, reaching Sarah in Kiriath-arba (Hebron), that precipitated her demise. Since she died at one hundred twenty-seven, having borne Isaac at ninety (17:17), the son must have been thirty-seven at the time of his being bound on the altar for sacrifice. An alternative midrashic calculation makes Isaac twenty-six (*Gen. Rab.* 56:8),[19] and a pre-rabbinic Jewish tradition, fifteen (*Jub.* 17:15–16),[20] at the time of the aqedah. If any of these is correct or close to it, then we have to assume that Isaac asks his question in Gen 22:7 out of either stupidity or a desire to probe his father's mind. Though the middle patriarch does not strike one as an intellectual giant (see, for example, 27:18–28), the first possibility would seem out of place in a narrative of this degree of tension and power: the beloved and favored son whom Abraham is prepared to sacrifice is surely not a dolt who fails to notice the absence of the sheep only after a trek into the wilderness of three days' duration.

But why Isaac does raise the issue is one of those great ambiguities "suggested by the silence and the fragmentary speeches," to reappropriate Auerbach's words. Perhaps Isaac wishes to let his father know that he recognizes—and accepts—his role in the great drama unfolding: he knows that he is the one to be offered on the mountain, and yet, as is said of the suffering servant in Isa 53:7, "Like a sheep being led to slaughter / . . . he did not open his mouth." If this be the point of Isaac's question in Gen 22:7, then the second occurrence of the sentence "And the two walked together" (v 8) is infinitely more meaningful than the first (v 6). For the first time these words appear, Abraham has just assured his two attendants that he and Isaac will, after an act of worship, return to them. But by the second time, Isaac has accepted his own mandated role as victim. And the two of them still walked together, or to render the Hebrew *yaḥdāw* more literally, "as one." In the words of the midrash, "the one to bind, the other to be bound; the one to slaughter, the other to be slaughtered" (*Gen. Rab.* 56:4), yet the two went as one, the father and the son undivided in their obedience to God. If the point of Gen 22:6–8 is indeed to expose Isaac's resolute acceptance of his fate, then these verses begin the long trajectory that culminates in the medieval Jewish notion that the aqedah is as much a test of Isaac as of Abraham—Isaac the archetypical martyr in a race exemplary for its martyrs.[21] One influential point on that trajectory is the Gospel notion that the death of Jesus of Nazareth was voluntary.[22]

If in Gen 22:7 Isaac is accepting his sacrificial role, it remains unclear why, in the next verse, Abraham answers as he does: "God will see to the sheep for His burnt offering, my son" (v 8). On Kierkegaard's interpretation of Abraham as the knight of faith, whose trust in the divine promise is here being put to the test, the answer is of a piece with his assurance to the attendants that he and Isaac will return (v 5): believing "by virtue of the absurd," as Kierkegaard puts it, he reiterates his astonishing faith "that God would not require Isaac"[23]—except this time he affirms his faith to the very son he is preparing to sacrifice. On this reading, Abraham's words in v 8 confirm his candor in speaking those of v 5. He tells the attendants that "we will worship and we will return to you," not in order to forestall their protest or his own loss of nerve, but because his faith in the promise centering on Isaac remains unshakable even as he obeys God's gruesome command to slaughter his beloved son. And now he tells Isaac the same thing, that God will provide the sheep, and Isaac, if he is really the adult that Jewish tradition has usually seen in him, tacitly signals his participation in the faith of Abraham by walking together with his father to the hill on which that faith will soon be either vindicated or discredited.

But, here again, the silence of which Auerbach speaks cautions against confidence about Abraham's motivations. We cannot be sure what he is thinking and what he is feeling when he answers Isaac's poignant query about the sheep to be slaughtered atop the unspecified mountain. It could be that the same motivations that we speculated underlay his words to the attendants in Gen 22:5 also underlie his answer to Isaac in v 8. Perhaps he worries that

Isaac will *not* share his faith, and, worse, flee the scene so that Abraham will fail the test after all. This possibility is raised in the midrash:

> Rabbi Isaac said: At the moment that Abraham sought to bind his son Isaac, he said to him, "Father, I am a young man and I am fearful that my body will tremble out of fear of the knife and I cause you sorrow, so that the slaughter will be rendered unfit and this will not be accredited to you as a sacrifice. Therefore, bind me very tightly." Immediately: "he bound his son Isaac" [Gen 22:9]. Can one bind a man thirty-seven years old (another version: twenty-six years old) without his consent? (*Gen. Rab.* 56:8)

The beauty in Rabbi Isaac's comment is that it recognizes both Isaac's informed consent and the possibility that the victim may lose his resolve nonetheless. Generating the comment is the oddity of the very act from which the aqedah receives its name. Why does Abraham bind Isaac at all? The ordinary procedure for the burnt offering is to slay the victim first, then to flay and section it, and finally to lay the pieces over the burning wood as "an offering by fire of pleasing odor to the LORD" (Lev 1:3–9). Abraham's act of tying Isaac to the altar, atop the wood, is altogether anomalous. The explanation for the anomaly may well lie in the simple fact that the aqedah is the only account we have of the procedure for a *human* sacrifice. Perhaps in this instance, for precisely the reason that Rabbi Isaac highlights, it was standard procedure to tie the victim down before the slaughter. One could, however, take a somewhat different tack from the rabbi's and suggest that the motivation for the binding lies not in any request of Isaac's, but in Abraham's fear that his son will render the sacrifice unfit precisely because he does not share his father's unshakable resolve to do the will of God at any price, or in Kierkegaard's terms, his father's absolute faith in the promise that requires that Isaac live. If this be so, then Abraham's answer in v 8—"God will see to the sheep for His burnt offering, my son"—is an attempt to keep Isaac in the dark, lest the sacrifice not take place and Abraham prove disobedient to his Lord.[24] It is the verbal equivalent of tying Isaac to the altar.

Isaac's question in Gen 22:7 and Abraham's answer in the following verse must be interpreted very differently if the son is only a small child. In that case, the question exposes not Isaac's consent to his fate, but almost the opposite, his naiveté about what awaits him at the end of the journey with his father. That he is old enough to speak in sentences and to carry the wood is indisputable but does not establish that he comprehends what is about to take place. Indeed, we must raise the possibility that Isaac is too young to understand death, a point that reaches an almost unbearable intensity when one considers that to all appearances, it is death that awaits him and him alone when he and his father reach their appointed destination. In that case, Abraham's reply in v 8 may still be an expression of his boundless faith. But it may also be the only answer that Isaac can grasp, and his father's offering it may be the kindest thing he can do under the circumstances—a white lie that puts the little boy at ease and prevents the father from having to articulate the horrendous deed that he is about to perpetrate. Some classical Jewish commentators are fond of the idea that Abraham's answer in v 8 is intended to appease Isaac without necessarily being altogether false. Rashi, for example, interprets the verse to mean " 'God will see to the sheep,' and if there is no sheep, 'for His burnt offering—my son.' " That is, either a sheep or Isaac will prove the victim. This interpretation, which Qimchi defends in detail, forces the natural division of the verse and cannot be sustained as plain sense. It does, however, capture nicely the very plausible notion that in Gen 22:8 Abraham is doing something other and much less pious than expressing Kierkegaardian faith in the absurd promise in which he trusts nonetheless. He may, instead, be giving voice to his uncertainty as to the results of his own extraordinary obedience. That God did indeed see to the sheep need not imply that Abraham knew that this would be the case, even if the knowledge at issue be by faith alone.

The climax of the story of the aqedah recalls the terms in which the action began, only with vastly heightened intensity:

> [9] They arrived at the place of which God had told him. Abraham built an altar there; he laid out the wood; he bound his son Isaac; he laid him on the altar, on top of the wood. [10] And Abraham picked up the knife to slay his son. [11] Then an angel of the LORD called to him from heaven: "Abraham! Abraham!" And he answered, "Here I am." [12] And he said, "Do not raise your hand against the boy, or do anything to him. For now I know that you fear God, since you have not withheld your son, your favored one, from Me." (Gen 22:9–12)

"The place of which God had told him" in v 9 (*hammāqôm 'ăšer 'āmar-lô hā'ĕlōhîm*) echoes precisely the term for the destination of Abraham's journey in v 3, itself a slight variant of the wording at the end of the command to sacrifice Isaac in v 2: The Patriarch is doing precisely what he intended, which is precisely what he was commanded to do. His consistency is total. If the command is not to be fulfilled, this will have to happen by God's change of mind, not that of his obedient servant. Abraham's laying (*wayyāśem*) Isaac "on the altar, on top of the wood" (v 9) is an entirely consistent reversal of the touching report in v 6, that Abraham "put [*wayyāśem*] [the wood for the burnt offering] on his son Isaac." The situation has now come full circle, and Isaac takes the place of the sheep about whose absence he inquired in v 7. Willingly or not, he has, by carrying the wood, made possible the death that now seems his inexorable fate.

The call of the angel of the LORD in v 11 resumes the divine address of vv 1–2 even as it reverses it. Qimchi is surely right that the purpose of the double vocative—"Abraham! Abraham!"—is "that he hear quickly and refrain from slaying [Isaac]." As Ibn Ezra puts it, the angel calls the name "twice, as if in haste." The contrast with the initial divine address of v 1, with its single vocative, is patent and suggestive of the change of pace that has taken place. The narrative began with a sense of slowness, apparent even in the cadences of the sentence structure, especially in v 2: "Take your son, your favored one, the one whom you love, Isaac"[25] Abraham prepared for the journey not immediately, but only "early next morning" (v 3). Now the narrative ends in a rush, with a sense of suddenness, as the angel hurriedly tries to get the attention of the man absorbed in executing the divine command—and his beloved son. That remarkable absorption is reiterated in the twofold prohibition, "Do not raise your hand against the boy, or do anything to him" (v 12). Abraham's answer to the angelic call, "Here I am" (*hinnēnî*, v 11) recalls v 1, in which the Patriarch answers God's address with the identical word. Here, as there, Speiser's "Ready" better captures the sense of this almost untranslatable term than the pallid "Here I am."[26] And it bears reiteration that between Abraham's two declarations of his readiness to receive God's instructions (vv 1, 11) comes the same declaration in response to his son (*hinnennî*, v 7). But whereas his intention with regard to God's command is clear, the meaning of his answer to Isaac remains shrouded in tantalizing obscurity. Obscure though the reason be, however, it is abundantly clear from Abraham's reply in v 8 that he is not at all ready to tell Isaac the blunt truth about the sacrifice he is prepared to carry out on God's instructions.

God's reason for calling off the sacrifice is stated with unmistakable clarity in Gen 22:12: "For now I know that you fear God, since you have not withheld your son, your favored one, from Me." The test announced in v 1, then, is a test of which is stronger, Abraham's fear of God or his love of Isaac, and once the answer is in, the sacrifice therein commanded can be called off. "Your son, your favored one" in v 12 harks back to the initial fourfold designation of the victim in v 2, "your son, your favored one, the one whom you love, Isaac." The reduction to only two of these terms may be a further indication of the heightened pace of the narrative at its conclusion. It may also be the case that Abraham's fear of God, that is, his reverential obedience to YHWH, has altogether overwhelmed his love of Isaac in the sentence structure no less than in the event, so that "the one whom you love, Isaac" is no longer at issue. The only point is that which the entire trial aims to prove: that Abraham's obedience is absolute and uncompromising. Just as the trial begins with "God ['s] put[ting] Abraham to the test" with no mention of Isaac, so does it end with God's acknowledgment that Abraham fears him without any mention of Isaac's name or the countervailing force of his paternal affection for the beloved son whom he has refused to withhold (v 12).

In this first angelic address (Gen 22:11–12), no reward for Abraham's definitive proof of his fear of God is specified. Perhaps we are to understand the possibility of continued life with Isaac as the reward. Or, perhaps the specification of a reward would have undercut the whole point of the trial, to demonstrate the completeness and utter selflessness of Abraham's devotion to his God. The matter is different in the second angelic address:

> [15]The angel of the LORD called to Abraham a second time from heaven, [16]and said, "By Myself I swear, the LORD declares: Because you have done this and have not withheld your son, your favored one, [17]I will bestow My blessing upon you and make your descendants as numerous as the stars of heaven and the sands on the seashore; and your descendants shall seize the gates of their foes. [18]All the nations of the earth shall bless themselves by your descendants, because you have obeyed My command." (Gen 22:15–18)

Beginning where the first speech left off, "because you have done this and have not withheld your son, your favored one" (v 15; cf. v 12), this second address makes Abraham's binding of Isaac for sacrifice into the basis for a renewal of the covenantal promise of nation, land ("your descendants shall seize the gates of their foes," v 17), and blessing. In so doing, it gives the story of the aqedah an ending that, like its beginning, recalls the first speech of God to Abram. That speech directed him to "go forth" (lek-lĕkā) from his homeland and his family to an unspecified land (12:1–3), and the aqedah began with the order to "go forth" (lek-lĕkā) to an unspecified height in the mysterious land of Moriah and thereon to give up his son (22:2), even as he had given up his "native land and [his] father's house" years before (12:1, 4). At that point, the promise of nation and blessing, as well as that of land soon to follow (v 7), rested on a foundation of pure grace. In the Bible, unlike the midrash, no prior deed is reported that could possibly explain this astonishing promise. But for the rabbis there is a problem with this: the special grace to Abraham thus makes his God vulnerable to the charge of arbitrariness, a charge that is recognized in the midrash but emphatically refuted there:

"Some time afterward God put Abraham to the test [*nissâ*]" [Gen 22:1]. It is written, "You have given[27] those who fear You (*lîrē'êkā*) because of Your truth a banner [*nēs*] for rallying [*lĕhitnôsēs*]" [Ps 60:6]—trial upon trial [*nissāyôn 'ahar nissāyôn*], exaltation upon exaltation in order to test them [*lĕnassôtām*] in the world and to exalt them in the world like the flag [*nēs*] of a ship. And why all this? "[B]ecause of Your truth [*qōšet*]": in order that God's attribute of justice may be verified [*titqaššēt*] in the world. For if someone says to you, "Whom He wishes to enrich, He enriches; whom He wishes to impoverish, He impoverishes, and whom He wishes He makes king—when He wished, He made Abraham rich, when He wished He made him king—" then you can answer him and say to him, "Can you do what our father Abraham did?" "What did he do?" You can say to him, "Now Abraham was a hundred years old when his son Isaac was born to him" [Gen 21:5]. Yet after all this anguish, it was said to him, "Take your son, your favored one," etc. [22:2], and he did not resist. Hence, "You have given those who fear You because of Your truth a banner [*nēs*] for rallying [*lĕhitnôsēs*]" [Ps 60:6] and, "God put Abraham to the test [*nissâ*]" [Gen 22:2]. (*Gen. Rab.* 55:1)

The midrash plays upon the similarity in sound between the Hebrew words for "test" (*nissâ*) and "trial" (*nissāyôn*), on the one hand, and those for "flag" (*nēs*) and "rallying" (*hitnôsēs*) on the other. The application of Ps 60:6 to the aqedah is generated not only by these near-homophonies, but also by the term "those who fear [God]" (*lîrē'êkā*) in the psalm and the angelic announcement in Gen 22:12 that Abraham is one of them (*yĕrē' 'ĕlōhîm*). The larger theological point is that the trials of the righteous serve to demonstrate not God's injustice, as many think to be the case, but quite the opposite, the fairness of his choices. For those choices are not mere whims, evidence of the arbitrariness of providence, and the proof is that those chosen, like Abraham, for exaltation, are able to pass the brutal tests to which God subjects them and thus to vindicate the grace he has shown them. The trials that appear to be their humiliation are, in fact, the means of their exaltation, proof positive that their special destiny is based on other than caprice. The trials of the righteous mediate the contradiction between God's grace and his justice. They also make sense of the combination of humiliations and exaltations in the lives of the chosen.

The sensitivity of the midrash quoted above to the charge that the God of Israel is capricious finds its parallel within the story of the aqedah only in Gen 22:15–18, the second speech of the angel of YHWH to Abraham. The clear purpose of this speech is to renew the great promise of nation, blessing, and land on the basis of Abraham's willingness to donate Isaac for sacrifice. As in the midrash, so in the second angelic address, the aqedah demonstrates retroactively the rightness of God's ostensibly arbitrary singling out of Abram for the most exalted of destinies.[28] The language of this oracle draws the aqedah and the promise together beautifully. "Because [you] have not withheld your son, your favored one" (v 16) echoes both the first angelic oracle (v 12) and the original command to sacrifice Isaac (v 2), and the bestowal of the blessing in v 17 (*kî-bārēk 'ăbārekĕkā*) echoes the initial promises to him in 12:1–3 (cf. *wa'ăbārekĕkā*, v 2). The promise to make Abraham's "descendants as numerous as the stars of the heaven and the sands on the seashore" recalls not only that original promise, but also the subsequent assurances of plenteous offspring in 13:16 ("I will make your offspring as the dust of the earth") and 15:5 ("Look toward heaven and count the stars . . . So shall your offspring be."). "I will . . . make your descendants . . . numerous" (*wĕharbâ 'arbeh 'et-zar-'ăkā*) in 22:17 echoes the angelic promise to Hagar after her first expulsion, "I will greatly increase your offspring" (*harbâ 'arbeh 'et-zar'ēk*, 16:10). The promise thus draws an implicit analogy between Abraham's willingness to sacrifice Isaac and the suffering of Hagar that prompted YHWH to console her with the announcement of Ishmael's birth and manner of life (16:11–12). If the greatness of the Ishmaelite nation is founded upon the affliction of the slavewoman who was their matriarch, the greatness of the Israelite nation, according to 22:15–18, rests upon Abraham's surrender of Isaac for sacrifice to YHWH. As we have had occasion to note, the only other attestation of the expression *harbâ 'arbeh* is in 3:16, when YHWH greatly multiplies the primal woman's pangs of childbearing. Whether this distribution is coincidence or deliberate is impossible to know. From the standpoint of intertextual connections, however, it clearly suggests that Hagar's submission to affliction and Abraham's unstinting conformity to the horrendous command of his God counteract "Man's First Disobedience," the sin of eating the forbidden fruit in the Garden of Eden. The effect of all the superabundant allusiveness of the second angelic address in Gen 22:15–18 is to reconceive the aqedah as a foundational act. It is not only that the binding of Isaac vindicates God's mysterious singling out of Abram. It is also the case that Abraham's obedience to the God who demands the death of his beloved son now becomes the basis for the blessedness of the people descended from him through that very son. The idea that the binding of Isaac continues to exert influence throughout the generations is, in different ways, basic both to rabbinic Judaism and to Christianity.[29] But it is in the angel's second speech to Abraham in Gen 22:15–18 that this enormously important idea is first attested.

The oracle in Gen 22:15–18 also serves to confirm Kierkegaard's paradoxical point that Abraham retains Isaac and the promise that centers on him only because of his willingness to carry out the command to immolate his beloved son. Against Kierkegaard, however, it must again be noted that it is far from clear in the text that Abraham obeyed because of *faith* in the promise. Indeed, the renewal of the Abrahamic promise to Isaac after his father's death suggests that the promise rested primarily on *obedience*, quite apart from faith in its realization:

> ¹There was a famine in the land—aside from the previous famine that had occurred in the days of Abraham—and Isaac went to Abimelech, king of the Philistines, in Gerar. ²The LORD had appeared to him and said, "Do not go down to Egypt, stay in the land which I point out to you. ³Reside in this land, and I will be with you and bless you; I will assign all these lands to you and to your offspring, fulfilling the oath that I swore to your father Abraham. ⁴I will make your descendants as numerous as the stars of heaven, and give to your descendants all these lands, so that all the nations of the earth shall bless themselves by your offspring—inasmuch as Abraham obeyed Me and kept My charge: My commandments, My laws, and My teachings. (Gen 26:1–5)

The reverberations of the story of Abraham in these five verses are legion. In v 1, the reverberation is an explicit reference: Isaac finds himself faced with famine, as did his father (12:10). Only this time he must break with his father's precedent and avoid the ominous descent into Egypt (26:2). "The land which I point out to you" (*hā'āreṣ 'ăšer 'ōmar 'ēlêkā*) recalls both "the land that I will show you" (*hā'āreṣ 'ăšer 'arekkā*) at the beginning of the story of Abraham (12:1) and "one of the heights that I will point out to you ('*aḥad hehārîm 'ăšer 'ōmar 'ēlêkā*) near its end, at the onset of the aqedah (22:2). The explicit conception of the promise to Abraham as an oath [*šĕbū'â*] in 26:3 suggests the second angelic promise in 22:16, "By Myself I swear . . . [*nišba'tî*]." The closest connection of the oracle to Isaac in 26:2b-5 with the second angelic address to Abraham in 22:15–18, however, is the reason given for the devolution of the promise of progeny, blessing, and land to Isaac: Abraham's superlative obedience to YHWH's directives (26:5). Abraham may have been the knight of faith that Kierkegaard, like most Christian and Jewish thinkers, have seen in him. But texts like Gen 22:1–19 and 26:2b-5 stress another side of the Patriarch— Abraham as the knight of observance, rigorously keeping his divine master's charge. For the ongoing Jewish tradition, one item in that enormous charge, ironically, is the Pentateuchal prohibition on child sacrifice.[30]

N B

Through the aqedah, Abraham surrenders his beloved son to the God who made his miraculous conception possible. The natural father hands over the son born outside the course of nature to the divine father whose due he is.

The divine father exercises his prerogative to decline the offering he demanded, Isaac is allowed to live, and a sheep takes his place over the fire. But
the Isaac who survives the aqedah is no longer the "boy" (Gen 22:5) who
accompanied his father on that fateful journey to Moriah. He is, instead, a
man ready for marriage, a point brought out nicely by the genealogy that
follows the aqedah, with the words "Bethuel being the father of Rebekah"
(22:23). The point is underscored by a subtle item of diction as well. The
angel's second address to Abraham promises him that "your descendants shall
seize the gates of their foes" (*wĕyīrāš zarᶜăkā 'ēt šaᶜar 'ōyĕbāyw*, 22:17), and,
when two chapters later, Rebekah's family blesses the maiden as she is about
to leave for Canaan and marriage to Isaac, they say, "May your offspring
seize / the gates of their foes" (*wĕyîrāš zarᶜēk 'et šaᶜar śōnĕ'āyw*, 24:60). The
unusual blessing occurring only in these two texts,[31] we can reasonably surmise
that the narrator wishes to underscore yet again the providential character of
the match of Isaac with Rebekah. The Isaac who emerges from the aqedah
is less his father's son than a patriarch in his own right, about to marry and,
after years of childlessness reminiscent of his father's experience (25:20–21),
to beget the children who will themselves be a further fulfillment of the
irrevocable promise. All this offers further corroboration for Hugh C. White's
interpretation of the aqedah as an initiation ritual, in which "the child is made
to face his own imminent death and to accept it emotionally" as the essential
act in his "passage into independence and manhood."[32] But the aqedah is, let
us not forget, also and primarily an ordeal for Abraham, who, in order to
play his role in the providential drama, must surrender his son to God so that
the son may assume his own foreordained role.

  One paradox of the aqedah is that it is Abraham's willingness to give up
Isaac that insures the fulfillment of the promise that depends on Isaac. The
other paradox is this: though Abraham does not give up his son through
sacrifice, he gives him up nonetheless—to the God who gave Isaac life, ordered
him slaughtered, and finally grants him his exalted role in the divine plan.
The aqedah is not only about the aversion of a child sacrifice. It is also about
the profound and sublime meaning in the cultic norm that the beloved son
belongs to God: "You shall give Me the first-born among your sons" (Exod
22:28b).

Chapter Thirteen

The Beloved Son as Ruler and Servant   JOSEPH

The story of Joseph in Genesis 37–50 is not only the longest and most
intricate Israelite exemplar of the narrative of the death and resurrection of
the beloved son, but also the most explicit. In it is concentrated almost
every variation of the theme that first appeared in the little tale of Cain and
Abel and has been growing and becoming more involved and more
complex throughout the Book of Genesis. The story of Joseph thus not
only concludes the book and links the Patriarchal narratives to those of the
people Israel in Egypt for which they serve as archetypes; it is also the
crescendo to the theme of the beloved son, which it presents in
extraordinarily polished literary form. It is arguably the most sophisticated   So too
narrative in the Jewish or the Christian Bibles.   in
   It is the belovedness of Joseph to his father that calls forth his brothers'   Qur'an
jealousy and, ultimately, their attempt to do away with him:

> ²At seventeen years of age, Joseph tended the flocks with his brothers,
> as a helper to the sons of his father's wives Bilhah and Zilpah. And
> Joseph brought bad reports of them to their father. ³Now Israel loved
> Joseph best of all his sons, for he was the child of his old age; and he
> had made him an ornamented tunic. ⁴And when his brothers saw that
> their father loved him more than any of his brothers, they hated him so
> that they could not speak a friendly word to him. (Gen 37:2b-4)

In a mere two and a half verses, the narrator here sets up the problematic
of Joseph's status, which is, in turn, the force that sets the story—and its
hero—on its uncertain way. Joseph is not only one of the youngest of the
brood but the son given the most menial task—to assist the sons of his
father's wives', the slaves Bilhah and Zilpah. The narrative thus begins
with a curious and suspect inversion: the son of a free woman—nay, Jacob/
Israel's son by his favorite wife and the only one he is ever said to love
(29:18)—has been relegated to a rank beneath even that of his half-brothers

by the slave-women. Contradicting this humiliation, however, is the exalted implication of Joseph's pastoral livelihood. "Shepherd" is, in fact, a term that in the ancient Near East often denoted the ruler. Long before this narrative was composed, Mesopotamian kings had already described themselves as "shepherds" of their people.[1] In the Hebrew Bible, two shepherds in particular, Moses and David, are noteworthy for the transition they make from the literal to the metaphorical forms of their vocation.[2] In the case of Moses, the wording of the verse that introduces his divine call to leadership and the deliverance of his afflicted people is strikingly reminiscent of the beginning of the Joseph story:

> Now Moses, tending the flock of his father-in-law Jethro . . .
> (*ûmōšeh hāyâ rōʿeh ʾet-ṣōʾn yitrô ḥōtĕnô*) (Exod 3:1)
> At seventeen years of age, Joseph tended the flocks with his
> brothers . . .
> (*yôsēp ben-šĕbaʿ-ʿeśrēh šānâ hāyâ rōʿeh ʾet-ʾeḥāyw baṣṣōʾn*) (Gen 37:2b)

That the similarity in wording is not coincidence is corroborated by the remarkable parallels in the lives of the two shepherds-turned-rulers: both are separated from their families early on, both survive conspiracies to murder them, both endure exile, both marry the daughters of foreign priests, both have two sons, and the two leaders, one dead and one alive, leave Egypt together (Exod 13:19). But most important, both of them are commissioned by God to lead and provision an unruly people with a pronounced proclivity to reject their leaders. It is striking that we hear the same note at the very onset of the narrative that will bring Israel down to Egypt as we shall hear at the onset of the narrative that will bring them back up to Canaan. This movement of the people of Israel down and up is pre-enacted in the story of Joseph, which begins with the hero in the most menial status—yet a status with royal implications. The rest of the narrative will work out the humiliations he suffers and the exalted status he attains. Both are signaled in that one section of a single verse with which the great novella begins: "At seventeen years of age, Joseph tended the flocks with his brothers, as a helper to the sons of his father's wives Bilhah and Zilpah" (Gen 37:2b). The story of Joseph will be the story of how the lowest brother becomes the highest, and the literal shepherd becomes the metaphorical shepherd. In the process, not only he but his brothers and father—indeed, the entire world—will be transformed in ways that cannot be foreseen at the outset of the narrative and continue to astonish.

The analogy with David, the other great shepherd-turned-ruler in the

Hebrew Bible, is also illuminating. Like Joseph in Genesis 37, David is introduced as the little brother of the brood:

> [11] Then Samuel asked Jesse, "Are these [seven] all the boys you have?" He replied, "There is still the youngest; he is tending the flock [*rō'eh baṣṣō'n*]." And Samuel said to Jesse, "Send someone to bring him, for we will not sit down to eat until he gets here." [12] So they sent and brought him. He was ruddy-cheeked, bright-eyed, and handsome. And the LORD said, "Rise and anoint him, for this is the one." [13] Samuel took the horn of oil and anointed him in the presence of his brothers; and the spirit of the LORD gripped David from that day on. (1 Sam 16:11–13)

In a few verses, 1 Samuel presents the theme that, in the case of Joseph, will occupy the last quarter of the Book of Genesis: the last shall be first, the youngest brother shall rule his elders. "For not as man sees [does the LORD see]"[3] (v 7), and in the calculus of the supernatural God, governance is better entrusted to a humble shepherd-boy than to those to whom nature seems to have awarded a prior claim upon it. In the case of David, it is the idealized picture of the humble shepherd elevated to kingship yet never shorn of his pastoral simplicity that the tradition continued to celebrate:

> [70] He chose David, His servant,
>   and took him from the sheepfolds.
> [71] He brought him from minding the nursing ewes
>   to tend His people Jacob, Israel, His very own.
> [72] He tended them with blameless heart;
>   with skillful hands he led them. (Ps 78:70–72; cf. Mic 5:1–5; Ezek 34:23–30; 37:24–28)

The ancient image of the king as shepherd expresses the perennial idea that the ruler is to be the servant of his people: his exaltation above his subjects is inseparable from his selfless devotion to their welfare.[4] It is, indeed, precisely his service of the people that, differentiating between authority and domination, legitimates the king's rule and enables his subjects to do him homage without loss of face. But it is precisely this subordination of the chosen ruler to his future subjects that is sorely missing as the story of Joseph opens.

In addition to his pastoral vocation and his status as the first-born son of the beloved Rachel, another element in the introduction to the story of Joseph hints at the reversal of the boy's present lowly status: "Israel loved Joseph best of all his sons" (Gen 37:3). The last time we heard of a father's love for his younger son, the context was the life-threatening ordeal that would end with the beloved son's ascent to his exalted role as second patriarch of Israel:

"Take your son, your favored one, the one whom you love, Isaac" (22:2).[5] The echo of this command at the onset of the Joseph story suggests that this son, too, will confront his own near-death and, like Isaac, surviving it, attain to great eminence. But certainty is not given us, at least not in biblical narrative, and it cannot be forgotten that Jacob/Israel himself was not the son whom his father loved. That honor belonged, instead, to his older brother, Esau, for it was Rebekah and YHWH who preferred the younger twin (Gen 25:28; Mal 1:2–3). For his usurpation of his older brother's blessing, inspired by his mother and blessed by providence, Jacob has already paid dearly. First, he met at the hands of his father-in-law the very fate he had inflicted on his father: Laban, having substituted Leah for Rachel, invoked the rule that Jacob had violated with regard to Esau: "It is not the practice in our place to marry off the younger before the older" (Gen 29:26). In fact, the price may have been higher still. For the beloved Rachel died in giving birth to Benjamin, the last of the beloved sons in Genesis (35:18; 44:20; Deut 33:12). What is more, Jacob cannot be dissociated from her early death. "Anyone with whom you find your gods shall not remain alive!" Jacob challenges Laban (Gen 31:32), unaware that the culprit was none other than Rachel (v 19). Laban fails to find the icons because Rachel pulls the wool over her father's eyes much as her husband had done to his own father many years earlier (v 35; 27:18–29). And so when she dies giving birth to the youngest son of all, the last of the beloved sons in Genesis, we have a sense that the price for the multiple trickeries has at last been exacted. That price is death. Now at the onset of the story of Joseph, we are left in doubt about the meaning of this love of Jacob's toward Joseph. Is it like Abraham's for Isaac, portending a horrific near-loss of the beloved son but also his exaltation to eminence? Or is it like Jacob's last love, his love for Rachel, portending an early death for the one preferred over his older siblings?

Jacob's love for Joseph is the direct cause of the older brothers' animosity toward the beloved son (Gen 37:4) and thus the indirect cause of their plot to do away with him (vv 18–27). Most immediately, this recalls Esau's resolve to kill Jacob (27:41) and thus hints at an eventual happy resolution to the estrangement of brother from brother—though only after many years and many changes, not the least of which are the changes in the character of the beloved younger son himself. But less immediately and more ominously, the brothers' resentment of Joseph in 37:4 suggests Cain's rage at Abel and thus portends the tragic death of the younger son favored unfairly. The unfairness of Joseph's being preferred is immediately underscored in the account of his two dreams, the first about the brothers' sheaves bowing low to his, the second about the sun, the moon, and eleven stars bowing down to him directly (vv

5–11). The dreams are transparent: they predict his domination first over his brothers, then over the entire family, and first under cover, so to speak—their sheaves bowing to his *sheaf*—but then directly—the heavenly bodies bowing not to his star, but to *him*. That this is what happens as the tale unfolds should not be taken to exonerate Joseph from the charges of brashness and arrogance in his youth. For he does not know, apparently, that these dreams are from God, and even if he does, why report them to the family? His failure to anticipate the readily understandable hostility that the dream-reports evoke shows him to be indiscreet and insensitive to those he would rule—and thus unworthy to rule after all. What neither Joseph in his arrogance nor his brothers and father in their outrage anticipate is the actual circumstances by which he will come to assume dominance over the family, circumstances in which they, not he, are threatened with death, and he acts to keep them alive—the circumstances in which the ruler becomes the servant of the ruled and domination yields to legitimate authority.

The resentful brothers' effort to rid themselves of their would-be ruler takes first one, then another form. They initially resolve to kill him, leaving him in a pit and pretending that he was mauled by a wild animal (Gen 37:20). But when an Ishmaelite caravan appears, Judah dissuades them by pointing to the gain that would ensue from the sale of their offensive junior and, not without a touch of contradiction, to the fact that "after all, he is our brother, our own flesh" (vv 26–27). A careful reading of v 28 leaves us in doubt as to whether the brothers ever had the opportunity to put Judah's proposal into effect: When Midianite traders pass by, they pull Joseph out of the pit. They sell Joseph for twenty pieces of silver to the Ishmaelites, who bring Joseph to Egypt. (Gen 37:28)

If the "Midianite traders" are the same as the Ishmaelite caravanners, as source critics usually maintain, the difference being only documentary, then it is Joseph's brothers who pull the boy out of the pit. If the two are not the same, however, then the Midianites have beaten the sons of Israel to the draw, selling the abandoned boy to the Ishmaelites before his brothers could get back to him, and the subject of "sold" would be the Midianite traders, not the brothers. The view of the source critics that we have here the interweaving of two documents, one in which the brothers sell Joseph to Ishmaelites and another in which they sell him to Midianites, is probably correct. The effect of the interweaving, however, leaves open the possibility that neither antecedent document allowed—that the brothers left the scene of the crime uncertain as to the fate of the boy they had first planned to kill.[6] It may well be that they came to believe the alibi that they had contrived: "a savage beast devoured him" (v 20). At all events, the documentary source that has Reuben, the first-born, planning "to save [Joseph] from [his other brothers] and restore him to his father" (v 22) shows Reuben distraught upon returning to find the pit empty (vv 29–30). His plan, more daring but also more responsible, as befits the first-born, fails altogether, and Judah's strategy, more modest but also less moral, may have failed as well. In the redacted text that now confronts us, all the brothers can be said to know for sure is that the favored son has disappeared and is unlikely ever to be restored to his loving father.

As in the case of Rachel's death, so in the case of Joseph's ominous disappearance, Jacob bears an indirect responsibility. In the case of the beloved wife, he could surely plead inadvertency: "Jacob, of course, did not know that Rachel had stolen [Laban's household icons]" (Gen 31:32). In the case of the boy who is both her first-born and his beloved son, the moral dimension is cloudier:

> [12]One time, when his brothers had gone to pasture their father's flock at Shechem, [13]Israel said to Joseph, "Your brothers are pasturing at Shechem. Come, I will send you to them." He answered, "I am ready [*hinnēnî*]." [14]And he said to him, "Go and see how your brothers are and how the flocks are faring, and bring me back word [*wahăšîbēnî dābār*]." So he sent him from the valley of Hebron. (Gen 37:12–14)

The passage follows immediately upon the account of the father and brother's ungracious reception of Joseph's second dream, in which the sun, the moon, and eleven stars bow down directly to him. "So his brothers were wrought up with him," we are told, "and his father kept the matter [*dābār*] in mind." (v 11) Now if this translation of the obscure last clause is correct, then Jacob/ Israel could not have "kept the matter in mind" very long, or, if he did, he failed to assess the gravity of the estrangement that Joseph's report of his dreams of grandeur had produced. For no sooner are we told this than the doting father sends his beloved son, (clad, it turns out, in the "ornamented tunic"—or, traditionally, "the coat of many colors"—that symbolized his favored status) directly into the hands of the brothers seething with jealousy. The boy is to bring back word (*wahăšîbēnî dābār*) of the brothers, but the last "word" (*dābār*) about the brothers was that they are wrought up with jealousy about Joseph's undeserved status (v 11). The one who will attempt "to bring something back" to Jacob is not Joseph, but Reuben, who tries but fails to restore the beloved son to his father [*lahăšîbô 'el-'ābîw*, v 22), and the word that does come back to Jacob comes not from Joseph about the brothers, but from the brothers about Joseph. It comes in the form of the ornamented tunic dipped in goat's blood and deciphered by the old man himself: "A savage beast has devoured him! Joseph was torn by a beast!" (v 33).

The affinities of the story with the binding of Isaac in Genesis 22 are striking, though the relationship is in some important respects one of inversion. Abraham intends to slay the boy but consequently sees his son spared in the nick of time. Jacob intends to send his son away and to receive him again in short order, but consequently finds that the boy has, to all appearances, been slain, for Reuben fails to act in the nick of time and cannot restore the doomed son to his doting father. In the case of Abraham, the father willingly sacrifices the ram in Isaac's stead: the animal takes the place of the child and symbolizes the restoration of his life. In Jacob's case, the goat's blood substitutes for Joseph, not (so far as Jacob knows) because the son has been spared but because he has been mauled to death: the slain animal symbolizes the loss of the beloved son. In Genesis 22, the father intends the loss of the son but is happily enabled to avert it. In chapter 37, the father intends to keep the son but must confront the stark tragedy of his bloody death.

But alongside these inversions of the aqedah, or perhaps it is better to say beneath them, there are profound continuities. For Jacob's beloved son's death is only symbolized: unbeknownst to him and possibly to the brothers as well, Joseph has indeed been spared. The goat dies, but the son lives and will yet be restored to his father. Moreover, as in the case of the aqedah, so here, the son who undergoes the symbolic death is the first-born of his father's preferred wife, the son whom he loves. Note that the word *hinnēnî* ("I am ready") in 37:13 establishes a connection with the aqedah that is verbal and not merely thematic.[7] This is, it will be recalled, the very word with which Abraham answered God's call in Genesis 22:1, Isaac's in 22:7, and the angel's in 22:11. It is also the very word with which Esau answered his father Isaac's call in 27:1, when the second Patriarch was unwittingly about to designate not his first-born Esau, but his younger son Jacob, as the dominant person of the next generation, the one to whom his own brothers and even whole nations will bow down (v 29). In a sense, the two stories, that of Abraham-Isaac and that of Isaac-Jacob, flow together in the tale of Jacob and Joseph: the father sends his beloved son to his death but finds him alive after all, dominant not only over his older brothers but over whole nations, who live or die according to his word alone.

The two ways in which the jealous brothers attempt to do away with Joseph recall the old Ugaritic myths of Baal, in which, as we have noted,[8] the young god is variously swallowed by Mot ("Death") or turned over to Prince Yamm ("Sea") as a slave. Indeed, Jacob's dispatch of Joseph to the hands of brothers bristling with resentment, who then seek to sell him into slavery, exhibits striking similarities to the Ugaritic text in which El, the father of the gods, betrays Baal into servitude to Yamm. Retrospectively, it is hard to avoid the conclusion that the biblical narrative is, in part, a histo-ricization of the older Canaanite myth. But it must also be noted once more that prospectively, the Joseph story is a pre-enactment of the fate of the Israelites in Egypt, where the king condemns them to slavery and then to genocide in the form of the death of the sons (Exod 1:8–11, 15–22)—the inverse order of Joseph's treatment at the hands of his older brothers.

The symbolic death that Joseph undergoes takes the form of a threefold downward movement. The movement begins with his descent into the pit into which his brothers cast him at Reuben's behest (Gen 37:18–24). The text goes out of its way to note that "the pit [*bôr*] was empty; there was no water in it" (v 24), a sure sign that the boy would not long survive. In truth, the pit is a symbol of the grave, and the same word can denote both:

> ² I extol You, O LORD,
> for You have lifted me up,
> and not let my enemies rejoice over me.
> ³ O LORD, My God,
> I cried out to You,
> and You healed me.
> ⁴ O LORD, You brought me up from Sheol,
> preserved me from going down [*yordî*] into the Pit [*bôr*].
>
> ⁹ I called to You, O LORD;
> to my God I made appeal,
> ¹⁰ "What is to be gained from my death [*mab-beṣaʿ bĕdāmî*]
> from my descent into the Pit?
> Can dust praise you?
> Can it declare Your faithfulness? (Ps 30:2–4, 9–10)

The resonances of the psalmist's words here with the story of Joseph in Gen 37:18–28 are impressive. Both the speaking voice of the psalm and the boy Joseph are thrown into a pit and left for dead, but then lifted out and thus saved from certain perdition. The psalmist's appeal to God—"What is to be gained from my death?" (*mab-beṣaʿ bĕdāmî*, Ps 30:10) is remarkably close in wording to Judah's appeal to his brothers' mercenary interest: "What do we gain by killing our brother and covering up his blood?" (*mab-beṣaʿ kî nahărōg 'et-'āḥînû wĕkissînû 'et-dāmô*, Gen 37:26). The psalmist's praise of God for "not let[ting] my enemies rejoice over me" (Ps 30:2) suggests the macabre scene of Joseph's brothers' sitting down to a meal immediately after casting the boy into the pit (Gen 37:25). They ate and drank while their little brother, their father's darling, languished without even water. Yet, through a providential combination of Reuben's and Judah's different plans to save the boy, his life was indeed saved, and like the speaking voice of Psalm 30, he was brought up from the underworld itself. As he tells his brothers at the end of the amazing tale, "Although you intended me harm, God intended it for good, so as to bring about the present result—the survival of many people" (Gen 50:20). But at the end of chapter 37, much guilt remains to be expiated, and many transformations to be worked before that happy result can be realized.

The second downward movement in Joseph's prolonged symbolic death is his descent to Egypt, where he is sold on the slave market:

> When Joseph was taken down [*hûrad*] to Egypt, a certain Egyptian, Potiphar, a courtier of Pharaoh and his chief steward, bought him from the Ishmaelites who had brought him there. (Gen 39:1)

Earlier, the other source, the one that knows Midianite tradesmen rather than Ishmaelite caravanners, had reported the same data (37:36). The verses immediately preceding had detailed Jacob's grief upon concluding that a wild animal had ripped apart the son of his old age:

> [34] Jacob rent his clothes, put sackcloth on his loins, and observed mourning for his son many days. [35] All his sons and daughters sought to comfort him; but he refused to be comforted, saying, "No, I will go down ['*ērēd*] mourning for my son in Sheol." Thus his father bewailed him. (Gen 37:34–35)

The use of the verb *yārad* ("go down, descend") in these passages establishes a bond between Joseph's descent into Egypt and Jacob's own death. The latter will take place only after he has indeed gone down to his son, except that the destination will be Egypt and not the underworld (Sheol) and the mood will be one of joy and not grief. It is telling that when Jacob is at last told that Joseph is still alive, his reaction is couched in the language of resurrection:

> [25] They went up from Egypt and came to their father Jacob in the land of Canaan. [26] And they told him, "Joseph is still alive; yes, he is ruler over the whole land of Egypt." His heart went numb, for he did not believe them. [27] But when they recounted all that Joseph had said to them, and when he saw the wagons that Joseph had sent to transport him, the spirit of their father revived [*wattĕḥî*]. [28] "Enough!" said Israel. "My son Joseph is still alive. I must go and see him before I die." (Gen 45:25–28)

To be separated from Joseph is, for Jacob, to be dead, and to be together with him is to live again. The point is nicely brought home by the sequence of events in Gen 45:26b–27. First, Jacob's heart goes numb, recapitulating his response to the evident demise of Joseph in 37:34–35, when he refuses to be comforted and speaks only of his own approaching death. But then, in 45:27, the sight of the wagons that have come with his older sons reverses the sight of the bloody ornamented tunic they brought him in chapter 37, and Jacob, emotionally dead these many years, comes back to life, for he knows that Joseph remains alive after all. The sequence powerfully confirms Judah's words about the relationship of Jacob with his other son by Rachel, the baby of the family, Benjamin: "his own life is bound up with his [son's]" (44:30). Like Joseph, Benjamin is the son of Jacob's old age and beloved of his father (v 20). He is, in short, the substitute for Joseph, and if he does not return to his father, Judah points out, the father will surely die (v 31). It is thus through the experience of Jacob that the meaning of Joseph's fate is interpreted. The son's descent into Egypt is a kind of death; his ascent to rulership, a kind of resurrection. Whereas the pit is a metaphor of Sheol in the case of Joseph's first descent, in the case of his second, the metaphor is Egypt, or, to be more precise, slavery in Egypt. Each descent is a manifestation of his symbolic death, and with each, Joseph moves farther from the source of his vitality— his family and his native land.

The last element in Joseph's threefold symbolic death is his descent into prison after Potiphar's wife falsely accuses him of sexual impropriety (Gen 39:20). The affinity of this third symbolic death with the second is obvious, imprisonment being close kin to slavery. The affinity with the first element in the threefold pattern, the descent into the pit, is more subtle but no less real. It is signified by the use of the term *bôr* (literally, "pit") to denote the place of his confinement (41:14). For all his glory as majordomo to the Pharaoh's chief steward, Joseph has now come full circle, finding himself once again in the pit from which he had been pulled up only to be sold into slavery. Now he is not only a slave, but a prisoner, not only rejected by his family, but condemned by his master and forced to spend years of his life beneath ground. The cost of chosenness has never been clearer: the chosen son has become the rejected brother, his life has turned into a living death, and the exaltation of which he dreamt has become a nightmare of humiliation from which it seems impossible that he will ever awaken.

Over against these three descents—into the pit, into slavery in Egypt, and into prison—stand a series of ascents: out of the pit, out of slavery, out of prison, and, ultimately, after Joseph's death, out of Egypt and up to the promised land in which his life began (Exod 13:19). The process of ascent reaches its climax when Joshua reinters Joseph's bones in Shechem: at last the beloved son reaches the destination to which his father sent him on that fateful day in his youth (Josh 24:32; Gen 37:12).[9] The source of these ascents, the text goes out of its way to tell us, is YHWH. It is he who ensures that Joseph's enslavement is mild, so that even as Potiphar's slave he is already the ruler of his master's house:

> ² The LORD was with Joseph, and he was a successful man; and he stayed in the house of his Egyptian master. ³ And when his master saw that the LORD was with him and that the LORD lent success to everything he undertook, ⁴ he took a liking to Joseph. He made him his personal attendant and put him in charge of his household and of all he owned. . . . ⁶ He left all that he had in Joseph's hands and, with him there, he paid attention to nothing save the food he ate. (Gen 39:2–4, 6a)

The same causation accounts for Joseph's eerie success even in prison, where, apparently in short order, he is put in charge of his fellow inmates:

> ²⁰ . . . But even while he was in prison, ²¹ the LORD was with Joseph: He extended kindness to him and disposed the chief jailer favorably toward him. ²² The chief jailer put in Joseph's charge all the prisoners who were in that prison, and he was the one to carry out everything that was done there. ²³ The chief jailer did not supervise anything that was in Joseph's charge, because the LORD was with him, and whatever he did the LORD made successful. (Gen 39:20b-23)

Even within the restrictions of his humiliations, Joseph meets with exaltation. His slavemaster turns out to be the king's chief steward, and Joseph becomes his majordomo. In jail, he likewise becomes second to the warden, and like the slavemaster, the warden declines to exercise oversight, for he knows that Joseph's success is assured (39:6, 22–23). The pattern repeats and reaches its crescendo in Joseph's ascent to the prime ministership. Here, too, it is God who stands behind the chosen son's rise to eminence, for he ascends on the strength of his charismatic gift of dream-interpretation. "Not I!" Joseph rejoins when Pharaoh attributes the gift to him, "God will see to Pharaoh's welfare" (41:16; cf. 40:8). At this point Joseph articulates what we have known for some time, that he owes his success not to himself but to the mysterious grace of God. With this explicit acknowledgment of the role of providence, Joseph attains his highest station, becoming second only to Pharaoh (41:40).

The pattern reappears too many times to be coincidental. In each situation, Joseph rapidly ascends to the rank of second in command and enjoys in practice the powers of his superior denied him in theory. In Potiphar's house and in Pharaoh's palace, only one thing differentiates his master from Joseph, the wife in the first instance (Gen 39:9) and the throne in the second (41:40). Indeed, it is precisely Joseph's stout refusal to yield to the wife's seductions that sets in motion the chain of events that brings him near the throne. The threefold pattern of ascent to the rank of second in command is a reenactment of the situation at the opening of the tale, when Joseph is presented in the role of the beloved son of Jacob (37:3). Though the brothers conspire to destroy the relationship, it continually re-forms, in whatever circumstances are at hand—in Potiphar's household, in prison, in Pharaoh's court. And the brothers' conspiracy is only the first of the factors militating against Joseph's retention of his exalted status. It is soon followed by Potiphar's wife's slander and the chief cupbearer's forgetfulness (39:11–18; 40:23). Yet each threat is overcome, for, with God's help, Joseph always lands on his feet and immediately captures the high ground, until he finds himself in the loftiest post a commoner could hold, prime minister to the king of Egypt.

Even if we lacked the editorial comments to the effect that "the LORD was with Joseph, and he was a successful man" (Gen 39:2), we would suspect that the continual reemergence of the unlikely pattern of ascent after humiliation was owing to the hidden hand of providence. The editorial comments and Joseph's own acknowledgments of God's role in his life only underscore the point that his status as the beloved son is not owing to his father's inegalitarian affections alone. On the contrary, Jacob's nearly lethal favoritism is itself only a reflection of God's mysterious choice of Joseph. It is the first natural manifestation of the supernatural favor that accompanies Joseph throughout his life. What the brothers take for paternal arbitrariness turns out to be divine grace, and in acting against it, they have condemned themselves to a fate not unlike the one they conspired to inflict upon their little brother, a fate of destitution, exile, subservience, and separation—literal and metaphorical—from their grieving father. What they will discover to their astonishment is that the very favor they had set themselves against has absorbed their own conspiracy and employed it to the benefit of the entire family. Of the harm the brothers intended, God will make good use, redeeming the family of its estrangements and ensuring the survival of a great people (45:5; 50:20).

The story of Joseph is the most sustained and the most profound exploration in the Hebrew Bible of the problematics of chosenness, one of the central theological concepts not only of ancient Israel, but of rabbinic Judaism and Christianity as well. The problematic derives from the disparity between the frailty of the human ego and the mysterious operations of the choosing Deity. Human nature, the story makes clear, is not constituted so as to facilitate the acceptance of chosenness. The one chosen is sorely tempted to interpret his special status as a mandate for domination: such is the impression that Joseph's father and brothers reasonably receive from the little brother's insensitive report of his two dreams. Those not chosen are unlikely to view their status with grace and quiet acceptance. The fratricidal jealousy of Joseph's older brothers reaches a new level of fiendishness, but after the examples of Cain and Esau it comes as no surprise. If the challenge of the chosen is to bear their exalted status with humility and altruism, the challenge of the unchosen—and chosenness is meaningless unless some are *not* chosen—is to play their subordinate role with grace and with due regard for the common good. In the story of Joseph, the principal symbol of the common good is the figure in the family who stands above the fraternal discord that has ripped it apart: the Patriarch Jacob. It is in his demeanor that the well-being of the family is communicated, as if by the chorus in a Greek tragedy, and at the end of the opening act, when he is absorbed in inconsolable grief, it is clear that neither the chosen nor the unchosen have met their distinctive but equally arduous challenges. Chosenness seems to have proven fatal not only for the chosen, but also for the common good, leaving in emotional ruin the family it has touched.

The two-sidedness of chosenness is brought out with great effect in our first glimpse of Joseph in Egypt. Because "the LORD was with Joseph" in Potiphar's house, he met with great success and won the favor of his Godfearing master. This brought him to a position of such eminence in the household that Potiphar "paid attention to nothing save the food that he ate" (Gen 39:1–6). As in the cases of Moses, David, and other important figures in the Hebrew Bible (Exod 2:2; 1 Sam 16:12), the grace of God exhibits a bodily manifestation in Joseph's physical beauty: "Now Joseph was well built and handsome" (Gen 39:6). It is this attractiveness, of course, that elicits Potiphar's wife's attempts at seduction and thus indirectly leads to Joseph's imprisonment after the enraged noble lady prefers her mendacious charge (vv 19–20). As we have seen, the story discloses a point of great moment for the intepretation of the larger narrative: that Joseph meets with favor wherever he goes demonstrates that he is possessed of a divine charism. His father's preference for him in the opening scene of the novella was not owing to paternal caprice after all.

There are two critical differences between Genesis 37 and 39, however. In chapter 37, there is, first, no reference to God and therefore no reason to believe that Joseph's two dreams of receiving obeisance express anything higher than his own ego. Second, but related to the first difference, is a little noticed but exceedingly important point about the dreams themselves: in them Joseph displays deference to no one, not to his brothers nor even—and here the hubris would be outrageous to the ancient Israelite audience—to his father. Instead, all bow to Joseph, and Joseph bows to no one. The contrast with chapter 39 is most evident in Joseph's reply to his insistent mistress's proposition:

⁸But he refused. He said to his master's wife, "Look, with me here, my master gives no thought to anything in this house, and all that he owns he has placed in my hands. ⁹He wields no more authority in this house than I, and he has withheld nothing from me except yourself, since you are his wife. How then could I do this most wicked thing, and sin before God?" (Gen 39:8–9)

The element that in Genesis 37 had proved nearly fatal—Joseph's utter insubordination—is here reversed, as the young man refuses to set himself highest in the household by appropriating the one symbol of his master's continuing supremacy, his wife. Elsewhere in the Hebrew Bible, the appropriation of a ruler's wife announces a claim upon the throne and thus constitutes an act of rebellion (e.g., 1 Kgs 2:13–25).¹⁰ It is precisely this that Joseph, withstanding great temptation, explicitly and emphatically refuses to do. Whether his God-given success could have reached as far as an attempt on Potiphar's authority remains, of course, an open question. What is beyond doubt, however, is that Joseph accepts in chapter 39 the subordination that proved conspicuously absent in his dreams of grandeur in chapter 37. He recognizes that his ascent rests upon the trust that a higher power has placed in him. When he refuses the proposition from the lady of the house, Joseph also refuses to betray the trust upon which his meteoric rise is founded. The irony is that this very refusal initiates his next movement of descent, into prison (39:19–20). The special favor of God brings with it both exaltation and humiliation. But the two are not evenly balanced, for the descent into prison is the last of the downward movements in Joseph's life and sets the scene for his most extraordinary exaltation, into the court of Pharaoh, where he will spend the rest of his life.

It remains unclear whether Joseph recognizes already in Genesis 39 the point that he will articulate so powerfully at the end of the tale: his life unfolds according to the design of providence (45:8; 50:19–20). What is undeniable is that he cites his fear of God as one of his two reasons for refusing his master's wife's brazen advances, along with the trust that his master has placed in him (39:9). This is the first of several instances in which Joseph mentions God. It is telling that most of them occur at points in the story when Joseph might have arrogated powers that he pointedly insists are not properly his (40:8; 41:16; 45:5–8; 50:19–20). In short, the note of subordination that the episode in Potiphar's house introduces is more than social: it is also religious. Joseph's refusal of his master's wife's proposition is more than self-interested: it is also devout. The young man who will not encroach upon his master's prerogative will also not sin against God. Even if he does not recognize that the latter is at least as much involved in his ascent as the former, Joseph's double sub-ordination in 39:9 stands in stark contrast with his stance in chapter 37, when even his father bows to him and God is not on his lips and, to all appearances, far from his heart as well.

Between these two sequences centered upon Joseph (Genesis 37 and 39) falls another in which Joseph is never mentioned, the story of Judah and Tamar in chapter 38. Among biblical scholars, there is a broad and durable consensus that this intervening narrative is without relevance to the novella of Joseph in which it now appears. It is, according to the majority of historical critics, a piece of lore about another son of Jacob that the chronology of the generations required to be placed toward the end of Genesis, and no spot was less inappropriate than that between the sale of Joseph and his ascent to eminence in the household of his Egyptian master. As E. A. Speiser puts it: "The narrative is a completely independent unit. It has no connection with the drama of Joseph, which it interrupts at the conclusion of Act I."[11] Claus Westermann, so different from Speiser in method and focus, nonetheless agrees: "The narrative of Judah and Tamar has not been inserted into the Joseph story; it has nothing to do with it but rather is an insertion into the Jacob story."[12] As Walter Brueggemann puts it in his recent commentary: "This peculiar chapter stands alone, without connection to its context. It is isolated in every way and is most enigmatic."[13] But the strongest language is that of Bruce Vawter, who, in words more suggestive of burglary or rape than of literary composition, speaks of "the forcible entry of chapter 38 into the surrounding J version of the story of Joseph." The motivation for this invasive move is, according to Vawter, J's discomfort "with the 'wisdom' genre of the Joseph traditions" and his preference for "the content and method of the saga sources."[14] In this view, the interpolation of Genesis 38 is not a mindless act of redaction, as Speiser, Westermann, and Brueggemann imply, but rather a deliberate counterpoint to the story into which it has been spliced. This is the last and most extreme point in the trajectory of opinion that sees in the story of Judah and Tamar a unit completely independent of the Joseph narrative.

It is not a trajectory without plausibility. Genesis 38 not only lacks any mention of Joseph or the catastrophic events of chapter 37; it also serves genealogical purposes relative to the royal tribe of the south, the tribe of Judah, and thus stands in contrast to the Joseph story, which has its tribal associations with the north, specifically with Manasseh and Ephraim, Joseph's two sons. But even on internal grounds, chapter 38 does not mesh with the novella of Joseph's fall and rise. For as the historical critics are wont to point out,[15] between the two notices of Potiphar's purchase of the Hebrew boy

(37:36; 39:1), Judah manages to marry, father three sons (all of whom reach marriageable age), and then to have a set of twins by his daughter-in-law. The evidence is overwhelming that the germ out of which Genesis 38 has developed is independent of the tale into which it has been set. The chronology alone requires that this be acknowledged.

The original independence of the story of Judah and Tamar from the tale of Joseph does not, however, compel us to accept the idea that Genesis 38 has been composed in obliviousness to the only environment in which it now appears. The possibility exists that an originally unrelated story has been told with its relationship to the surrounding material very much in mind. Alternatively, it is possible that the placement of chapter 38 between 37 and 39 is indeed owing entirely to a redactor—not the mindless one that most source critics seem to detect, however, but one who recognized both verbal and thematic affinities between the stories of Joseph and Judah. If so, his literary instincts are plainly superior to that of most source critics, for the latter, even in our day, still manage to miss those affinities.[16]

Some of these have been astutely demonstrated by Robert Alter, a scholar of comparative literature. Alter notes, for example, that the statement with which Genesis 38 opens—that "Judah left [wayyēred] his brothers" (v 1)—employs an odd use of the verb for "the purpose of connecting this separation of one brother from the rest with Joseph's, transmitted with the same verb-root."[17] For, as Alter notes, the next chapter, which tells of Joseph in Potiphar's house, opens with the statement that "Joseph was taken down [hûrad] to Egypt" (39:1). He might have noted as well the use of the same root in the preceding chapter also, in which it defines the purpose of the Ishmaelite caravan—to take down [lĕhôrîd] to Egypt their cargo of delicacies, soon to include a Hebrew boy to sell on the slave market (37:25). The point was already noticed in Talmudic times. "Why were these two passages juxtaposed?" asks the midrash (Gen. Rab. 85:2). "In order," answers Rabbi Eleazar, "to juxtapose the one descent [yĕrîdâ] with the other descent [yĕrîdâ]," that is, Judah's with Joseph's. But Rabbi Yochanan proposes an alternative, this one, too, rooted in an unusual turn of phrase: "in order to juxtapose the one instance of 'examine' [hakker-nā'] with the other instance of 'examine' [hakker-nā']," that is, Joseph's brothers' imperative to their father with reference to the bloodied tunic (37:32) and Tamar's imperative to Judah with reference to his seal, cord, and staff (38:25) (a point not lost on Alter either).[18] Rabbi Yochanan's observation is acute: These are the only attestations of hakker-nā' in the entire Hebrew Bible. The odds that they should stand in adjacent chapters by pure coincidence are not high. In the rabbi's mind, the events of chapter 38 are punishment for those of chapter 37:

Rabbi Yochanan said: The Holy One (blessed be he) said to Judah: You said to your father, "Examine" [37:32]. By your life, Tamar will say to you, "Examine"! [38:25]. (*Gen. Rab.* 85:11)

Rabbi Simon ben Lakish, a contemporary of Rabbi Yochanan and his brother-in-law, makes a similar observation regarding the kid from the flock with which Judah pays for the services of the woman he takes for a prostitute, though she is actually his daughter-in-law:

The Holy One (blessed be he) said to Judah: You deceived your father with a kid goat [37:31–33]. By your life, Tamar will deceive you with a kid goat [38:17,23]. (*Gen. Rab.* 85:9).

And, once again, Alter develops the observation in the mode of modern formalist literary interpretation:

Judah with Tamar after Judah with his brothers is an exemplary narrative instance of the deceiver deceived, and since he was the one who proposed selling Joseph into slavery instead of killing him (Gen. 37:26–27), he can easily be thought of as the leader of the brothers in the deception practiced on their father. Now he becomes their surrogate in being subject to a bizarre but peculiarly fitting principle of retaliation, taken in by a piece of attire, as his father was . . . The narrator shows him exposed through the symbols of his legal self given in pledge for a kid (*gedi ʿizim*), as before Jacob had been tricked by the garment emblematic of his love for Joseph which had been dipped in the blood of a goat (*seʿir ʿizim*).[19]

Here it bears mention again that it was through two goats of the flock (*gĕdāyê ʿizzîm*) that Jacob had deceived his own father, Isaac. Rebekah, it will be recalled, used the goats for the tasty dish that the blind old man mistook for Esau's venison, and she clothed her smooth-skinned son in the hides of the same animals in order to perpetrate the same momentous act of impersonation (Gen 27:5–17). It is as though some strange karmic force keeps this act of deception in continual ricochet, dooming the chosen family to re-experience it in succeeding generations and even within the same generation. The substitution of the animal for the son, however, is not always negative. Rather, these are the negative instances that correspond to the positive substitutions—the ram for Isaac (22:13) and, ultimately, the paschal lamb for the first-born sons of all Israel (Exod 12:13). The last is surely the most significant of the instances: it is the blood of the lamb that, as it were, deceives the Destroyer and enables the doomed first-born to live and be redeemed from exile and slavery (v 23).

One last answer to that midrashic question, "Why were these two passages juxtaposed?" must be noted. It was, said Rabbi Samuel bar Nachman, "in order to juxtapose Tamar's deed with Potiphar's wife's deed" (*Gen. Rab.* 85:2). The rabbi's reason—that both acted out of religious motives, Potiphar's wife having learned through astrology that she would be an ancestress of Joseph's descendants[20]—need not detain us. What Samuel bar Nachman's observation does bring out is the juxtaposition of the two instances of seduction, Tamar's successful seduction of Judah for motives grounded in religious law (Deut 25:5–10) and Potiphar's wife's unsuccessful attempt to seduce Joseph for motives that are in violation of religious law, indeed of the Decalogue itself (Exod 20:13). And here again articles of attire play a critical role. For just as it is Judah's seal, cord, and staff that serve to indict him (Gen 38:18, 25), so it is Joseph's cloak that Potiphar's wife employs as evidence for her false charge against the chaste steward of her husband's estate (39:11–18). Whereas Judah's articles of attire testify to his moral and religious laxity, Joseph's cloak witnesses to his probity and his fear of sin. It also witnesses to the trials of the beloved son, who is, first, hated by his brothers because of their father's favoritism toward him, symbolized by the ornamented tunic, and second, defamed by his mistress because of his chastity, symbolized by the garment that she grabs as he flees her advances and Potiphar's house.

"Why were these two passages juxtaposed?" The question would not have been asked if the abruptness of the transitions of Genesis 38 with the chapters on each side of it were not glaringly obvious. The answers the rabbis of the midrash offer to their own question expose continuities that lie deep beneath the incongruity of chapter 38 with both the incident that precedes it—the sale of Joseph—and that which follows—the episode in Potiphar's house. Some of these continuities are broadly thematic. A brother separates from the family and goes down in more senses than the geographical. Articles of attire are used for purposes of deception: Joseph's ornamented tunic in Genesis 37, Tamar's widow's garb and Judah's seal, cord, and staff in the following chapter, and Joseph's cloak in Genesis 39. A woman attempts the seduction of the man separated from his family, for righteous purposes and with success in Genesis 38, for sinful purposes and without success in chapter 39. Other continuities are verbal, most strikingly the peculiarity of the expression *hakker-nā'* to Genesis 37 and 38 within the entire Hebrew Bible. And so the insights of ancient midrash and modern literary criticism shed an old/new light on the passage that almost all historical critics regard as "a completely independent unit" (Speiser) and at least one even regards as having effected a "forcible entry" (Vawter) into the story of Joseph. By means of the narrative analogies that it employs, the episode of Judah and Tamar actually plays a critical role in the unfolding of the Joseph story in which it now appears.

For purposes of our investigation, another element of narrative analogy, one to which none of these midrashic observations points, is, however, preeminent. Alter comes close to it when he observes that the tales of Judah and of Joseph both are "about the election through some devious twist of destiny of a younger son to carry on the line."[21] What he has in mind is Joseph's status as the "next to the youngest" and Judah's as "the fourthborn" of Jacob's brood. This is indeed important, and the emergence of kings from precisely these two tribes is a point of no small consequence in the interpretation of the story of Joseph. But so long as we keep our focus on Joseph, we shall miss another analogy to Judah in the extended story, and this is the analogy between Judah's predicament in chapter 38 and Jacob's when the story shifts its focus back to him, the predicament of the father reluctant to give up his son even though only so doing will ensure the survival of the family line.[22]

In Genesis 38, Judah having in short order lost his first two sons, Er and Onan, is understandably reluctant to surrender his third and last son Shelah for marriage to Tamar, as traditional family law requires (Deut 25:5–10). By refusing to hand over Shelah, Judah is willy-nilly ensuring that "the name [of the dead brothers will] be blotted out in Israel," in contravention of the Levirate law (v 6). What is more, since his own wife has died (Gen 38:12), he has no other children, and Tamar has a legal claim upon Shelah, the chance that Judah's line itself will continue is gravely imperiled. This makes of Judah a kind of negative antipode to Abraham as the aqedah is interpreted in the second angelic oracle of Genesis 22 (vv 15–18). Abraham, it will be recalled, is there blessed with innumerable progeny precisely because he did not withhold his son, his only son, surrendering him to what seemed certain death. But Judah now confronts a childless future and a name blotted out in Israel because he refuses to surrender Shelah to the woman with whom marriage has spelt death for two of his sons already. Here we once again confront the great paradox that lies at the heart of our inquiry: the son's presence can be enjoyed and the family preserved only if the son is given up to death itself.

Such are things if we look back to Abraham. If we look forward a few chapters to Jacob, we find him in a predicament even more strikingly analogous to Judah's in Genesis 38. At the end of chapter 42, the brothers, with the exception of Joseph's stand-in, Benjamin, have returned to their father after buying grain in Egypt. But they have come back without Simeon and with the money they had taken for the purchase, suggesting perhaps that they had indeed paid for the foodstuff but also sold Simeon to make up for the expenditure. Having deceived their father about their conspiracy to kill or to sell Joseph, they now inadvertently give the equally deceptive impression that they have sold Simeon, if not killed him, and this understandably induces Jacob to refuse to surrender Benjamin, as is imperative if Simeon is to be released (vv 35–38). Having lost two sons, a father is, in short, once again adamant about not surrendering a third, very much as in the episode of Judah and Tamar in chapter 38: "Their father Jacob said to them, 'It is always me that you bereave: Joseph is no more and Simeon is no more, and now you would take away Benjamin. These things always happen to me!' " (Gen 42:36). Reuben's typically ineffective attempt to break the deadlock between the father and the other sons only underscores the analogy between Jacob and Judah: "Then Reuben said to his father, 'You may kill my two sons if I do not bring him back to you. Put him in my care, and I will return him to you' " (Gen 42:37). As the previous verse clarified with poignance, the loss of two sons is precisely Jacob's problem. The loss of two grandsons will hardly solve it. Reuben's foolish words do, however, perform an important function: they remind the reader of the last incident in which a father had seen two sons killed and therefore withheld the third, the incident of Judah and Tamar. And in so doing, Reuben's offer reminds the reader also of what is at stake if the father persists in his refusal to give up his beloved son. For what is at stake in these years of worldwide famine is the survival of the family, nay, life itself: only if life is risked can it continue. It is the risk of the loss of the beloved Benjamin that Jacob cannot accept: "But he said, 'My son must not go down with you, for his brother is dead and he alone is left. If he meets with disaster on the journey you are taking, you will send my white head to Sheol in grief' " (Gen 42:38).

The irony is that when Jacob does finally surrender his beloved son Benjamin, he receives anew not only Simeon, but even Joseph, whom he has given up for dead. His courageous willingness to expose Benjamin to the risk of death restores Joseph to him alive.

It is Judah's offer to stand surety for Benjamin that moves Jacob from adamant refusal to reluctant agreement to part with his youngest son:

> [8]Then Judah said to his father Israel, "Send the boy in my care, and let us be on our way, that we may live and not die—you and we and our children. [9]I myself will be surety for him; you may hold me responsible; if I do not bring him back to you and set him before you, I shall stand guilty before you forever. [10]For we could have been there and back twice if we had not dawdled." (Gen 43:8–10)

Judah's repetition of the same offer (44:32–34) brings the entire tale to its climax: it prevents the enslavement of Benjamin and, by destroying Joseph's carefully constructed persona, forces him to reveal himself to his brothers, for he "could no longer control himself" (45:1). The enormous power behind Judah's offer derives from the complicated set of substitutions that it articulates. Judah will be the substitute for Benjamin, accepting upon himself the slavery to which Joseph has sentenced his younger brother. But Benjamin is himself a substitute, standing in for that other beloved son and child of Rachel and Jacob's old age, Joseph (44:20; 37:3). And Joseph and Benjamin are both, in some deeper sense, substitutes for their father and thus paradigms for the people Israel. We have already seen that the deceptive report of Joseph's death leads Jacob to speak of his own and that the report of Joseph's survival, doubtful but true, brings about the old man's revivification (37:34–35; 45:25–28). This is because, as Judah puts it with reference to Jacob and Benjamin, "his own life is bound up with his" (44:30). The son beloved of his mother and his God in the previous generation, Jacob is, in the last analysis, one with his own two beloved sons of his favored wife, Joseph and Benjamin. He shares their fate, enacting in his own life the symbolic death that his love for them has occasioned. By offering to take Benjamin's place—to bear his brother's sentence of slavery in Egypt—Judah has at long last made good his crime of proposing the sale of Joseph, taking the place of the one who takes Joseph's place. He has also made good his offense against his father, now preferring lifetime slavery, as he puts it to Joseph, over "send[ing] the white head of your servant our father down to Sheol in grief" (v 31). As in the case of King Mesha of Moab (2 Kgs 3:27), the son once again takes the place of the father: Judah endures willingly the symbolic death realized in slavery in order to spare his father the symbolic death realized in a life of grief and despondency. The paradox is that this very willingness breaks the impasse in the family: Joseph drops his disguise, neither Benjamin nor Judah is enslaved, yet Jacob is redeemed nonetheless from his own death-like state of continuous mourning for his beloved son, and the fractured family is reunited and reconciled.

That it is Judah who effects this total reversal is a point of high significance. From the historian's vantage point, this is undoubtedly to be associated with Judah's role as the preeminent tribe of the south, the tribe from which kings of the House of Jesse hail. Indeed, the first two of those kings, David and Solomon, reigned over a united kingdom of north and south (that is, Joseph and Judah), and the memory of this unity remained alive and served in some circles as an ideal (Ezek 37:15–23). From the vantage point of narrative analysis, however, the key point is that it is Judah's experience in Genesis 38, the incident with Tamar, that prepares him to play the great substitutionary role that reverses the decline in the family fortune. He can empathize with Jacob—indeed, take his place—because his own loss of two sons and his unwillingness to surrender the third have taught him a lesson. Moreover, it is in chapter 38 that he first learns to play the role of a substitute, taking the place of Shelah with shameful results as he will, six chapters later, take the place of Benjamin with the most honorable of results—the healing of a family gravely wounded, the family chosen by God and wounded by his very act of choosing. Whereas Reuben offered the lives of his two *sons* as surety (42:37), Judah, as always more realistic and more effective, offered *himself*. He has, in the process, accepted in the name of the brothers the very prospect that first evoked their fateful conspiracy against Joseph. He has freely accepted Joseph's rule and his own status as the unfavored brother doing obeisance to the beloved son.

Joseph has also undergone a process of transformation, one so massive that one may wonder whether the man to whom the brothers bow is still the same person as the boy with the grandiose dreams. We have observed that beginning already in Potiphar's house, Joseph affirms his own subordination to God and master in a way hardly to be anticipated on the basis of those dreams in Genesis 37. A comparison of the dreams by which he ascends with those by which he fell is most revealing. He falls, as we have seen, through the report of two dreams of domination—his brothers and even his father prostrating themselves before him. The next set of two dreams, which begin his ascent from the prison/pit (40:1–19), expresses beautifully the ambiguity and jeopardy of Joseph's position as he interprets them. The first dream is that of Pharaoh's cupbearer. It means, according to Joseph's inspired interpretation, that the man will be pardoned and restored to his eminent office: literally, "Pharaoh will lift [his] head" (v 13). The second, the dream of the Pharaoh's baker, is superficially similar, except that the baker sees the birds eating the bread from a basket on his head where the cupbearer had seen Pharaoh accepting the cup from his servant's hand (vv 16–17; cf. v 11). Joseph interprets this dream, with fitting cleverness, in similar language to the first but with the opposite meaning: Pharaoh will lift the baker's head as well, but not, as in the case of the cupbearer, with the sense of pardoning him.[23] Rather, the baker will be decapitated and impaled (v 19).

The episode advances the plot in several important ways. It establishes Joseph as a master of dream interpretation and not simply a dreamer and makes us wonder what the proper interpretation of his own two dreams is. Were they dreams of ascent, like the cupbearer's, or dreams of doom, like the baker's? So far, they have spelt only doom, and the sense that this is their true meaning is reinforced when the cupbearer, his dream come true exactly as Joseph interpreted it, forgets the Hebrew boy and his moving request to be mentioned to Pharaoh (v 23). But the episode of the dreams of Pharaoh's courtiers also establishes that Joseph's ability to interpret is a gift from God, whom he pointedly credits (v 8). This reinforces the theological point made at the outset of the previous chapter: because YHWH is with Joseph, he meets with success (39:1–6). And, that being the case, the cupbearer's forgetfulness may prove no more definitive than his brothers' animosity or Potiphar's wife's slander. The second set of dreams, so similar yet opposite in meaning, bring to the fore the two-sidedness of Joseph's status as the beloved son. Like the cupbearer, he is the beneficiary of undeserved favor. But like the baker, he now knows that the language of favor is chillingly close to the language of doom.

It is Pharaoh's two dreams that cause the cupbearer to overcome his forgetfulness and lead most directly to Joseph's final ascent to eminence (Gen 41:9–13). The dreams themselves are, at one level, transparent: seven scrawny cows devouring seven sturdy ones and seven emaciated ears of grain devouring seven healthy ones indicate, as Joseph immediately divines, that seven years of famine will succeed seven of plenty (vv 17–33). Here again, however, it would be a capital error to interpret the dreams only with relevance to the one who dreams them, ignoring the suggestive commentary about the larger story that they provide. For the alternation of success and failure is not only the common pattern of Pharaoh's pair of dreams. It is also the pattern of Joseph's life, a life marked by meteoric ascents and precipitous plunges. The point of Joseph's unsolicited counsel to Pharaoh in vv 33–36 is that the downward movement can be overcome if only it is duly considered during the moments of dizzying success. Joseph is at just such a moment as he speaks to Pharaoh, and the consequence of his remarks is his own appointment as prime minister (vv 37–46). Joseph, in short, is doing for himself exactly what he advises Pharaoh to do for Egypt. His personal story merges at this moment with the national story of his adopted country. The union will be broken only with Joseph's last words, when he reaccepts and reaffirms his ancestral connection with the promised land: "When God has taken notice of you, you shall carry my bones from here" (50:25).

Pharaoh's pair of dreams, the last of the three sets, exhibits an important tangent with the first set, Joseph's own dreams (Gen 37:5–11). In each case, the strong yield to the weak—the sturdy cows to the scrawny, the healthy ears of grain to the emaciated ones, the older brothers and the father to the younger sibling. With this last pair of dreams, we at first seem to be back to where we began, Joseph's repeated expressions of self-subordination notwithstanding. A closer look, however, shows the matter to be otherwise. In this regard, a detail in Pharaoh's report of his dream to Joseph (41:17–23)—missing, interestingly, from the first report (vv 1–7)—is most revealing. When the lean cows have devoured the sturdy ones, Pharaoh tells Joseph, "One could not

tell that they had consumed them, for they looked just as bad as before" (v
21). As oblique commentary on the larger story of Joseph, this detail delivers
a message of high import: when the strong yield to the weak because they
have been devoured, the weak are none the stronger. Domination of the sort
anticipated on the basis of Joseph's own dreams does not benefit the one who
dominates. It may destroy its victims, but it does not enhance its putative
beneficiary. As the story in fact unfolds, Joseph does *not* devour his brothers.
Quite the opposite: he feeds them. And it is his succor that moves them from
jealousy to appreciation, from resentment of his chosenness to acceptance,
not only of the chosenness itself, but of his rule over them as well. The weak
and the strong have indeed exchanged positions, just as Joseph's dreams por-
tended, but now the weak brother who has become strong serves those who
do him homage, and the strong who have become weak gladly live by the
favor of the little brother whose favor they once so resented.

With this in mind, it is useful to reconsider the superficial impression,
shared by most commentators, that all six of the dreams in the story of Joseph
come true, thus confirming Joseph's possession of the charismatic gift of dream
interpretation. What this overgeneralization misses is the key difference between the first pair of dreams and the latter two pairs. In fact, Joseph never
interprets the first pair (Gen 37:5–11). They are his own dreams, the dreams
of a teenager, full of grandeur and with little or no deference to the respon-
sibilities that the ancient Israelite ethic associates with true greatness. The
interpretation, rather, comes from his brothers and his father (vv 8, 10), who
see only domination. What is more, the brothers and father, unlike Joseph
himself (Gen 40:8; 41:16, 25, 32), never ascribe their ability to decode the
dreams to God. It is their own doing, and the interpretation, insofar as it sees
only domination and not service, proves wrong.

They might have done better had they been as attentive to detail as Joseph
proves to be in differentiating the baker's dream from the cupbearer's. Had
they, like the thirteenth-century commentator Rabbi David Qimchi, given
the element of binding sheaves closer scrutiny, they might have suspected
that the imagery of grain is not irrelevant to Joseph's ascent. As Qimchi puts
it, it was "because of grain that he rose to greatness."[24] Furthermore, the image
of the brothers' sheaves bowing while Joseph's own remained upright (Gen
37:7) might have suggested that his supply of grain would be full when theirs
had already given out. The collapsed sheaves would then have foreshadowed
the brothers' empty sacks, and Joseph's upright sheaf would, by the same
logic, have suggested that his sack would be abundant when they were in dire
need.[25] Attention to detail on the part of the brothers might have led them
to suspect that domination was not quite the right term to describe their

eventual prostration to their younger brother. But Joseph does not seem to notice this, either. He offers no challenge to his brothers' and his father's interpretation of his dreams as a matter of domination and humiliation.

The tale of Joseph is thus a story of *legitimation*, and in more than one way. Most obviously, it tells of the legitimation of Joseph as the favored son of his doting father, Jacob. The father's infuriating preference for the son of his old age, it turns out, is no arbitrary act of favoritism, but only the first sign of the mysterious grace that encompasses the life of the beloved son. Yet Jacob's vindication does not come cheaply. Instead, it appears only at the end of a long and tortuous process in which the loving father had to endure the loss of his favored son—lost precisely because he had been favored. He also had to endure the humiliation of bowing before his own son (Gen 47:31), a prospect that he had once pronounced incredible (37:10). Yet now he bows with equanimity, assured that the son whose death he has already mourned will return the father's bones to the promised land, so that he may "lie down with [his own] fathers" and the continuity of the generations, so grievously imperiled in this story, may be unbroken after all (47:30). The doting father's preference for his younger son is not, therefore, vindicated in its original form. It is, rather, taken up into a higher plan and transformed accordingly. The son whom Jacob meant to send to his brothers he, in fact, sent into the hands of God, donating, as it were, his beloved son, the first-born of his beloved Rachel, to providence. But when providence gives him back his son, both father and son have themselves been transformed in ways that neither could have foreseen.

The story of Joseph is also, to some extent, a legitimation of the favor God extends to the son of Jacob's old age. Earlier, we saw that the second angelic address after the binding of Isaac recasts the old promise of progeny to Abraham as a consequence of the father's willingness to give up his son as a burnt offering (Gen 22:15–18). The promise, it turns out, rests on more than grace alone; it is not a whim of an arbitrary Deity. Now we can see that not only Jacob's but also God's favor to Joseph is not unrelated to the moral and intellectual mettle of the favored son himself. Instead, it comes to the man who, in conspicuous contradistinction to his brother Judah (chap. 38), will resist sexual temptation because of his fear of God and gratitude to his master (39:9), the same man who will provide abundant proof of his managerial genius in Potiphar's house (v 5), in prison (vv 22–23), and, most important, in Pharaoh's court (41:39–40). As always in the Hebrew Bible, we have here a theology too subtle to be done justice by the familiar Christian dichotomy of grace versus works. Joseph succeeds because of God's favor, but God's favor comes to the man who, because of his mounting strength of character and self-knowledge, is able to put it to the proper use. If the favor bestowed upon Joseph brings the family to catastrophe, it also ensures that the family will survive an even worse catastrophe, the seven years of famine:

> [18] His brothers went to him themselves, flung themselves before him, and said, "We are prepared to be your slaves." [19] But Joseph said to them, "Have no fear! Am I a substitute for God? [20] Besides, although you intended me harm, God intended it for good, so as to bring about the present result— the survival of many people." (Gen 50:18–20)

The choice of Joseph is the engine both of the decline in the family's fortunes and of its ascent from the pit of jealousy, conspiracy, deception, despondency, and, ultimately, destitution into which it had fallen. But the family ascends farther than it had declined. The chosenness of Joseph proves more an asset than a liability, and the wisdom and justice of the God who chose him, so easily doubted at the beginning of the tale, are richly vindicated at its end.

Finally, the tale of Joseph is a legitimation of Joseph's *authority*, the lordship over his brothers, his premonition of which set the family onto its precipitous descent. That which legitimates Joseph's authority is the critical element of which his dreams betrayed no premonition whatsoever: his service for those he would rule, his deliverance from dire affliction of those who do him obeisance. Just as his father's initial favor suggested preference without merit, so did Joseph's own dreams suggest lordship without authority (Gen 37:2–11). But just as the favor encompassing Joseph's life comes to be joined with his superlative moral and administrative accomplishments, so does his lordship over his brothers come into being only in a situation in which he saves them— the very ones who once plotted his death—from certain starvation. The multiple ruptures in the family are healed only when Joseph's dreams of receiving his family's homage are realized in a situation of legitimate authority and his brothers' egalitarian resentment gives way to acceptance, grateful and gracious, of Joseph's unique position.

The midrash asks why the Decalogue first appears only in Exodus and not, as one would expect given its importance, at the beginning of the Torah. The answer, characteristically, comes in the form of a parable:

> A king who entered a province said to the people: May I be your king? But the people said to him: Have you done anything good for us that you should rule over us? What did he do for them? He built the city wall for them, he brought in the water supply for them, and he fought their battles. Then when he said to them: May I be your king? They said to him: Yes, yes. Likewise, God. He brought the Israelites out of Egypt, divided the

sea for them, sent down the manna for them, brought up the well for them, brought the quails for them. He fought for them the battle with Amalek. Then He said to them: May I be your king? And they said to Him: Yes, yes. (*Mekilta de-Rabbi Ishmael*, Baḥōdeš 5)[26]

One might add, "Likewise, Joseph." When he first broached the possibility of his ruling over his family, the response was swift and unambiguous: "Do you mean to reign over us? Do you mean to rule over us? . . . Are we to come, I and your mother and your brothers, and bow low to you to the ground?" (Gen 37:8, 10). But when through his reorganization of the Egyptian economy he saves the lives of those who so scoffed at him, their scorn yields to submission, and the beloved son who would rule now also serves.

Part III
The Beloved Son Between Zion and Golgotha

Saturn did not spare his own children; so, where other people's were concerned, he naturally persisted in not sparing them. Tertullian

He who did not spare his own Son but handed him over for us all; how will he not also give us everything else along with him? Rom 8:32

Chapter Fourteen

The Rewritten Aqedah of Jewish Tradition

The extraordinary prominence of the story of the binding of Isaac in Gen
22:1–19 in rabbinic Judaism stands in stark contrast to the utter absence of
direct references to it anywhere else in the Hebrew Bible. In part, the
difference reflects the greater emphasis upon the Patriarchs in rabbinic
theology than in the thinking of the prophets and the other non-
Pentateuchal biblical authors. This explanation, in turn, reflects an even
deeper difference between the forms of biblical religion and those of the
rabbis: because in rabbinic theology the Pentateuch was preeminent over
the rest of the Bible and prior to it not only in date of authorship but in
value as well, even relatively brief and uneventful episodes in the
Pentateuch can command more extensive attention in rabbinic literature
than non-Pentateuchal passages that are longer and seemingly more
momentous. The intensely exegetical character of rabbinic Judaism, which
it inherited from its Second Temple forebears, ensured that the relative
obscurity of the aqedah within the Hebrew Bible would not be the last
word of Jewish tradition on the question of the righteous father's
willingness to sacrifice his beloved son. That willingness, together with the
son's glad and unqualified acceptance of his own divinely mandated death,
became a theme of enormous import in Judaism in the Roman period,
including the forms of Judaism that served as the matrix of Christianity.

A foretaste of the importance of the aqedah in post-biblical Judaism can
be gotten, however, in the two biblical passages that betray exegetical
interest in the episode even before the canon was closed or, for that matter,
the Pentateuch completed. The first of these passages is Gen 22:15–18, the
second angelic address at the aqedah, which we have examined in chapters
11 and 12. It converts the standing promise to Abraham of innumerable
progeny into a consequence of the near-sacrifice of Isaac: "Because you
have done this and have not withheld your son, your favored one, I will

bestow My blessing upon you" (vv 16b-17). This is a transformation of enormous import. It renders the very existence of the Abrahamic peoples dependent upon their ancestor's obedience to the fearsome directive to make of his beloved son a burnt offering to his God. The aqedah, in short, has become a foundational act, and its consequences extend to every generation of those whose father is Abraham. Our people exists and perdures, the Israelite narrator seems to be saying, only because of the incomparable act of obedience and faith that the patriarch-to-be carried out on a certain unnamed mountain in the land of Moriah. In light of the interpretive move that the second angelic address evidences, it is hardly a source of wonderment that, at least since biblical times, Jewish thinkers have continually pondered the troubling story of the binding of Isaac. Nor is it surprising that the pondering is usually most intense when the existence of the Jews is threatened, and their survival, to all appearances, miraculous.

Our second passage betrays an exegetical interest in the aqedah in a manner less direct. This is the verse that denotes as "Mount Moriah" the mountain on which Solomon built his temple and which David had acquired from the Jebusites (2 Chr 3:1). As we have had occasion to observe,[1] there is an opinion among scholars that "the land of Moriah" in Gen 22:2 is not original to the narrative of the aqedah but was interpolated in Second Temple times in an effort to associate Abraham's altar with David and Solomon's foundation of the great shrine atop Zion, the Temple Mount here named Moriah. Whether or not this be so, we must see in the name "Moriah" an effort to endow Abraham's great act of obedience and faith with ongoing significance: the slaughter that he showed himself prepared to carry out was the first of innumerable sacrifices to be performed on that site. The hope accompanying this etiological move is the same whether "Moriah" is original to Gen 22:2 or to 2 Chr 3:1. It is the hope that just as Abraham's intention met with divine favor and secured a rich blessing on his descendants, so would their own acts of service in the Temple prove acceptable to God and merit his continued good will toward them. Here, too, the aqedah has become a foundational narrative. What rests upon it is the elaborate and incalculably important system of divine worship in the Temple on which the religious life of the people Israel increasingly centered. In the one word "Moriah" in 2 Chr 3:1 lies the germ of the rabbinic notion that the aqedah is the origin of the daily lamb offerings (the *těmîdîm*) and, less directly but more portentously, of the passover sacrifice as well.

The paschal connection will prove central to the parallel Christian belief that the eucharist is a reenactment of Jesus' final meal before his sacrificial death. Both the Jewish and the Christian systems of sacrifice come to be seen as founded upon a father's willingness to surrender his beloved son and the son's unstinting acceptance of the sacrificial role he has been assigned in the great drama of redemption. Though this is more obviously and more centrally the case in Christianity, it holds for Judaism more than is generally recognized. The Christian doctrine is incomprehensible apart from the history of Jewish biblical interpretation.

These developments stand toward the end of a long history of exegesis of the life of Abraham. It is revealing that in the great liturgical composition that is Neh 9:5b–37, a text almost certainly from the fifth century B.C.E., there is still no mention of the binding of Isaac. What is there deemed memorable in Abraham's life is God's election of him, his exodus from Ur, his change of name, his proving faithful to YHWH (the beginning of v 8 being an interpretive paraphrase of Gen 15:6), and his receipt of a covenant promising the land to his descendants (vv 7–8). In the Wisdom of Joshua ben Sira, however, a Jewish book known in Christian circles as Ecclesiasticus and dating to the early second century B.C.E., we read of Abraham that "when tested he was found loyal" and therefore received God's promise by oath to provide blessing and countless progeny with vast holdings (Sir 44:20–21). The test in question, which is reported directly after Abraham's circumcision (v 20), is surely the aqedah (cf. Gen 22:1). Ben Sira's postponement of the blessing until after the test reflects the reinterpretation of the life of Abraham that first emerges in the second angelic address (Gen 22:15–18).

A century later, in 1 Maccabees (another book of what came to be known in some communities as the Apocrypha), when Mattathias, the patriarch of the Hasmonean clan, exhorts his sons on his deathbed to remain zealous for the Torah, his first exemplum is an earlier patriarch. "Was not Abraham found faithful in trial," he asks rhetorically, "and it was reputed to him as uprightness?" (1 Macc 2:52). The latter phrase is patently dependent on the assertion in Gen 15:6 that "because [Abram] put his trust in the LORD, He reckoned it to his merit," or, more literally, if less accurately, "reputed it to him as uprightness." This, in turn, raises the interesting possibility that the conjunction of testing and faithfulness in Sir 44:20 arises from the same application of Gen 15:6 to the aqedah: the binding of Isaac has supplanted Abraham's trust in the covenantal promise of Gen 15:4–5 as the supreme example of his faith in God. These two books of the Apocrypha, ben Sira and 1 Maccabees, attest to an exegetical tradition alive in the second and first centuries B.C.E. according to which Abraham's faithfulness, altogether unmentioned in Gen 22:1–19, has become the central point of the aqedah.

One final passage in the Apocrypha deserves mention. This is the verse from the account of the manifestations of Wisdom in the history of redemption in the Wisdom of Solomon, a book that seems to date from about the late first century B.C.E. or early first century C.E. It was Wisdom, the book relates, that "knew the just man, kept him blameless before God, and preserved him resolute against pity for his child" (Wis 10:5). This is one of only two points from the life of Abraham deemed worthy of mention, the other being Wisdom's rescue of the Patriarch from the destruction of the Cities of the Plain (v 6). It is in the Wisdom of Solomon that we find the most explicit reference to the aqedah in the Apocrypha, a point owing to the increasing interest in the episode in Judaism in the first century. This is an interest that is evident from a broad array of sources of various genres and different locales.[2]

But long before that momentous first century of the common era, a transformation of inestimable significance had come about in the interpretation of the aqedah. It is in the Book of Jubilees, which dates to the middle of the second century B.C.E., that we find the earliest evidence for the new thinking. To the account of the binding of Isaac in Genesis 22, Jubilees has prefixed a scene of the heavenly council in debate, and, as is the wont of this book so preoccupied with calendrical matters, it has even specified the date on which the scene took place:

> [15]And it came to pass in the seventh week, in its first year, in the first month, in that jubilee, on the twelfth of that month, that words came in heaven concerning Abraham that he was faithful in everything which was told him and he loved the LORD and was faithful in all affliction. [16]And Prince Mastema came and he said before God, "Behold, Abraham loves Isaac, his son. And he is more pleased with him than everything. Tell him to offer him [as] a burnt offering upon the altar. And you will see whether he will do this thing. And you will know whether he is faithful in everything in which you test him." (Jub 17:15–16)[3]

The twelfth day of the first month is, of course, three days before the paschal lamb is to be offered, for that sacrifice took place at twilight after the fourteenth (Exod 12:6; Lev 23:5). It would seem that Jubilees has made the eminently reasonable assumption that Abraham bound Isaac over the altar immediately upon his arrival at the designated spot after his three-day journey (Gen 22:4; Jub 18:3). This, in turn, means that the aqedah has been transformed into an etiology of Passover, or, to be more precise, that Passover, like other Pentateuchal festivals in Jubilees, has acquired what Mircea Eliade calls "the prestige of origins"[4]: its root lies in the life of the very first Jew. That Jubilees interprets the aqedah as the etiology of a feast is made explicit at the conclusion of its retelling of Genesis 22:

[17]And Abraham went to his young men and they got up and went [to] Beer-sheba together. And Abraham dwelt by the Well of the Oath. [18]And he named it "the feast of the LORD" according to the seven days during which he went and returned in peace. [19]And thus it is ordained and written in the heavenly tablets concerning Israel and his seed to observe this festival seven days with festal joy. (Jub 18:17–19)

The only seven-day festival in the first month is, of course, Passover (Lev 23:5–8). Jubilees seems to derive its duration, for which the Hebrew Bible gives no etiology, from Abraham's journey—three days to the mountain, three to return, and one day (the Sabbath) without travel. The journey begins on the twelfth rather than on the evening after the fourteenth (i.e., the beginning of the fifteenth) precisely so that the binding of Isaac will coincide with the date on which the paschal lamb will be offered.[5] Isaac has become the lamb of God, as it were, and Passover, an implication of the aqedah, a commemoration of Abraham's refusal to spare his own son when God demanded he be sacrificed.[6] It is to be an annual week of rejoicing based on the happy fact that Isaac was not ultimately killed.

That the aqedah and Passover should have come into an inextricable association is hardly surprising. Indeed, one wonders why the association first appears only in the mid-second century B.C.E. and whether Jubilees does not depend here upon an older tradition still. For, as we have had occasion to observe, both the near-sacrifice of Isaac in Genesis 22 and the sparing of the Israelite first-born sons in the tenth plague upon Egypt in Exodus 12–13 reflect a cultic institution, pre-Israelite in origin and evident among the Phoenicians, which allows for the substitution of an animal for the child marked for sacred slaughter—*agnum pro vikario*, as a North African inscription puts it, "a lamb as a substitute."[7] Jubilees thus only makes textually explicit a relationship that had always lain in the deep structure of Israelite culture. This was a culture *"deep structure"* profoundly imbued with the conviction that the first-born son belonged to God and thus overjoyed that God might accept a sheep in the son's stead. This conviction and its attendant joy continue to live, in significantly different ways, in both the Jewish and the Christian traditions.

The motivation for the aqedah that Jubilees furnishes is the innuendo of Prince Mastema that Abraham's love for God and faithfulness to him are subordinate to his love for Isaac. The only way God can disprove Mastema's impugning of Abraham is to order the Patriarch to offer up his son. Only then will it become known which stands higher in Abraham's calculus of value, his love for God or his love for Isaac.

The scene in heaven that Jubilees prefixes to its retelling of Genesis 22 is self-evidently an adaptation of the prologue of the Book of Job, in which a heavenly Adversary, or Satan, impugns Job's motivation for maintaining his blamelessness (Job 1–2). It is, Satan tells God, a matter of self-interest rather than authentic service, for blamelessness has always paid Job handsome dividends. "But lay Your hand upon all that he has and he will surely blaspheme You to Your face" (1:11). The effect of this transference of the motif of the prologue to Job to the aqedah is to provide a ready answer to a question that also bothered the rabbis of the midrash: what provoked this gruesome test, what could have been "these things" on which the aqedah logically followed (Gen 22:1; see *Gen. Rab.* 55:4)?[8] The answer of Jubilees has its own weighty midrashic logic and must not be judged arbitrary. For surely it is not unrelated that as a consequence of the heavenly Adversary's accusation, Job loses his children—but receives a new set in the end and lives "to see four generations of sons and grandsons" (Job 1:18–19; 42:13–16). This quite naturally suggests an analogy with the story of Abraham's willingness to sacrifice his beloved son, a story that closes, revealingly, not with the son dead, but with his life spared and with a genealogy of the family from which his son's wife—and the mother of Abraham's prime lineage—derives (Gen 22:20–24). It also merits mention that among the many parallels between Abraham and Job is to be numbered the language that describes the spiritual posture of each upon his death. Despite the trials they had endured, both die "old and contented" (*zāqēn wĕśābēaʿ*, Gen 25:8; *zāqēn ûśĕbaʿ yāmîm*, Job 42:17). There is, in sum, abundant and potent midrashic logic behind Jubilees' interlacing of God's tests of his two faithful servants, Job and Abraham.

The name of the heavenly adversary in Jub 17:15–16 provides another clue as to the origin of this prologue to the aqedah and also another and subtler connection with Passover. The Hebrew word *maśṭēmâ* derives from a root meaning "hostility, enmity." The prince with this name in Jubilees is one of a number of demonic figures prominent in the book (see, for example, 1:20). That the aqedah should have been a stinging rebuke to such a figure makes sense in terms of the worldview of Judaism in the late Second Temple period, a worldview with an acute sense of the factors impeding obedience and faithfulness and of the corollary necessity for herculean efforts at every level to overcome these impediments. Although the point is often missed, an analogous figure appears in the biblical account of the tenth plague upon the Egyptians. This is the mysterious "Destroyer" (*maśḥît*) who is deflected from the houses of the Israelites only because of their slaughter of the paschal lamb and their apotropaic manipulation of its blood (Exod 12:21–23). To be sure, the mission of the Destroyer originates more directly in the will of God than the mission of Prince Mastema, and once they have performed the paschal rites as instructed, the Israelites benefit from the Destroyer in a way that renders the term "demonic" somewhat problematic. It is the case, nonetheless, that Israel's scrupulous obedience to God's command concerning the yearling male lamb constitutes a setback, if not quite a stinging rebuke, to the Destroyer, whom it compels to abandon part of his mission of destruction—the part involving the Israelite first-born.

If an identification of the Destroyer with the Devil had been made by the time of Jubilees,[9] the application of the scene in heaven in Job 1–2 to the prologue to the aqedah in Jub 17:15–16 is readily understood. The test to which Abraham is subjected would then be the suggestion of the demonic figure defeated by the rites adumbrated in Abraham's obedient action—the slaughter of the paschal lamb and the placement of its blood on the doorposts and the lintels of the Israelites' houses in Egypt. Abraham pre-enacts his descendants' destiny, obeying God's command in a way that defeats the supernatural forces of destruction and, paradoxically, enables his first-born son to survive. We have had occasion to observe that some items in the story of Abraham in Genesis foreshadow the fate of the people Israel in Egypt (see chapter 10). Jubilees has made one of them explicit—his sacrifice of a sheep in place of his first-born and beloved son on the night after the fourteenth day of the first month. Abraham becomes the originator of Passover, and Passover becomes one massive footnote to the faithful obedience of the world's first Jew.

The idea that the salvation of the nation should hinge upon a father's willingness to surrender his son harks back to Canaanite and Israelite themes already of hoary antiquity by the time Jubilees was written. Most obviously, it recalls the story of Joseph, in which it is only Jacob's willingness to hand over his beloved son Benjamin that saves the family from starvation—and Simeon from lifelong imprisonment in Egypt (see chapter 13). But it also recalls the story of Mesha, king of Moab, who was able to break the deadly Israelite siege against him only by making his first-born son and heir apparent into a burnt offering (2 Kgs 3:24–27). It is this gruesome deed that causes a "great wrath" (*qeṣep gādôl*) to fall upon Israel and thus forces their retreat (see chapter 1). By founding the story of Passover upon the aqedah, Jubilees makes a father's willingness to give up his son and heir a key ingredient of Israel's redemption from Egypt. Once again the wrath of God falls upon the enemy, this time in the form of the Destroyer's execution of the tenth and climactic plague upon the Egyptians. The functional equivalence of the Destroyer and the "great wrath" should not be missed, nor should the Canaanite affinities of the paschal theology and rites. A holiday whose origins lie in a father's willingness to surrender his beloved son for a sacrificial death ends in the redemption of his descendants' first-born sons from the grip of death.

Jewish literature later than Jubilees continues the identification of Isaac and the paschal lamb that is there only implicit. Particularly noteworthy is a comment in the *Mekilta de-Rabbi Ishmael*, a midrashic work redacted most likely about the end of the fourth century C.E., on Exod 12:13b: "When I see the blood [of the paschal lamb] I will pass over you, so that no plague will destroy you when I strike the land of Egypt":

> I see the blood of the binding of Isaac. For it is said, "And Abraham named that site Adonai-Yireh [the LORD will see]," etc. [Gen 22:14]. Further on its says, "[God sent an angel to Jerusalem to destroy it,] but as he was about to wreak destruction, the LORD saw and renounced further punishment," etc. [1 Chr 21:15]. What did he see? He saw the blood of the binding of Isaac, as it is written, "God will see to the sheep," etc. [Gen 22:8]. (*Mekilta de-Rabbi Ishmael*, Pisḥā' 7).

Here, the blood of Isaac has displaced the blood of the lamb that dies so that the Israelites may be freed from bondage in Egypt. As the biblical text itself would have it, there is, of course, an enormous difference between Abraham's beloved son and the paschal lamb he here replaces: unlike the blood of the lamb, Isaac's was never shed, for in his case, the sacrifice was called off in the nick of time (Gen 22:12). It may be, as some suggest,[10] that our midrash simply assumes that because of Abraham and Isaac's willingness to go through with the offering, God views it as if it had taken place: where others see the blood of the paschal lamb, God alone sees the blood that would without question have been shed had he not canceled his gruesome command to Abraham. It is also possible and, in my judgment, more probable that, like some other rabbinic texts, this midrash assumes against the plain sense of Genesis 22 that some of Isaac's blood—perhaps even all of it—was indeed shed at the aqedah. In either case, it is the blood of Isaac that procures deliverance for the Israelite first-born from the lethal plague that the Destroyer is about to unleash. The father's refusal to spare his son has become a paradigm of the saving act, and the paschal lamb has become a cipher for the beloved son.

The second text that the midrash in the *Mekilta de-Rabbi Ishmael* cites is in some respects even more revealing of the transformation that the aqedah has undergone. This is the passage that treats the great plague on Jerusalem in the time of David. As in the case of Gen 22:14 and 22:8, the immediate connection is the word "saw": "the LORD saw [*rā'â*] and renounced further punishment" (1 Chr 21:15). This rather naturally links with the words "when

I see [*wĕrā'ìtí*] the blood [I will pass over you]" in Exod 12:13 and suggests that it is blood that YHWH "saw" in 1 Chr 21:15, in which the direct object is oddly omitted. There are, however, further connections with the aqedah. One is the incident itself, which serves as the foundation legend for the Jerusalem Temple. For this is not only the spot at which the angel appeared, "standing between heaven and earth" (v 16), and where David at the angel's behest builds an altar (vv 18, 26). It is also the spot on which the Temple will stand (1 Chr 22:1). This is, it will be recalled, none other than the site that Chronicles calls "Mount Moriah" (2 Chr 3:1). The mountain on which the angel is seen is thus identified with the mountain named Adonai-Yireh ("The LORD will see") in Gen 22:14, playing on Gen 22:8: "God will see [*yir'eh*] to the sheep for His burnt offering, my son." The oddly unspecified object of "saw" in 1 Chr 21:15 must then, by a strict but thoroughly midrashic logic, be none other than the blood of Isaac. And, once again, whether the son's blood was thought to have been literally shed or not, it is this blood that God sees when he renounces punishment and spares Israel from devastation. The aqedah/passover sacrifice has become the efficient cause of Israel's rescue from affliction throughout history.

The identification of Isaac's blood with that of the paschal lamb made in the first observation of our midrash is also to be detected in its second observation, the explanation of God's mysterious decision to renounce the punishment that he had initiated. The key, as is usual in midrash, is the phrasing:

> God sent an angel to Jerusalem to destroy it [*lĕhašḥîtāh*], but as he was about to wreak destruction [*kĕhašḥît*], the LORD saw and renounced further punishment and said to the destroying [*hammašḥît*] angel, "Enough! Stay your hand." (1 Chr 21:15a)

The prominence of the verb *hišḥît* here is remarkable: three occurrences in one verse. The last of these, *hammašḥît*, is identical with the name of the obscure agent of destruction in the tenth plague (Exod 12:23); the only difference is that here the word modifies the noun "angel," a term that in the parlance of the Hebrew Bible encompasses agents of either benign or maleficent mission. Jerusalem, in short, was spared from the pestilence that befell it in the days of David only because of God's rebuke of the *mašḥît*. To the rabbinic midrashist, this means that the two rescues are of the same origin: what God "saw" in 1 Chr 21:15 is the blood that saved the Israelite first-born. The first observation of our midrash establishes this to have been "the blood of the binding of Isaac."

The attribution of Jerusalem's deliverance from plague to the blood of Isaac rests, however, upon more than just the midrashic comment on the clause "when I see the blood" in Exod 12:13. It also rests upon the striking parallels between the aqedah and the story of the pestilence in Jerusalem in the time of David. Both stories are, or at least have become, etiologies of the Temple of Solomon. In each case, God halts a slaughter at the last moment, in the one instance through the angel's sudden order to Abraham, "Do not raise your hand against the boy" (Gen 22:12), in the other through God's order to the destroying angel after seventy thousand had fallen, "Enough! Stay your hand" (1 Chr 21:15). In each instance, the human protagonist builds an altar on the site known to both sources as Moriah (Gen 22:9; 1 Chr 21:26; 2 Chr 3:1). One key difference between the two narratives is that the motivation for the aqedah is unknown, whereas the pestilence in Jerusalem results from Satan's inciting David to conduct a census (1 Chr 21:1). Combined, these two related etiologies of the Jerusalem Temple result in something like Jub 17:15–16: the aqedah originates in a challenge by a diabolical figure. Then identifying the "destroying angel" of 1 Chr 21:15 with the "Destroyer" of Exod 12:13, as the diction and the context readily allow, one has something like our midrash from the *Mekilta de-Rabbi Ishmael:* what saved Jerusalem from the pestilence was the blood of the binding of Isaac. According to this text, a line runs from Abraham's great act of obedience to the deliverance of Jerusalem from pestilence in the days of King David. It must not be overlooked that this line runs through the tenth plague upon the Egyptians and the corollary sparing of the Israelite first-born. For, as the midrash would have it, where the text of Exodus speaks of the blood of the lamb, God saw the blood of Isaac. This piece of rabbinic exegesis makes a particularly direct use of the identification of Abraham's beloved son with the paschal lamb, an identification that first appears in Jubilees—but there only obliquely, by implication alone.

Some will find this tight and enduring association of the aqedah with Passover, and of Isaac with the paschal lamb surprising, since Genesis 22 has long been read in synagogues not on Passover but on Rosh Hashanah, the great autumn New Year's festival, where since Amoraic times it has served as the Torah lection for the second day of the feast (*b. Meg* 31a). The association of the aqedah with Rosh Hashanah underlies, for example, midrashim in which Abraham's vision of the ram "caught in the thicket by its horns" (v 13) is seen as the origin of the blowing of the shofar, the ram's horn solemnly sounded on New Year's Day.[11] As Rabbi Abbahu, who lived in the land of Israel in the third century C.E., put it:

Why do we blow the horn of a ram? The Holy One (blessed be he) said: "Blow the ram's horn before me so that I may remember for your benefit the binding of Isaac, son of Abraham, and account it to you as if you had bound yourselves before me." (*b. Roš. Haš.* 16a)

Rabbi Abbahu's assumption here is that acts of self-sacrifice in the imitation of Isaac will assist Jews in securing the gracious acquittal for which they petition God on Rosh Hashanah.

Despite this profound and increasingly central involvement with Rosh Hashanah, the story of the binding of Isaac never lost its ancient association with Passover even in rabbinic Judaism:

> "This month shall mark for you [the beginning of the months; it shall be the first of the months of the year for you]" [Exod 12:2]. "Happy the nation whose God is the LORD, / the people He has chosen to be His own" [Ps 33:12]. After the Holy One (blessed be he) had chosen his world, he established the order of the new moons and the new years. And when he chose Jacob and his sons, he established the new moon of redemption, in which Israel was redeemed from Egypt and in which they will in the future be redeemed, as it is said, "I will show him wondrous deeds / As in the days when you sallied forth from the land of Egypt" [Mic 7:15]. This is the month in which Isaac was born and in which he was bound. (*Exod. Rab.* 15:11)

This midrash does more than simply associate the aqedah with Passover after the manner of Jubilees.[12] It also makes the binding of Isaac into an archetype of redemption and thus a foreshadowing of the eschatological deliverance, the new Exodus. Isaac's descendants will be redeemed in the same month in which he was bound over the altar, the month that is first not only in order of enumeration, but, more profoundly, in order of importance to the history of redemption.

The ongoing redemptive effects of the aqedah and its importance in Jewish worship underlie an illuminating midrash on Lev 22:27. The verse itself deals with an item of cultic law, to all appearances of no special import:

> When an ox or a sheep or a goat is born, it shall stay seven days with its mother, and from the eighth day on it shall be acceptable as an offering by fire to the LORD. (Lev 22:27)

In a tradition evident in Palestinian Targumim, or Aramaic biblical translations, the three animals mentioned here are understood to refer to events in the lives of the three Patriarchs. The ox is a commemoration of the calf that Abraham rushed to prepare for his three divine visitors (Gen 18:7–8). The goat, similarly, is associated with the kids with which Jacob deceived his father and usurped his older brother's blessing (27:9, 14–16). In the explanation of the sheep, however, we find a midrashic comment most germane to our present investigation:

> Immediately [after Abraham provided the meal to his visitors] it was announced about Sarah that she would give birth to Isaac. After this [i.e., Isaac's birth], the lamb was chosen in order to recall the merit of the special [yĕḥîdā'] man who was bound on one of the mountains like a lamb as a burnt offering upon the altar. [God] redeemed him in his goodness and mercy, and when his descendants shall pray, they shall say in their time of distress, "Answer us at this time and listen to the cry of our prayer and remember for our benefit the binding of Isaac our father." (*Tg. Neof.* to Lev 22:27)[13]

It is here that we have the tightest and most explicit identification of Isaac with the sacrificial lamb. The animal, in fact, has become the symbol of the "special," "favored," or "only" son (however one renders *yāḥîd* in Gen 22:2, 12, and 16, reflected in *yĕḥîdā'* in this Targum) who was bound on the altar. The continuing sign of Isaac's having become like a lamb is that the lamb becomes like Isaac—a symbol of God's merciful bounty for those in affliction. As God redeemed the lamb-like Isaac awaiting slaughter upon the altar, so might he redeem his descendants, the Jews, when they invoke the memory of Abraham and Isaac's superlative obedience.

It is interesting that in the formulation of the Targum Neofiti to Lev 22:27, the lamb in question is not distinctively paschal. Rather, the association of Isaac with the paschal lamb, first discernible (though in an oblique way) in Jubilees 17–18, has now been generalized to include *all* lambs that Israel is enjoined to offer upon the altar of their God. Since it is virtually certain that Jubilees predates this and related Targumim, it is safe to conclude that the origin of the lamb symbolism of Isaac lies in the aqedah as an etiology of Passover. In a sense, the tradition has come full circle. Originally, the aqedah had no connection to the passover sacrifice, the two stories being, in fact, two variant historicizations of a long-standing and widespread Canaanite practice of child sacrifice potentially realized through an animal substitute. Then, at some point in the Second Temple period but, in any event, certainly by the time of Jubilees, the aqedah became a foundation story for Passover. Now, in midrashim like that on Lev 22:27, the aqedah is once again independent of paschal associations. It has become the basis of God's election of the sheep as a sacrificial animal, alongside the ox and the goat.

The generalization of the liturgical implications of the aqedah results in a new etiology. The daily sheep offering, like the paschal sacrifice before it, comes to be seen as a kind of reenactment of the binding of Isaac:

> In the case of a ram, it says, "[It shall be slaughtered] on the north side [of the altar] in the presence of the LORD" [Lev 1:11]. They said: When our father Abraham bound Isaac his son, the Holy One (blessed be he) established the institution of the two lambs, one in the morning and one in the evening. Why so much? Because when Israel would sacrifice the daily offering on the altar and recite this verse ("on the north side in the presence of the LORD"), the Holy One (blessed by he) would remember the binding of Isaac.
>
> I call heaven and earth to witness against me: Whenever anyone— Gentile or Jew, man or woman, male or female slave, reads this verse ("on the north side in the presence of the LORD"), the Holy One (blessed be he) remembers the binding of Isaac, as it is written: "on the north side in the presence of the LORD" (*Lev. Rab.* 2:11).[14]

In the first part of this midrash, the aqedah has become the origin of the daily offering of two yearling lambs, specified in Exod 29:38–42 and Num 28:3b–8. The full effect of the sacrifice now depends, however, upon its accompaniment by the recitation of the words in Lev 1:11, "on the north side [*ṣāpōnâ*] in the presence of the LORD." The underlying assumption seems to be that *ṣāpōnâ* should be understood not only as a word for "north," but also as a form of the root *ṣpn*, meaning to hide or store away. Indeed, the consonantal text, which is all that was written in rabbinic times, allows the word in question to be read as the feminine passive participle *ṣěpūnâ*, "hidden." The aqedah— a feminine noun—is hidden away in the presence of God but can be brought to his attention by imitating Abraham's sacrifice of a sheep and reciting the bivalent expression in Lev 1:11. On the basis of the overall rabbinic theology of the aqedah, it is certain that the effect of God's bringing the event to mind is an effluence of divine grace upon the worshipers and the establishment of reconciliation in place of estrangement. It is worthy of note that the second form of the midrash cited above goes out of its way to universalize the availability of this grace. So long as the key expression is recited, the personal status of the one doing so is of no consequence. This midrash is emphatic: the benefits won in the aqedah are open even to those who are not descended from Abraham.[15]

The emphasis in the midrash cited above upon the recitation of those words in Lev 1:11 tends to confirm what the overall context suggests: the text comes from an age in which animal sacrifice is no longer available and prayer (among other spiritual practices) must substitute for it. For here the efficacy of the burnt offering is rendered dependent, at least in part, upon the recitation of the law prescribing the manner of its performance. In the second form of the midrash, the actual offering is unmentioned, and the theurgic practice is limited to the recitation alone.

In the Talmud, the idea occurs that certain statutory prayers derive their authority from the laws of sacrifice in the Torah. In the case of the "prayer" par excellence, the *Shemoneh Esreh*, Rabbi Joshua ben Levi, who lived in the land of Israel in the third century c.e., said, "The prayers were instituted to correspond to the daily offerings" (*b. Ber.* 26b). The offering of two lambs every day, one in the morning and one at twilight (Exod 29:39; Num 28:4), is replaced by the recitation of the *Shemoneh Esreh* as a statutory obligation during the hours that tradition had fixed as the period for the lamb offerings. If, in accordance with the midrash in *Lev. Rab.* 2:11, one were to see the daily lamb offering as an effective symbolic reenactment of the aqedah, then one would have to say that the recitation of the *Shemoneh Esreh* is, in turn, founded upon the binding of Isaac. This conclusion, though logical, goes beyond the data in our hands. It does, however, bring to light a certain overlooked continuity between Judaism and Christianity. For in some Christian communions, most conspicuously the Roman Catholic, the eucharist is seen not only as a commemoration of the Last Supper ("Do this in remembrance of me," 1 Cor 11:24), but as a ceremony of prayer and feasting that is also and most importantly *sacrifice*, an effective reenactment of Jesus' atoning death.[16] In their different ways, both the *Shemoneh Esreh* and the mass have roots in the sacrificial ordinances of the Torah and a substantial debt to post-biblical Jewish exegesis of the story of the binding of Isaac. The indisputable differences between the two great liturgical practices should not be allowed to obscure their profound commonalities.

From one perspective, the rabbinic extension of the etiological function of the aqedah to cover all lambs sacrificed and not merely the paschal offering returns the story to where it began: a narrative without a direct association with Passover but with a pointed etiological connection to the Temple in Jerusalem. Abraham's unequaled act of faithful obedience on Moriah/Zion validates and gives meaning to the worship that takes place on the mountain where God can be seen. From another point of view, the aqedah separated anew from Passover becomes, however, another narrative. For now the sheep is only a reminder of Abraham's great deed and no longer a substitute for the beloved son, the first-born who belongs to God, as it is in the Passover legend. When every sheep offered is a theurgic recollection of the binding of Isaac, it becomes easier to lose sight of the crucial point that the aqedah is a legacy of a world in which God might choose to exercise his right to the first-born among a man's sons (see chapter 1).

Our conspectus of the transformation of the aqedah in its Second Temple and early rabbinic retelling requires us to qualify the identification of Isaac with the lamb, paschal and other, with material that moves in quite another direction. For one badly misunderstands the character of this transformation if one thinks that Isaac was imagined to have been willing to go to his appointed demise sheep-like, without awareness or choice. The truth is much the opposite. At the same time that Jewish writers and teachers were filling out the lines that run from Isaac to the paschal and daily lamb offerings, some of them were also subtly but steadily transforming the aqedah from the story of Abraham's offering of his son into one of Isaac's self-sacrifice in the service of the God of his father. His brush with death was increasingly viewed as self-conscious and freely chosen. The offered becomes the co-offerer of the near-sacrifice of the beloved son.

An early example of this extraordinary revisioning of the aqedah appears in 4 Maccabees, a profound work of Jewish philosophy in narrative form, of uncertain provenance and a likely date of composition between 18 and 55 c.e.[17] This book centers upon a decree of the Seleucid emperor Antiochus IV Epiphanes about 167 b.c.e. that every Jew must eat pork and meat sacrificed to idols. The Jews are, however, offered an alternative to these violations of their religion: they can be delivered into torture and then death (5:1–3). Antiochus' decree, in short, presents the Jews with the stark choice of a painful death in fidelity to the Torah or continued life granted them only because of their apostasy. It celebrates those who withstand horrific torture with astonishing bravery and choose death over faithlessness to the divine law. Among those who fall in this precious category are a certain mother and her seven sons, each of whom delivers himself, before his execution, of a highly polished oration on the demands of piety and the virtue of absolute loyalty to the law of God. At one illuminating point, the narrator of 4 Maccabees relates a scene in which the brothers call upon each other to stay the course and not buckle under the pressure of impending death:

> [10]"Courage, brother!" said one, and another, [11]"Hold on nobly." [12]And another, recalling the past, said, "Remember whence you came and at the hand of what father Isaac gave himself to be sacrificed for piety's sake." (4 Macc 13:10–12)[18]

The allusion to the aqedah is hardly surprising in a work suffused with scriptural exempla and in which the Abrahamic origins of the Jews are prominently displayed. These are, after all, the "seven sons of the daughter of

Abraham" (18:20), that is, heroic Jews born of an equally heroic Jewess. What is especially worthy of note, however, is the way the context requires an identification of the sons not with Abraham but with Isaac. For they must confront the loss not only of those dearest to them, but of their own lives as well. In order to fit into the Abrahamic paradigm, their martyrdom requires a refocusing of the aqedah on Isaac rather than on his father and a reconception of Isaac's death as one he *chooses* in complete freedom, and not, as Genesis 22 allows one to think, one in which he is only a naive victim, a sheep led to the shambles. The seed of the all-important notion of Isaac's near-death as voluntary lies in the Jewish theology of martyrdom as it emerges in the aftermath of the Seleucid persecutions. It was a seed that would be watered by the blood of Jewish martyrs throughout the ages, from those dark days of the Second Temple to the time of the First Crusade, when devout Christians massacred Jewish communities in the Rhineland (1096 c.e.)—and beyond.

By recreating the aqedah as the story of Isaac as a prototype of the Jewish martyr, 4 Maccabees and literature like it have both undermined and reinforced the association of Abraham's beloved son with the sacrificial lamb. The undermining is obvious: the lamb has no understanding of what awaits it and no volition with which to choose a sanctifying death over an unholy life. The reinforcement, which is more subtle, derives from another essential aspect of the Jewish theology of martyrdom, the conception of the martyr's demise as sacrificial and redemptive. This is nowhere stated with more poignance than in the peroration on the seven sons that appears near the end of 4 Maccabees:

> [17] The tyrant himself and his whole council were astonished at their endurance, [18] on account of which they now stand beside the divine throne and live the life of the age of blessing. [19] For Moses says, *All the holy ones are under your hands* [Deut 33:3]. [20] These then, having consecrated themselves for the sake of God, are now honored not only with this distinction but also by the fact that through them our enemies did not prevail against our nation, [21] and the tyrant was punished and our land purified, since they became, as it were, a ransom for the sin of our nation. [22] Through the blood of these righteous ones and through the propitiation of their death the divine providence rescued Israel, which had been shamefully treated. (4 Macc 17:17–22)[19]

The affirmation that the endurance of the martyrs has exalted them into the upper world and granted them a position near the throne of glory is best understood as a logical development out of an older Israelite theology. This was a theology that promised blessing and success for those who, resisting temptation, remained faithful to YHWH and obedient to his commandments (e.g., Lev 26:3–13). In the case of those who die the death of martyrs, the old theology had to undergo an adjustment, for their failure, in a worldly sense, is a consequence of the very behavior that the Torah commands and commends. The adjustment of 4 Maccabees is to call the worldly criteria of success into question. The passage 17:17–19 interprets the ostensible defeat of the martyrs as an actual victory: with their life's blood the martyrs have purchased their exalted place in the upper world where they enjoy the blessing that the tradition once promised them and cruel happenstance denied them on earth.[20]

If the martyrs' deaths had benefited only themselves, the full measure of self-sacrifice that is its distinguishing characteristic would, our text seems to suggest, be undermined. For 4 Macc 17:20–22 carries the interpretation of their deaths beyond the exploration of the consequence for the martyrs themselves. It was, these verses tell us, death on behalf of the rest of Israel, whom it benefited by eliciting God's compassion and ultimately his rescue of the downtrodden nation. The language in which this enormous benefit is described is unabashedly cultic. The term for "propitiation" (*hilastērion*) in v 22, for example, is the word that the Septuagint uses for the cover of the Ark of the Covenant (Hebrew, *kappōret*), on which the high priest sprinkles the blood of the bull as a sin offering (Lev 16:14). It is worthy of note that it is also the term that Paul was to use when he wrote that "God set [Jesus] forth as an expiation, through faith, by his blood" (Rom 3:25).

The book known as 4 Maccabees and the Jewish theology of martyrdom for which it is one of the earliest witnesses is more democratic than Paul. To *all* Jews who die the consecrated death it applies the language of propitiation or expiation that Paul was to apply to Jesus alone. Isaac, in 4 Maccabees, both is and is not thus a spiritual forebear of Jesus as reinterpreted by Paul and kindred Christians. Isaac is a forebear of Jesus in that, as a martyr, he helps bring reconciliation and redemption. He is not a forebear of Jesus, however, in that his death is not *uniquely and exclusively* redemptive: it is one scriptural example, albeit an especially poignant one, of the sort of death that the author asks of Jews facing the horrific choice of martyrdom or violation of the Torah. One other point of comparison must not go unmentioned here: the norms for which 4 Maccabees calls upon Jews to be willing to give their lives are the very ones that Paul believed to have been set aside by the new aeon inaugurated by the death and reported resurrection of Jesus.

The idea that Isaac was bound over the altar by his own free choice soon transcended the theology of martyrdom that most probably served as its matrix. A case in point is the *Biblical Antiquities*, a book ascribed to Philo of

Alexandria but not of his authorship, preserved in Latin but most likely composed in Hebrew some time in the first century c.e.[21] The *Biblical Antiquities* presents two texts relevant to our subject. The first directly recounts the conversation of Abraham and Isaac on their trek to Moriah:

> But the son said to the father, "Hear me, father. If a lamb of the flock is accepted as sacrifice to the LORD with an odor of sweetness and if for the wicked deeds of men animals are appointed to be killed, but man is designed to inherit the world, how then do you now say to me, 'Come and inherit life without limit and time without measure'? Yet have I not been born into the world to be offered as a sacrifice to him who made me? Now my blessedness will be above that of all men, because there will be nothing like this; and about me future generations will be instructed and through me the peoples will understand that the LORD has made the soul of a man worthy to be a sacrifice." (*Bib. Ant.* 32:3)

Isaac's comments here show him overcoming the suspicion that his impending death at the hands of Abraham will reduce him to the level of an animal. On the contrary, he comes to see that his acceptability for sacrifice is a unique honor: it demonstrates the dignity of the human race for all future generations.

The other allusion to the aqedah in the *Biblical Antiquities* of Pseudo-Philo is even more explicit about Isaac's active role. It comes from the mouth of Jephthah's daughter (here given the name of Seilah), who, as we have seen,[22] has much in common with the intended victim of the aqedah:

> [2]*And* Seilah *his daughter said to him*, "and who is there who would be sad in death, seeing the people freed? Or do you not remember what happened in the days of our fathers when the father placed the son as a holocaust, and he did not refuse him but gladly gave consent to him, and the one being offered was ready and the one who was offering was rejoicing? [3]And now do not annul everything you have vowed, but carry it out." (*Bib. Ant.* 40:2–3)[23]

The point could not be clearer: Isaac *agreed* to be sacrificed and contemplated with utter joy his transformation into a holocaust, that is, a burnt offering. It is worthy of note that by recounting the allusion to the aqedah in the mouth of Seilah rather than Jephthah, the narrator has also shifted the focus from Abraham, the hero of the biblical story, to Isaac, the son who with joy and equanimity now looks upon his impending immolation.

Before leaving the Jewish sources from the first century c.e. that emphasize Isaac's choice to be bound as a sacrifice, attention must be given to the retelling of the aqedah that appears in Flavius Josephus' *Jewish Antiquities*, a work composed at the end of that century. Abraham loved Isaac passionately (*hyperēgapa*), Josephus tells us, because he was his only son (*monogenē*), granted him as a gift of God in his old age (*JA* 1:222). Ordered to sacrifice his beloved son, Abraham explains to the chosen victim his reason for compliance. It is obviously God's intention, he tells Isaac, that the son should die not as most people do, "by sickness or war or by any of the calamities that commonly befall mankind, but amid prayers and sacrificial ceremonies" will God receive the soul of the beloved son and keep it near himself. "And for me," Abraham concludes, "you shall be a protector and stay of my old age—to which end above all I nurtured you—by giving me God instead of yourself" (*JA* 1:230–231).[24] Again, though martyrdom is not the context here, the cultic resonances should not be missed. The death that has been decreed for Isaac is sacrificial in character. It draws Abraham closer to God, for, by playing his assigned role in bringing it about, Abraham chooses God over what he otherwise most loves—his only son, Isaac.

Most germane to our present discussion is Isaac's response to his father's speech:

> The son of such a father could not but be brave-hearted, and Isaac received these words with joy. He exclaimed that he deserved never to have been born at all, were he to reject the decision of God and of his father and not readily resign himself to what was the will of both, seeing that, were this the resolution of his father alone, it would have been impious to disobey; and with that he rushed to the altar and his doom. (*JA* 1:232)

The doom, of course, never comes to be, for God explains to Abraham that he felt "no craving for human blood," but only wanted to test his obedience (1:233). It is not hard to detect Josephus' apologetic intentions in his rewriting of the aqedah. He clearly wishes his cultured Greek-speaking readership to think of the aqedah in terms other than that of a child sacrifice narrowly averted and to view Judaism as a lofty philosophy rather than a barbarian cult founded by a man who would gladly kill his own son. Josephus accomplishes these goals by putting in Abraham's mouth a carefully reasoned explanation of his behavior and in Isaac's, a statement of unqualified assent. But the notion that Isaac (here presented as twenty-five years old in *JA* 1:227) gladly accepts his role in the aqedah is not exclusively a figment of Josephus' apologetic motives.[25] It is, as we have seen, a feature prominent in other Jewish retellings from the period, works composed for internal consumption and surely reflecting generations of midrashic development. One of the engines driving this development was the greater sense of the accountability of the individual in Hellenistic Judaism as opposed to earlier periods in the history of the religion of Israel. This made it less feasible to retell the aqedah with Isaac as a mere appendage to Abraham, as the biblical narrative arguably suggests. When precisely this transformation of the story began is impossible to say. It may be implicit even in Jubilees, which seems to assign Isaac the age of fourteen at the time of his binding[26]—an age when he doubtless could have understood what was about to happen to him and escape if he chose to. In Genesis 22, his age is unspecified.

Isaac's glad and unstinting participation in the aqedah is a legacy of earlier forms of Judaism that the rabbinic movement developed further. Particularly illuminating is the comment of the *Sifre Deuteronomy*, a relatively early midrashic collection, on Deut 6:5: "You shall love the LORD your God with all your heart and with all your soul and with all your might." In the *Sifre Deuteronomy*, Rabbi Meir, a figure of the mid-second century C.E., applies the three common nouns in this verse to the three patriarchs. "With all your soul" thus recalls the patriarch of the middle generation: "[You shall love the LORD your God] with all your soul"—like Isaac, who bound himself upon the altar. (*Sifre Deut.* 32) In Rabbi Meir's retelling, Abraham's binding of Isaac as a sacrificial offering is transformed into Isaac's binding of himself: child sacrifice has been sublimated into self-sacrifice. And it is this note of self-sacrifice that God hears, according to Rabbi Abbahu in the third century, when Israel sounds the ram's horn in hopes of bringing the aqedah to God's remembrance (*b. Roš. Haš.* 16a).[27] The Jew is enjoined to imitate not only Abraham, but Isaac as well.

We have already examined an exemplar of the last of the salient changes that the aqedah underwent in ancient Jewish tradition. This is the startling transformation by which a story in which the father is explicitly forbidden to "do anything to" his beloved son (Gen 22:12) metamorphosed into one in which he wounds or even kills the lad. "When I see the blood I will pass over you," God announces to Israel enslaved, with incontrovertible reference to the paschal lamb (Exod 12:13). But the *Mekilta de-Rabbi Ishmael* glosses: "I see the blood of the binding of Isaac" (Pishā' 7).

This notion that Isaac's blood was in some sense shed is not confined to rabbinic sources. The *Biblical Antiquities* of Pseudo-Philo also makes an allusion to the blood of Isaac, though hardly one that specifies just what happened at that all-important instant:

> And he brought him to be placed on the altar, but I gave him back to his father and, because he did not refuse, his offering was acceptable before me, and on account of his blood, I chose them. (*Bib. Ant.* 18:5)

What this obscure text excludes is any possibility that Isaac was indeed slain. It remains unclear, nonetheless, exactly how far the new sacrifice of Isaac proceeded. A minimalist position both accords best with the plain sense of Genesis 22 and offends the modern sensibility least: though Abraham did nothing to his son bound upon the altar, God accounts his willingness to go through with the act as if he had, in fact, shed his blood. Abraham's binding his son and taking the butcher's knife in hand thus constitute, in God's eyes, the full equivalent of the sacrifice that, thankfully, never took place. Isaac's symbolic death at the hand of his loving father has the theological value of a real death.

Ancient midrash would not be ancient if it never offended modern sensibilities, nor would it be midrash if it always conformed to the plain sense of the biblical passage it interprets. The minimalist position, though it may indeed fit the two references to the blood of Isaac that have been mentioned, fails utterly when it confronts a passage like the following:

> Rabbi Joshua says: "God spoke to Moses and said to him ['I am the LORD']" [Exod 6:2]. The Holy One (blessed be he) said to Moses, "I can be trusted to pay out the reward of Isaac son of Abraham, who gave a quarter of [a *lōg* of] blood upon the altar and to whom I said:
>
> [¹⁰ Let the nations not say, "Where is their God?"
> Before our eyes let it be known among the nations
>   that You avenge the spilled blood of Your servants.
> ¹¹Let the groans of the prisoners reach You;]
>   reprieve those condemned to death
>   as befits Your great strength. [Ps 79:10–11]
>
> I am trying to bring them out of Egypt, and you say to me, "[Please, O Lord], make someone else Your agent"? [Exod 4:13] (*Mekilta de Rabbi Shimon ben Yochai*, Wā'ērā')²⁸

This text suggests that a bolder reading of the other allusions to the blood of Isaac may be in order, for it makes clear that some of his vital fluid was indeed shed. The point of the quotation from Psalm 79 is to render the Exodus from Egypt a consequence of the aqedah. Because of the "spilled blood" of God's servant Isaac, the groan of the captive Israelites reaches God and induces him to grant them a reprieve. The term "prisoners" recalls the first of Pharaoh's schemes for dealing with the Israelite threat: enslavement. "Those condemned to death" suggests the second: genocide (Exod 1).²⁹ Both are reversed when God vindicates the blood shed by his faithful servant Isaac and liberates the people Israel from Egypt.

Underlying this powerful, multilayered midrash is, once again, a conception of Isaac as a martyr: he gives his blood so that God, in avenging him, may redeem his descendants from bondage and death. How much he gives remains unclear. A quarter *lōg* is a small amount and suggests a token donation. But a Talmudic text seems to say that the same measure is all the blood a person has (*b. Soṭa* 5a), and the possibility cannot be disallowed that our midrash portrays Isaac as a man who gave every ounce of his vital fluid—a true and not just a would-be martyr. The notion of a token donation of blood fits the context of *Bib. Ant.* 18:5 at least as well as the minimalist idea of God's accounting the near-sacrifice of Isaac to Abraham as if the deed had come to pass. In the case of the anonymous midrash on the words "when I see the blood" (Exod 12:13), here, too, it is eminently plausible that the underlying assumption is that Isaac really did give some of his blood at the aqedah—or even all of it.

We have seen that the possible interpretations of the midrashic allusions to the blood of Isaac are three. The first is the minimalist view: no blood was spilled, but God graciously reckoned Abraham's and Isaac's devout *intention* as the equivalent of the bloody *deed*. Next comes the intermediate position: Abraham drew a fraction of Isaac's lifeblood as a token of the sacrifice he was prepared to carry out. The third view is maximalist: the father slew his son, and the son gave up his life, in obedience to the command of God.

Some rabbinic texts speak not of Isaac's blood, but of his *ashes*, and it is here that the convenient intermediate interpretation seems quite forced. Either God views the aqedah as if Isaac had been reduced to ash in the sacrificial flames, though nothing of the sort actually transpired, or God sees the real ashes of Isaac as a poignant and potent testimony to the obedience of Abraham and his son—the latter an obedience even unto death. To be sure, some midrashim, usually found in late collections, do venture an intermediate position. They interpret "the ashes of Isaac" as referring to what remained of the ram sacrificed in his stead, which they sometimes report had itself always borne the name "Isaac."[30] Creative and charming though this interpretation be, it still bespeaks an anxiety to avoid associating Abraham with a human sacrifice—and with disobedience to the explicit and unambiguous prohibition delivered by none other than the angel of the LORD. It is, in short, probably only a pious harmonistic gloss on the eminently disquieting older phrase, "the ashes of Isaac."

As long as one restricts oneself to the wording of the passages themselves, the texts that speak of "the ashes of Isaac" are generally amenable to the minimalist reading. Our first example includes a close parallel to the passage in the *Mekilta de-Rabbi Ishmael* that tells of God's seeing the blood of Isaac during the pestilence with which he afflicted Jerusalem in the days of King David:

"[The LORD] said to the angel who was destroying the people, 'Enough [*rab*]!' [2 Sam 24:16]. Said Rabbi Eleazar: The Holy One (blessed be he) said to the angel, "Take for me the greatest man [*rab*] among them, who is capable of expiating many sins." At that moment there died Abishai son of Zeruiah, who alone was equal to the majority of the Sanhedrin.

"[But] as [the angel] was about to wreak destruction, the LORD saw and renounced further punishment" [1 Chr 21:15]. What did he see? Rav said: He saw our father Jacob, as it is written, "When he saw them Jacob said . . . " [Gen 32:3]. But Samuel said: It was the ashes of Isaac that he saw, as it is written, "God will see to the sheep [for His burnt offering, my son]" [Gen 22:8]. Rabbi Isaac Nappaha said: It was the money of atonement that he saw, as it is written, "You shall take the expiation money from the Israelites [and assign it to the service of the Tent of Meeting; it shall serve the Israelites as a reminder before the LORD, as expiation for your persons]" [Exod 30:16]. (*b. Ber.* 16b)

It is altogether unremarkable that most of the Talmudic figures quoted here understand the cessation of the pestilence in terms of their own theology of atonement. Rabbi Eleazar's comment is premised upon the crucial rabbinic notion that the death of the righteous atones for the sins of others. Rabbi Isaac Nappaha's assumes the equally traditional notion that a donation in substitution for death can have the same atoning effects. The comment of Samuel, head of a Babylonian academy in the early third century C.E., is more ambiguous. In form, it is highly reminiscent of the statement in the *Mekilta de-Rabbi Ishmael* that attributes both the salvific effect of the paschal lamb and the cessation of the pestilence in David's time to "the blood of the binding of Isaac." Here, as there, it remains unclear in what sense God "saw" the results of the aqedah. Perhaps God only regards the event *as if* it produced the ashes that have the atoning effects of which Rabbi Eleazar and Rabbi Isaac Nappaha speak—the equivalent of a sacrifice but not a literal one. Samuel's resort to Gen 22:8 as his prooftext only adds to the ambiguity. The connection may be nothing more than the verb *yir'eh* ("[God] will see") to explain what God "saw" (*rā'â*) when he "renounced further punishment" (1 Chr 21:15). But it may also be that Samuel thinks that what God "saw" is what Gen 22:8 predicts he will see—the sacrificial sheep offered by Abraham as the equivalent of his beloved son (v 13), though without the late embellishment that the animal, too, bore the name Isaac. A third possibility is that Samuel, like some later Jewish commentators, understood the end of Gen 22:8 to indicate that

Abraham's son was to be the burnt offering. If so, then the phrase "ashes of Isaac" implies that Samuel, unlike those commentators, thought Isaac had actually been immolated. This last possibility departs from the plain sense of Genesis 22, but no more than the midrash in which Abraham draws blood from his son. In fact, a certain overly literal reading of the biblical chapter can be pressed into service in support of the contention that Isaac was sacrificed (and later resurrected). The angel, after all, "called to Abraham a second time" (v 15), an indication that the instruction in the first address, not to harm the boy (v 12), had proven ineffective. The second angelic address only specifies the bright consequences of Abraham's not withholding his son (vv 16–18), leaving us to wonder what he had done to the boy between the angel's two speeches.[31] But we need not wonder long, for the last verse, if read in the same overly literal fashion, hints at the gruesome answer:

> Abraham then returned to his servants, and they departed together for Beer-sheba; and Abraham stayed in Beer-sheba. (Gen 22:19)

But what of his son? Isaac is unmentioned here, writes Abraham ibn Ezra (c. 1092–1167), because he was under his father's custody, "and anyone who says that he slaughtered him and left him and that afterwards he came back to life has said the opposite of the Scripture."[32] But as ibn Ezra understood better than most Jews of his generation or ours, to say the opposite of the Scripture is often precisely what midrash does. His rejection of the notion that Isaac was slain and resurrected stands, as we shall soon see, in marked contrast to the views of some of his contemporaries.

The ambiguity we find in Samuel's allusion to the ashes of Isaac bedevils all the comparable rabbinic texts. None of them seems able to resolve our pressing question of whether the ashes exist outside the mind of God and whether they derive from Isaac or from the ram offered as his stand-in. It may well be that one cause of the ambiguity is that the difference between the three possibilities is less to the rabbinic than to the modern mind. To say that God *accounts* Isaac as having been sacrificed can be, in rabbinic thought, the equivalent of saying he was indeed sacrificed, though not necessarily in ordinary reality: he may have been sacrificed according to the reckoning of a higher and infinitely more important reality than that of mundane life. And to say that it was the ashes of the ram rather than the son that God beholds is not to say that Isaac was not sacrificed. It is merely to say that the realization of the sacrifice of Isaac through the instrumentality of the animal was fully acceptable to the God who issued the gruesome command to Abraham to incinerate his beloved son.

A new and unexpected light is shed on these questions when one shifts the discussion from the texts about the ashes of Isaac to some other midrashim about the second patriarch, notably the following:

By the merit of Isaac who offered [*hiqrîb*] himself upon the altar, the Holy One (blessed be He) will in the future resurrect the dead, as it is written:

[²⁰ For He looks down from His holy height;
    the LORD beholds the earth from heaven]
 ²¹ to hear the groans of the prisoner,
 [to release those condemned to death.] [Ps 102:20–21] (*Pesikta de-Rab Kahana, zō't habbĕrākâ*)³³

That Isaac should be described as one "who offered himself upon the altar" is not surprising in light of the longstanding tendency to present him as a willing, indeed active participant in the aqedah. The problematic element is the precise meaning of the verb *hiqrîb*. The word, a causative from the root meaning "to be near, approach," is common in discussions of sacrifice in every period of the Hebrew language. Does it here mean that Isaac presented himself upon the altar for a sacrifice that was never consummated, at least in any mundane, empirical sense? Or does it mean that he sacrificed himself? In support of the latter interpretation, one can adduce the context. God's eschatological resurrection of the dead makes much sense as a consequence of the merit of one who put himself to death and was revived. It makes less sense as the consequence of the merit of one who only presented himself for a sacrifice that God called off in the nick of time. The prooftext from Psalm 102 can be made to speak for either understanding of *hiqrîb*. The part of v 21 actually quoted suggests that God, in response to Isaac's cry of pain, let him free from the bonds into which, as this midrash would have it, he had put himself. But the second half of that verse, with its mention of "those condemned to death" (*bĕnê tĕmûtâ*, literally, "sons of death," "dead ones") suggests a true resurrection and better fits the overall context. It is most germane that this expression occurs in only one other place, Ps 79:11, which, as we saw earlier in this chapter, is a prooftext for the idea that Isaac shed blood in the aqedah. This, too, supports the interpretation of *hiqrîb* as indicating a true sacrifice.

Sufficient ambiguity envelops the expression "the ashes of Isaac" as to permit a conjecture, but only a conjecture, about its meaning. It is reasonable to suspect that the pressure of Jewish martyrdom spawned the idea that Isaac, like the martyrs of a later age, went willingly to a death that was never called off but only miraculously reversed, a sign for the martyrs to follow who now sleep in the dust. Given the extreme precariousness in dating rabbinic literature, it is well-nigh impossible to say when this momentous and portentous transformation began. The absence of any evidence for it outside of rabbinic sources naturally suggests the lethal persecutions of Hadrian (c. 130–135 C.E.) as the terminus a quo, but the underlying exegetical moves may be older still. In any event, efforts were made to blunt the new idea that Isaac was immolated after all. This was an idea that clashed with Gen 22:12–13 but conformed to a certain reading not only of v 19 but also of v 15, in which the angel is constrained to call upon Abraham a second time, as if the first call had failed. That Isaac was indeed sacrificed was also an idea that may have stood too close to certain Christian narratives for the rabbis' comfort. These consideration may explain why "the ashes of Isaac" has been preserved as a set expression without the accompanying narrative that alone explains it. But the idea that Isaac underwent the same gruesome fate as his descendants, the Jewish martyrs, reappeared from time to time. Its most moving statement occurs in a poem by Rabbi Ephraim of Bonn, written some time after the Second Crusade (1146):

> *He made haste, he pinned him down with his knees,*
>   *He made his two arms strong.*
> *With steady hands he slaughtered him according to the rite,*
>   Full right was the slaughter.

> *Down upon him fell the resurrecting dew, and he revived*
>   *(The father) seized him (then) to slaughter him once more.*
> *Scripture, bear witness! Well-grounded is the fact:*
>   And the Lord called Abraham, even a second time from heaven.[34]

Ephraim's older contemporary, ibn Ezra, would have to counter that Scripture cannot bear witness, for these ideas are "the opposite of the Scripture." The retort is tragically simple: which better captures the reality of the Jewish martyrs of the twelfth or any other century, the plain sense of Genesis 22 beloved of ibn Ezra, or the rewritten aqedah of Jewish tradition?

Such, then, are the transformations that the episode in Gen 22:1–19 underwent in the periods of the late Second Temple and the Talmud. Never directly referred to within the Hebrew Bible, the aqedah had, by early in the second century B.C.E., emerged as a supreme moment in the life of Abraham. Soon thereafter it had already become a foundation story for the festival of Passover, with the near-sacrifice of Isaac foreshadowing the literal slaughter of the lamb. The association of Abraham's beloved son with the paschal lamb continued to grow in the rabbinic period, and eventually the aqedah became an etiology even of lamb offerings that were not paschal. At the same time, Isaac's role in the drama was becoming increasingly active. He was reconceived as a willing participant, freely and gladly choosing, like a martyr, to give up his life in obedience to the heavenly decree, and, again like a martyr, his choice was seen as effecting atonement for the many. This transformation, already in evidence in the first century C.E., gathered force in the rabbinic period. Eventually, it became possible to allude to the aqedah without mention of the hero of the biblical story, Abraham: Isaac bound himself and offered himself upon the altar. Moreover, the sacrifice to which he had given joyful assent was imagined, in contradiction to the biblical report, to have in some sense taken place—in the reckoning of God, through a token shedding of blood, or even literally, with Isaac reduced to ashes and then raised to life anew by the power of the God who is master over death as well as life.

Not all these transformations proceeded at the same pace, nor should the new conceptions that they yielded be thought to have been endowed with the normative force of dogma. Jewish tradition has always been too multifarious, argumentative, and decentralized for this to have been the case. Nor should our choice of topics mislead us into imagining that the aqedah alone occupied center stage in the theology of the periods discussed. This was, instead, an honor it shared with a number of other Pentateuchal episodes—the splitting of the sea, for example, or the revelation at Sinai, the incident of the golden calf, the report of the scouts, the rebellion of Korah, the prophecy of Balaam, the death of Moses. It is clear, nonetheless, that on any short list of the critical moments in the history of redemption according to the rabbis, the aqedah would merit a high rank, and certain key rabbinic conceptions of the episode are demonstrably pre-rabbinic. Notable among these are the associations with Passover and with martyrdom, both themes at the very center of the Christian adaptation of the aqedah that will occupy our attention in the following chapters.

thus, post-biblical readings set up Passover + martyrdom, thus setting up Xian reading

Chapter Fifteen

The Displacement of Isaac and the Birth of the Church

The identification of Jesus of Nazareth with "the beloved son" on which our discussion has focused comes early in the Synoptic Gospels. It is first made through a heavenly announcement during Jesus' ablution at the hands of John the Baptizer:

> "You are my beloved son; with you I am well pleased." (Mark 1:11; cf. Matt 3:17; Luke 3:22; 2 Pet 1:17)

The wording recalls the designation of Isaac in the aqedah, wherein the Hebrew term *yāḥîd* ("favored one") is consistently rendered in the Septuagint as *agapētos*, "beloved" (Gen 22:2, 12, 16), the very term that appears in this heavenly announcement.[1] "Take your beloved son, the one you love," the Septuagint renders Gen 22:2, "and offer him up there as a burnt sacrifice." In light of the mounting importance of the aqedah in the Judaism of the Second Temple period, it is reasonable to suspect that the early audiences of the synoptic Gospels connected the belovedness of Jesus with his Passion and crucifixion. Jesus' gory death was not a negation of God's love (the Gospel was proclaiming), but a manifestation of it, evidence that Jesus was the beloved son first prefigured in Isaac. As we shall see, the point was vital to the self-definition of the nascent Christian community.

The announcement of Mark 1:11 (and the parallels) is no less indebted to another Jewish text with rich resonances[2]:

> This is My servant, whom I uphold,
> My chosen one, in whom I delight,
> I have put My spirit upon him,
> He shall teach the true way to the nations. (Isa 42:1)

This is only one of several passages in Isaiah 40–55 that speak of the enigmatic figure of "the servant of YHWH." The most developed of these is Isa 52:13–53:12, which depicts the servant as an innocent, humble, and submissive man who was, nonetheless, persecuted, perhaps even unto death. These persecutions were not meaningless, however: they served a redemptive role, for through them the servant atoned vicariously for those who maltreated him. Isa 52:13–53:12 came to exert an extraordinary influence upon the way that early Christians reconceived Jesus after his execution (see, for example, Acts 8:26–35), enabling him to accomplish through his death the cosmic transformations denied him in life. The identification of Jesus with the suffering servant of the Book of Isaiah thus became a mainstay of Christian exegesis. It was not shaken until the twelfth century, when Andrew of St. Victor, anticipating modern critical study, interpreted the servant as a representation of the Jewish people as they suffered during the Babylonian exile. In light of the longstanding Christian investment in the figure of the suffering servant, it is no cause for wonderment that some Christians reacted negatively to Andrew, accusing him of "judaizing."[3]

Whether the interlacing of Gen 22:2, 12, and 16 with Isa 42:1 was original to the evangelists or a legacy of prior Jewish exegesis is unknown.[4] Either way, the equation of Isaac with the suffering servant has its own potent midrashic logic. For if the binding of Isaac had already been reconceived as foreshadowing the sacrifice of the paschal lamb and the liberation and redemption that it heralds (Jub 17:15–18:19), the suffering unto death of the servant of YHWH had also been analogized to the condition of a sheep about to be slaughtered, and in Scripture itself:

> He was maltreated, yet he was submissive,
> He did not open his mouth;
> Like a sheep being led to slaughter,
> Like a ewe, dumb before those who shear her,
> He did not open his mouth. (Isa 53:7)

The servant's acceptance of his fate conforms, as we have seen, very much to the image of Isaac as it develops in some important Jewish sources from the first century C.E. That these two revered figures, both obedient unto death, should have been identified with each other and, in Christian sources, with Jesus after his humiliating demise, is hardly surprising. It may well be that the catalyst for this second midrashic equation was the prior identification of Jesus with the paschal lamb, an intertextual move that, as we shall discover, predates the composition of the Gospels.

The application to Jesus of the two not dissimilar Jewish traditions of Isaac and the suffering servant sounds an ominous note, easily missed by those who interpret God's love in sentimental fashion: like Isaac, the paschal lamb, and the suffering servant, Jesus will provide his father in heaven complete pleasure only when he has endured a brutal confrontation with nothing short of death itself. The midrashic equation underlying the heavenly announcement of Mark 1:11 and its parallels makes explicit the theology of chosenness that lies at the foundation of the already ancient and well-established idea of the beloved son: the chosen one is singled out for both exaltation and humiliation, for glory and for death, but the confrontation with death must come first.

It is in the proleptic glimpse of Jesus' future glory vouchsafed to his disciples that we next hear the identification of him as the beloved son in the Synoptic Gospels:

> Then a cloud came, casting a shadow over them; then from the cloud came a voice, "This is my beloved son. Listen to him." (Mark 9:7; cf. Matt 17:5; Luke 9:35)

In this narrative (Mark 9:2–8 and parallels), traditionally known as the Transfiguration, the last sentence adds a new note to the theme of the beloved son in the New Testament. Though marked for sacrifice and thus unspeakable humiliation, the son is also invested with *authority* and thus destined to receive the homage of others. In this case, the affinities with Isaac are less to the point than those with another of the beloved sons in Genesis, Joseph, whom "Israel loved . . . best of all his sons, for he was the child of his old age" (Gen 37:3). As we have argued in chapter 13, the tale of Joseph in Genesis 37–50 is, in part, the story of how its hero came to earn the privileged status that had been granted him in childhood, how, through multiple symbolic deaths (the first of which his father takes to be a literal death), Joseph was catapulted into a position to issue directives to his older brothers—and to see them heeded. We can go further: the Gospel story of the Transfiguration functions as a rough analogue to Joseph's report to his brothers and his father of his dreams of domination (37:5–11). In each case, the narrator presents us with a vision of the coming grandeur that seems preposterous at the moment—Joseph's brothers and parents prostrating themselves before him in Genesis, Jesus conversing with Moses and Elijah in the Gospels (Mark 9:4–6 and parallels). And, in each case, what falls between the vision and its realization is the crucial event—a confrontation with death, as the one designated as the beloved son is betrayed and abandoned, never to be seen again. Or so it would appear.

What the Joseph story more than any of the other tales of the beloved son contributes to the Gospels is the theme of the disbelief, resentment, and murderous hostility of the family of the one mysteriously chosen to rule. In the Christian story, this theme is concentrated in the figure of Judas, who betrays Jesus in exchange for thirty pieces of silver (Matt 26:14–16, 20–25,

47–56 and parallels). It would seem more than possible that the episode of Judas has been molded upon the sale of Joseph for twenty pieces of silver in Gen 37:26–28 (if "they" in v 28 is understood to be the brothers rather than the Midianite traders), an arrangement suggested by none other than his brother Judah. The names are the same. The number in Genesis correlates with Lev 27:5, which fixes the worth of a male between five and twenty years of age at twenty shekels. It will be recalled that Joseph is seventeen when he is sold into slavery (v 2).

The sum in the Gospels may derive from Zech 11:12, an obscure text in which a shepherd is paid thirty silver shekels. Note that in the same passage the shepherd breaks his staff named "Unity, in order to annul the brotherhood between Judah and Israel" (v 14). This alone would suggest (at least to the midrashic mind) some affinity with the story of Joseph, in which, as we have seen, Judah is Joseph's most important brother and the one among the twelve who takes the lead in healing the catastrophic rift in the family. Ezekiel 37:15–28 may have aided in the association of Zechariah 11 with Genesis 37, for in that passage God likewise speaks of two sticks, one representing Judah and one representing Joseph, and orders the prophet to join them, symbolizing the reunion of the separated brothers. In light of these biblical precedents, it was not an unlikely move for the Gospels to associate the fatal rift among the twelve disciples with the betrayal of Joseph, their father's beloved son and the one among the twelve destined to rule despite his brothers' enmity and perfidy.[5]

The theme of authority draws the traditions of the beloved son into relationship with another important stream in Jewish tradition, that of messianism. This stream originates within the royal theology of the Judean dynasty, the House of David. In the Hebrew Bible, its most characteristic literature centers on the divine commission to the Davidic king or heir-apparent, the latter in some cases only a newborn or even as yet unborn. The practical point of such literature is often to elicit homage for the king in a moment in which his rule seems shaky. Psalm 2, for example, paints a scenario in which nations and their rulers intrigue together "against the LORD and His anointed" (v 2), the last word being the Hebrew term of which "messiah" is simply a crude transliteration. In response, YHWH gives forth a mocking laugh from his heavenly throne, terrifying the conspirators with his reiteration of the threatened king's divine commission:

"But I have installed My king
on Zion, my holy mountain!" (Ps 2:6)

The king himself then speaks, reciting the terms of that commission:

⁷Let me tell of the decree:
the LORD said to me,
"You are My son,
I have fathered you this day.
⁸Ask it of Me,
and I will make the nations your domain;
your estate, the limits of the earth.
⁹You can smash them with an iron mace,
shatter them like potter's ware." (Ps 2:7–9)

The dominion of the king enthroned upon Zion is a function of his status as the son of YHWH.⁶ How literally this status was understood is difficult to know. A minimalist position would see in the decree rehearsed in v 7 only a metaphor that conveys the unique covenantal relationship of the Davidic king with Israel's ultimate suzerain, their God YHWH. For the language of fatherhood and sonship in the biblical world doubled as the terminology of suzerainty and vassalage (see, e.g., 2 Kgs 16:7 and Ps 89:27–29). A maximalist position would not deny the covenantal denotation, but it would see in this language something more than the frozen forms of diplomatic convention: it would see a living metaphor, a dynamic communication of the heavenly source of the earthly king's authority. The rule of the Davidic king enthroned upon Mount Zion is a manifestation of the universal dominion of the God of Israel. The former issues from the latter like a son from the father who begot him, and for those who refuse to "listen to him," as the story of the Transfiguration puts it in reference to the beloved son, this has catastrophic consequences.

The emphasis in some of the messianic oracles in the Hebrew Bible upon the birth of the king speaks persuasively for the maximalist interpretation of the divine sonship of the ruler from the House of David:

⁵For a child has been born to us,
A son has been given us,
And authority has settled on his shoulders.
He has been named
"The Mighty God is planning grace;
The Eternal Father, a peaceable ruler"—
⁶In token of abundant authority
And of peace without limit
Upon David's throne and kingdom,
That it might be firmly established
In justice and in equity
Now and evermore. (Isa 9:5–6)

The prince is not merely an ordinary person elevated to regal status through covenant with YHWH. He is, rather, a miraculous figure, and his accession is an event that transforms ordinary reality and ushers in the reign of justice traditionally associated with YHWH's own lordship. It is possible that oracles like the one excerpted above were recited not at the heir-apparent's literal birth, but upon his enthronement, at which point, as Psalm 2 would suggest, he assumed the status of God's son, exchanging, as it were, human for divine paternity.[7]

Regardless of the king's chronological age at the time, the miraculousness and giftedness of his birth establish another link with the tradition of the beloved son in the Book of Genesis. For, as we have observed, the men there so designated are rather consistently born to barren women—Isaac to Sarah, Jacob to Rebekah, Joseph to Rachel—and in each case the birth is owing to God's intervention. In the case of Isaac, the supernatural character is underscored through the emphasis placed upon his mother's advanced age at the time of his birth (Gen 18:11), ninety in the reckoning of the Priestly source (17:17).

The notion that heroic figures are born outside the course of nature, to barren mothers, is not unique to the account of Israel's origins. It can be found also in the stories of Samson and Samuel (Judges 13; 1 Samuel 1), two of the nation's most renowned deliverers. One function of these stories is to legitimate the special status of the person to whom miraculous birth is attributed. His authority is not something that he has usurped: a gracious providence has endowed him with it, thus to benefit the entire nation. As Isa 9:5 puts it, "a child has been born *to us,*/A son has been given *us*" (emphasis added). In the case of Isaac, Jacob, and perhaps Joseph as well, what the stories legitimate is the lineage that descends from them. Isaac and not Ishmael, Jacob and not Esau carry on the chosen line of their fathers. Given the royal connections of the tribe of Joseph in the north, the story of Joseph may originally have played a similar role, perhaps at the expense of the House of Judah, from which the Davidites hailed: the true monarchy is Josephite, not Judean. But given the emphasis in Genesis 37–50 on authority, one might also see in Joseph's birth to a barren woman something akin to the miraculous (re)birth of the Judean kings so prominent in the messianic oracles of the Hebrew Bible. Precisely because the beloved son rules by the grace of God, it is by that grace and in startling defiance of common experience that his birth comes about.

The New Testament equivalent of this Israelite notion of the birth of the beloved son to a barren woman is the story of the virgin birth of Jesus (Matt 1:18–25; Luke 1:26–38),[8] an idea whose prominence in later Christian dogma obscures the fact that it seems to have been unknown outside Matthew and Luke. In the former, the idea is midrashically linked to Isa 7:14, which speaks of a "young woman" (ʿalmâ) giving birth to a son named "Immanuel." The midrash in question seems to depend upon the Septuagint rendering of ʿalmâ as *parthenos*, a Greek word that often denotes a virgin (Matt 1:22–23). In the case of Luke, the idea of the Virgin Birth is associated with the titles "Son of the Most High" and "Son of God" and with Jesus' claims upon the Davidic throne (Luke 1:32–35). Underlying this is an extremely literal understanding of the Judean royal theology and its characterization of the Davidic king as YHWH's son. Within the overall structure of the Gospels, however, the two vocabularies of sonship, that of the beloved son and that of the Davidic king as the son of God, reinforce each other powerfully.[9] They yield a story in which the rejection, suffering, and death of the putatively Davidic figure is made to confirm rather than contradict his status as God's only begotten son.[10]

It would seem to have been the timing of Jesus' execution that accounts for the Gospels' identification of him with the beloved son. One of the few things upon which all four canonical Gospels agree is that his death occurred in the season of Passover. Precisely when within that season is another matter. According to the three Synoptics, Jesus was executed on the first day of Passover. Since Jewish festivals begin at sundown, this means that the Last Supper occurred on the evening the holy day began and thus likely had a paschal purpose (Matt 26:17–20; Mark 14:12–17; Luke 22:7–15). The Gospel according to John, however, dates the crucifixion to the day *before* Passover, that is, to the day at the end of which the festival would begin, with the sacrifice of the paschal lambs (John 13:1; 18:28). This would seem to mean that the Synoptics and John differ as to the year in which the trial of Jesus took place. The Synoptics assume a year in which Passover began on a Thursday evening, whereas John assumes one in which the holy day began on a Friday evening.

John's chronology therefore precludes his interpreting the Last Supper as paschal in a strict sense. Thus, the words of consecration prominent in the Synoptic accounts of the Last Supper ("Take this; this is my body . . . This is my blood" [Mark 14:23–24; cf. Matt 26:26–28; Luke 22:14–20]) are altogether missing from the Fourth Gospel. This should not be taken to mean, however, that John does not interpret the end of Jesus' life as sacrificial. It does mean that the association of Jesus' body with the paschal lamb will be made explicit not at the Last Supper but at Golgotha, on the cross itself:

> [31]Now since it was preparation day, in order that the bodies might not remain on the cross on the sabbath, for the sabbath day of that week was

a solemn one, the Jews asked Pilate that their legs be broken and they be taken down. ³²So the soldiers came and broke the legs of the first and then of the other one who was crucified with Jesus. ³³But when they came to Jesus and saw that he was already dead, they did not break his legs, ³⁴but one soldier thrust his lance into his side, and immediately blood and water flowed out. ³⁵An eyewitness has testified, and his testimony is true; he knows that he is speaking the truth, so that you also may (come to) believe. ³⁶For this happened so that the scripture passage might be fulfilled:

"Not a bone of it shall be broken." [Exodus 12:46; Num 9:12]
³⁷And again another passage says:
"They will look upon him whom they have pierced." [Zech 12:10]

(John 19:31–37)

The first scriptural quotation refers to the paschal lamb. It appears here in order to demonstrate that Jesus' passing away earlier than the two men with whom he was executed was providential. Had he remained alive and thus suffered the broken legs, he would have been rendered unfit to serve as the sacrificial offering of the first night of Passover. In John's thinking, Jesus' body has thus rather literally taken the place of the lamb consumed by the worshipers at the sacred Passover banquet. Regardless of the intention of the Romans and Jews who carried it out, the crucifixion of Jesus was, in the Johannine view, a *sacrifice*, the offering of the son of God in place of the paschal lamb.

The second scriptural quotation, Zech 12:10, is brought in order to make sense of the Roman soldier's thrusting his lance into the dead man's side: according to the evangelist, this, too, fulfills a prophecy. Here it is useful to remember that the relevance of a verse often extends beyond the words that the midrashist cites. In the case of Zech 12:10, it is highly suggestive to note the words that follow those cited in John 19:37:

. . . wailing over them as over a favorite son and showing bitter grief as over a first-born. (Zech 12:10c)

We have already had occasion to observe that the word here rendered "favorite son" (*yāḥîd*) seems to have been, at least on occasion, a technical term for the son sacrificed as a burnt offering. It is, once again, the term applied fully three times to Isaac in the *aqedah* (Gen 22:2, 12, 16). In the Septuagint to Zech 12:10, *yāḥîd* is rendered exactly as in the Septuagint to those three verses, *agapētos*, "beloved one." It would thus seem likely that John is here reflecting the old equation of the first-born and beloved son with the paschal lamb but asserting a relatively new equation as well—the Christian equation of the first-born and beloved son and paschal lamb with the figure of Jesus.

The threefold identification of the beloved son, the paschal lamb, and Jesus would seem also to underlie John's version of the baptism of Jesus:

> The next day he saw Jesus coming toward him and said, "Behold, the Lamb of God, who takes away the sin of the world." (John 1:29)

On the one hand, John the Baptizer's words upon first setting eyes on Jesus contrast markedly with the heavenly proclamation that the Synoptic Gospels all report at the same point in the story: "You are my beloved son; with you I am well pleased" (Mark 1:11; cf. Matt 3:17; Luke 3:22). If, on the other hand, the author(s) of the Fourth Gospel had assumed the equation of the beloved son with the paschal lamb, then the dissonance between the two proclamations, though still significant, is of lesser import. Here the end of John the Baptizer's little speech that opens with John 1:29 is revealing: "Now I have seen and testified that he is the Son of God" (v 34). The implication that the "Lamb of God" is to be equated with the "Son of God" once again takes us back to the ancient Israelite rite by which a sheep substitutes for the first-born son destined for sacrifice (Exod 34:20). This is a rite that, as we have seen, is crucial to both the binding of Isaac (Gen 22:13) and the Exodus from Egypt (Exod 13:11–15). In a certain sense, the dynamics underlying this ritual-mythical pattern come full circle in this New Testament material: the son takes the place of the sheep who took the place of the son. The Jewish parallels suggest, however, that the sheep and the son should never be conceived of as totally separate, that the ransom and the one redeemed were always tightly associated. Recall the late midrashim that report that the ram sacrificed in Isaac's stead was itself named "Isaac."

The Johannine account of the crucifixion of Jesus, with its explicit reference to Exod 12:46 (John 19:36), provides powerful additional evidence that the "Lamb of God" of John 1:29 is paschal. It might be retorted, nonetheless, that since the paschal lamb was never a sin offering, the clause "who takes away the sin of the world" argues for a different animal, such as the sheep of Lev 4:32–35, offered by a commoner in expiation of wrongdoing. The latter is, however, not necessarily a lamb, and we must not assume that the fine technicalities of sacrificial classification weighed heavily upon the minds of the evangelists as they drew upon biblical materials for their own purposes. More importantly, the unclassifiable passover sacrifice of Exodus 12 does indeed have much in common with a sin offering, for it is through the blood of the lamb that lethal calamity is deflected, as the mysterious Destroyer is prevented from working his dark designs upon the Israelite first-born (vv 21–

23). It is not at all hard to imagine that in the heated apocalyptic Judaism that served as the matrix of Christianity, the Destroyer would be transmuted into a personification of the Israelites' own mortal sins, and the blood of the paschal lamb would be seen as effecting not only escape from death, but purification from moral pollution as well.

A close analogy to the process here reconstructed is patent in Rev 12:10–11. There it is the blood of the lamb that overpowers the "accuser" (*katēgōr*, a title of Satan) and enables the Christ to come into power. Like Prince Mastema, the diabolical figure who institutes the aqedah (and thus, indirectly, Passover as well) in Jub 17:15–16, this "accuser" has a striking analogue and perhaps also his root in the eerie Destroyer of Exod 12:23. In all these instances, Jewish and Christian alike, it is the offering of the sheep or the son identified with it that defeats the demonic forces and brings blessing out of near-catastrophe, life out of the jaws of death.

As a reference to the Passover offering, the "Lamb of God" of John 1:29 correlates nicely with the explicit identification of Jesus with the paschal lamb in 19:36. The location of these two verses in the Gospel's narrative is telling: the man introduced as the lamb that takes away the sin of the world dies according to the laws governing the offering of the paschal sacrifice. Thus has the evangelist placed the earthly story of Jesus within brackets drawn from the story of Passover—the story of how the preternatural forces of death were foiled and the doomed first-born miraculously allowed to live.

Probably the earliest identification of Jesus with the paschal lamb occurs in a document that predates both the Synoptic and the Johannine Gospels:

> [6]Your boasting is not appropriate. Do you not know that a little yeast leavens all the dough? [7]Clear out the old yeast, so that you may become a fresh batch of dough, inasmuch as you are unleavened. For our paschal lamb, Christ, has been sacrificed. [8]Therefore, let us celebrate the feast, not with the old yeast, the yeast of malice and wickedness, but with the unleavened bread of sincerity and truth. (1 Cor 5:6–8)

Here the apostle Paul, writing in about the year 54 c.e., employs an allegory of the sort one finds occasionally among the rabbis but more frequently in Hellenistic Judaism. Its basis is the law of Passover in Exodus 12—not so unlikely a topic since Paul seems to be composing his letter to the Corinthians about the time of Passover and Easter.[11] His allegory identifies the leaven forbidden to be eaten or even seen during the week of Passover with boasting, malice, and wickedness and urges his correspondents to prepare for the holiday by ridding themselves of the proscribed substance, as Exod 12:15 mandates. The genesis of the allegory lies in the last clause of 1 Cor 5:7: "For our paschal lamb, Christ, has been sacrificed." It is the equation of Jesus with the paschal lamb, almost certainly already traditional by the time Paul wrote, that rids his little allegory of the odor of arbitrariness. If Jesus is the passover offering, then all those who are "in Christ" (to use a Pauline idiom) must be continually in the moral equivalent of the state of high ritual preparedness for Passover. Indeed, if the lamb/Christ has already been sacrificed, as the tense of the verb at the close of v 7 indicates, then such preparedness is doubly urgent, for the festival has begun though the leaven remains—an intolerably dangerous situation.

Given the threefold equation of the paschal lamb, the beloved son, and Jesus that we found lurking beneath the surface of the Gospel of John, we should not be surprised to find Paul identifying his Christ not only with the passover offering but also with Isaac, the beloved son par excellence of the Hebrew Bible (the only Bible Paul knew). Indeed, the boldness with which Paul projects Jesus (and the Church) into the story of Abraham is a midrashic tour de force that has affected Jewish-Christian relations ever since:

> [13]Christ ransomed us from the curse of the law by becoming a curse for us, for it is written, "Cursed be everyone who hangs on a tree," [14]that the blessing of Abraham might be extended to the Gentiles through Christ Jesus, so that we might receive the promise of the Spirit through faith.

> [15]Brothers, in human terms I say that no one can annul or amend even a human will once ratified. [16]Now the promises were made to Abraham and to his descendant. It does not say, "And to descendants," as referring to many, but as referring to one, who is Christ. (Gal 3:13–16)

Paul's midrash in v 16 turns upon his interpretation of the morphologically singular collective noun *ûlĕzarʿăkā* (Greek, *kai tō spermati sou*) in Gen 13:15 and 17:8 as therefore semantically singular as well: not "to your offspring" in the sense of many people but "to your *one* offspring," whom Paul identifies as the Christ.

The association of the individual Isaac with the collective noun *zeraʿ*, "offspring," is familiar from the Book of Genesis. Recall God's reassurance to Abraham when Sarah insists on the expulsion of Hagar and Ishmael: "Whatever Sarah tells you, do as she says, for it is through Isaac that offspring will be continued for you" (Gen 21:12). It is as though Abraham's offspring through Ishmael are not really his *zeraʿ*, or at least not in the same way as those descended from his beloved younger son, Isaac. A discussion in the Talmud cites this verse to explain why the *halakhah* obligates Jews but not Edomites to practice circumcision:

"For it is in Isaac that offspring will be continued for you." Then the descendants of Esau should be obligated! "In Isaac"—not all of Isaac. (*b. Sanh.* 59b)[12]

In other words, because the Edomites, though descended from Isaac's son Esau, are not included within the subgroup of Isaac that the rabbis here think the preposition "in" implies, they are not included in the Abrahamic covenantal act that is circumcision. Abraham's real offspring are those descended from Isaac alone. Whereas Gen 21:12 excludes the Ishmaelites from the status of Abraham's prime lineage, the Talmudic discussion uses the same verse to exclude the Edomites. Both passages, however, presuppose the association of Isaac and the singular collective noun, *zeraʿ*, "offspring."

It is precisely this association that Paul ruptures when he glosses "and to your descendant" in Genesis with the words "who is Christ" (Gal 3:16): the beloved son to whom and about whom the ancient promises were made is no longer Isaac but Jesus, no longer the Israelite patriarch in whom the future of the Jewish nation is prefigured but the messiah of Christian belief whose mystical body is the Church. Paul's midrash on the one word *ûlĕzarʿăkā*, "and to your descendant(s)," exemplifies a familiar and uneventful Jewish exegetical technique.[13] But in it loom the future separation of Christianity from Judaism and their crystallization as mutually exclusive traditions.

Once Jesus has displaced Isaac, it follows that the promises and blessings that had been associated with the beloved son par excellence in Genesis must be available instead through the Christian messiah. This is, in fact, the implication of Paul's first clause in Gal 3:14, "that the blessing of Abraham might be extended to the Gentiles through Christ Jesus." In the Hebrew Bible, the exact words "blessing of Abraham" occur only in Gen 28:4, in a passage in which Isaac, having directed Jacob to avoid intermarriage, pronounces upon him the Abrahamic blessing of progeny and land (vv 1–4). It is surely relevant to Paul's purpose that this passage has to do with Isaac's confirmation of Jacob as his—and Abraham's—rightful heir. It is surely no less relevant that part of the Abrahamic blessing is that Jacob shall "become an assembly of peoples" (v 3). Given Paul's motivation in composing his letter to the Galatians, a passage like this must have held an enormous appeal for him. For his dominant purpose in this letter is to argue that Gentiles can inherit the status of descent from Abraham, and all the promises that go with it, without having to convert to Judaism (and become circumcised). The idea that the blessing of Abraham should entail that Jacob/Israel "become an assembly of peoples" fit Paul's polemical intentions beautifully. As he read Gen 28:1–4, it almost certainly implied precisely the possibility for which he was doing battle—that by be-

AQEDA = CRUCIFIC.

coming Christian, Gentiles could have the best of both worlds, retaining their non-Jewish identity and yet falling heir to the promises to Abraham.

"That the blessing of Abraham might be extended to the Gentiles through Christ Jesus" (Gal 3:14a) recalls another passage in Genesis as well, one much more focused on the relationship of Abraham and Isaac. This is the second angelic address toward the end of the story of the aqedah:

> [15] The angel of the LORD called to Abraham a second time from heaven, [16] and said, "by Myself I swear, the LORD declares: Because you have done this and have not withheld your son, your favored one, [17] I will bestow My blessing upon you and make your descendants as numerous as the stars of heaven and the sands on the seashore; and your descendants shall seize the gates of their foes. [18] All the nations of the earth shall bless themselves [alternatively, "be blessed"] by your descendants, because you have obeyed My command." (Gen 22:15–18)

In chapter 14, I observed that the effect of this speech is to make the blessing to Abraham contingent upon the aqedah. Abraham's willingness to sacrifice Isaac has become a foundational act, indeed the essential foundational act for the existence and destiny of the people Israel. As Paul read this text through his own particular christological lenses, the key point would probably have been this: it is the father's willingness to surrender his beloved and promised son unto death that extends the blessing of the Jews to "all the nations of the earth."

The equivalent for Jesus of the binding of Isaac is, once again, his crucifixion. It is undoubtedly this that underlies Paul's citation of Deuteronomy 21:23 (Gal 3:13). The law therein forbids allowing the impaled body of a person executed for a capital offense to remain on its stake overnight. The words that Paul (or the translation from which he is working) renders as "cursed be everyone who hangs upon a tree" are probably more accurately translated "an impaled body is an affront to God." In positioning this clause before his mention of the blessing of Abraham (v 14), Paul develops a polarity between the curse that, in his view, comes from biblical laws and the blessing that comes from biblical promises. This, too, befits one of his central objectives in composing the letter to the Galatians—to argue against those apostles who maintained that the laws of the Torah were still valid and in no way voided by the Christian revelation. Though far from an antinomian, Paul rather consistently associated the laws of the Torah with sin, curse, condemnation, and death, all of which are antithetical to those things he associated with Jesus. In the juxtaposition of Gal 3:13 and 3:14, we can thus hear a recapitulation of the whole movement of Pauline salvation history: from curse to blessing, from law to spirit and faith, from Israel to the Church, from the crucifixion to the blessings contingent upon it—ultimately, to use language not yet available in Paul's time, from Judaism to Christianity.

Nils Dahl has made the intriguing suggestion that the combination of the aqedah with the law of the impaled criminal in Gal 3:13–14 turns upon the equation of the man hanging on the tree in Deut 21:23 with the "ram caught in the thicket" of Gen 22:13. More problematic is Dahl's conclusion, that "here there is an element of typology, but the ram, rather than Isaac, is seen as a type of Christ."[14] If Paul does see a foreshadowing of his Christ in the ram, the ram, in turn, derives its significance for the history of redemption only from its status as a stand-in for Isaac. For the extension of the blessing of Abraham to the nations that is so important to the apostle to the Gentiles is a consequence not of Abraham's sacrifice of the ram, but of his unfaltering resolve to obey the command to offer his beloved son.

But even to speak of a typology of Isaac and Jesus here (rather than one of the ram and Jesus) has its difficulties and must be attended by important qualifications. An Isaac-Jesus typology does indeed develop in early Christian literature,[15] but it must not be projected into texts that move in another, and much more radical, direction. For Gal 3:13–14 cannot be detached from vv 15–16, and v 16 makes clear that Isaac does not foreshadow Jesus at all. Rather, Paul argues that the "descendant" who is the heir of the promise to Abraham *is not* and *never was* Isaac or the Jewish people collectively. His whole point about the putative semantic singularity of the word "and to your descendant" is to connect the promise with Jesus alone. The descendant of Abraham who is Isaac has disappeared from the story altogether. Paul never mentions his name. If Gal 3:13–16 is still to be seen as a typology, it is a typology of such intensity that the antitype has dislodged the archetype: in Paul's theology Jesus has so thoroughly displaced Isaac that even Genesis testifies not to the second of the Jewish patriarchs, but to the messiah of Christian belief. Paul's Jesus does not *manifest* Isaac. He *supersedes* him.

None of this is to deny that Isaac can function typologically in Paul's thinking. He is most explicitly a type, however, not of Jesus but of the Church, and it is in his interpretation of Isaac's conflict with Ishmael, and of Sarah's with Hagar, that we see the full boldness of Paul's appropriation of the traditions in Genesis about the beloved son:

> [21]Tell me, you who want to be under the law, do you not listen to the law? [22]For it is written that Abraham had two sons, one by the slave woman and the other by the freeborn woman. [23]The son of the slave woman was born naturally, the son of the freeborn through a promise. [24]Now this

is an allegory. These women represent two covenants. One was from Mount Sinai, bearing children for slavery; this is Hagar. [25] Hagar represents Sinai, a mountain in Arabia; it corresponds to the present Jerusalem, for she is in slavery along with her children. [26] But the Jerusalem above is freeborn, and she is our mother. [27] For it is written:

"Rejoice, you barren one who bore no
   children;
break forth and shout, you who were not in
   labor;
far more numerous are the children of the
   deserted one
than of her who has a husband." [Isa 54:1]

[28] Now you, brothers, like Isaac, are children of the promise. [29] But just as then the child of the flesh persecuted the child of the spirit, it is the same now. [30] But what does Scripture say?

"Drive out the slave woman and her son!
For the son of the slave woman shall not
share the inheritance with the son" [Gen 21:10]

of the freeborn. [31] Therefore, brothers, we are children not of the slave woman but of the freeborn woman. (Gal 4:21–31)

In this allegory, Hagar, the Egyptian slave woman, represents two closely related images of bondage. The first is the site of the giving of the Torah, Mount Sinai, which, lying somewhere between the land of Israel and Hagar's homeland, suggests the slave woman's abortive flight to freedom and her reenslavement (Genesis 16). The second is the earthly Jerusalem, where, in Paul's time, some form of Torah observance was normative for the Church. The first great innovation in Paul's reading of Genesis is this identification of Hagar's slavery with Torah. It bears mention that in rabbinic literature, Torah and Mount Sinai often represent true freedom (and the other positives that Paul associates exclusively with Jesus). [16]

The other mother in Paul's allegory is obviously Sarah, the freeborn woman whom he associates with a heavenly Jerusalem not obligated by the Torah. Sarah's infertility, miraculously overcome in accordance with God's promise, leads Paul to associate her son Isaac with promise and spirit. This, in turn, makes Hagar's son Ishmael, born through the altogether natural means of surrogate motherhood, a "child of the flesh." The rivalry of Ishmael and Isaac, and of Hagar and Sarah (Gen 21:9–10), is thus allegorized into a stark opposition between slavery, Torah, and flesh, on the one hand, and freedom, promise, and spirit, on the other. Ishmael's persecution of Isaac, attested in ancient Jewish interpretation of Gen 21:9,[17] thus becomes a figure for those Jewish Christians who opposed Paul's message of a Torah-less Gospel and sought, instead, to evangelize the Galatians into Torah-observant Christianity. It was this that Paul considered a perversion of the Gospel and urged his Galatian correspondents to avoid (Gal 1:6–9; 5:1).

The second major innovation in Paul's allegory of Hagar and Sarah, Ishmael and Isaac, lies in his association of Sarah and Isaac with a Torah-less religion, that is, with a form of Judaism in which the injunctive dimension of the Torah has been voided. If we had only Gal 4:21–31 and lacked the antecedent Pentateuchal texts, we would never have guessed that it was actually *Isaac's* descendants rather than Ishmael's who stood at Mount Sinai and received what in Pentateuchal and later Jewish thinking alike is regarded as the incomparable blessing that is the Torah of Moses. With his reading of Genesis 21, Paul thus effects a startling inversion, one fraught with significance for the future character of the Church and, needless to say, for its relation to the Jews into our own day.[18] The literal descendants of Sarah and Isaac have become the moral and spiritual progeny of Hagar and Ishmael. Isaac has ceased to be the first critical link in the great chain that will lead from Abraham to redemption in the promised land. Instead, he has become a type for the possibility of a spiritual life of freedom apart from the Torah—more than that, in contradistinction to the Torah, which Paul now reinterprets as fleshly and enslaving rather than spiritual and liberating, as the rabbinic tradition would continue to conceive it. For, whereas in the Pentateuch Mount Sinai is the first great *destination* of those freed in the Exodus (Exod 3:12), in Paul's Gospel Mount Sinai is the point of *departure* for the exodus, the equivalent of the house of bondage. "For freedom Christ set us free," he concludes his allegory; "so stand firm and do not submit again to the yoke of slavery" (Gal 5:1).

In the post-Enlightenment world, this freedom from Torah is often used to reinforce the portrayal of Paul as a universalist, a person, that is, to whom ethnic identity is of no account. Similarly, Paul's critique of Judaism as he knew it (or reconstructed it after his conversion) is seen as premised upon an opposition to particularism and exclusivism and a corollary affirmation of the natural dignity of all humanity, regardless of whether the individual is Jewish or Greek, slave or free, male or female (Gal 3:28). This line of thought has traditionally served powerfully to reinforce an image of Judaism as separatist, exclusivistic, and chauvinistic, in contradistinction to Christianity, which is thought to be integrationist, inclusive, and non-particularist. That this rejection of particularism should have fueled the lethal fires of anti-Semitism is one of the larger ironies of modern history.

A consideration of Pauline and other early Christian theology in its historical context immediately casts this convenient polarity into grave doubt. For in Paul's lifetime and for a significant period thereafter, it was actually Judaism that was the larger community, spread throughout the known world, with influence even in the centers of power, and attracting converts and semi-converts. The Christian Church, by contrast, was a very new sect, small and beleaguered. To attribute godliness and freedom to the Church—and especially, as Paul did, to the Torah-less subgroup within it—was hardly to strike a blow for universality and inclusiveness.

The allegory in Gal 4:21–5:1 shows us a different and more historically plausible picture of Paul. His point there is anything but the oneness of the human family or the irrelevance of belonging to Abraham rather than to the nations. He does not argue that Hagar and Sarah, Ishmael and Isaac, are ultimately one, nor that the distinction between Jew and Gentile has, through the Christ, yielded to an affirmation of their common humanity. All to the contrary, it is a point of capital import that it is Abraham, the father of the Jewish people, rather than Adam, the father of the human race, whose blessing Paul seeks to appropriate exegetically for the Church (Gal 3:29). In Paul's theology, one of the prime consequences of the Gospel is a grafting of the Gentiles onto the tree of Abraham *in place of the Jews*, who have been lopped off but are to be re-engrafted in the eschatological future when God's rage against them comes to an end (Rom 11:11–29).[19] Whereas Christian universalists like to imagine Paul's christology as offering a way out of Jewishness and into an undifferentiated humanness, the actual thrust of the theology of the apostle to the Gentiles is the reverse: the undifferentiated humanity that is the nations of the world, the "wild olive shoot" as Paul disparagingly terms them (v 17), can, through the Christ, become the equivalent of the Jews. Thus and only thus can they shed their worthless Gentile status and attain the only status that Paul thinks has value in the sight of God—the status of Isaac, the son promised to Abraham and conceived outside the course of nature, in contradistinction to Ishmael, the son of his wife's slave, conceived through the natural and perhaps not altogether honorable means of surrogate motherhood. Pauline ecclesiology is premised upon the possibility and the legitimacy of borrowed ethnicity—a very different thing from universalism or inclusiveness for its own sake.

For Paul, then, participation in the Christ is the equivalent of conversion to Judaism, but it is more than that: it is also the *only* means of conversion to Judaism, for the Jewish means—acceptance of the Torah and its commandments, symbolized in men by circumcision—have, in Paul's mind, ceased to be efficacious. For reasons that remain unclear, Paul insists that the two modes of conversion to the status of children of Abraham must not be combined: contrary to the Gospel of his opponents, Paul demands that a Gentile who comes into the Christ must not become circumcised and practice the Torah. To do so is to forfeit the precious status of the promised son—Isaac—and to fall into the carnality and subjugation of the offspring of Abraham whom Isaac displaced and superseded—Ishmael, son of Hagar the Egyptian slave-woman. The division between the circumcised and the uncircumcised, between Israel and the nations, and between those (of whatever origin) who have accepted the Torah and those who have not, has become the division between the baptized and the unbaptized, between the Church and the world, between those who have accepted the Gospel and those who have not. But in both the Jewish and the Pauline frameworks, the issue turns upon the question of which community can lay just claim upon the status of Abraham's beloved son. This could not be more different from the way modern universalists approach such matters.

At first glance, Paul's elaborate allegorical reading of Genesis 16 and 21 appears so forced as to suggest utter arbitrariness. The apostle to the Gentiles has, it would seem, a theological message to get across, and his choice of the rivalry of Isaac and Ishmael and their respective mothers as his prooftext is without an anchor in the text itself. I submit that the matter is quite the opposite: Paul focuses on Isaac's right of inheritance because, in his mind, the Church is to be identified with Isaac on grounds altogether independent of the particular texts about the expulsion of Hagar and Ishmael. For, as we have seen, Paul believes that Jesus was the promised son of Abraham that Jewish tradition had (and has) always interpreted as Isaac. Moreover, Paul points out on more than one occasion that the Church is the body of Christ and individual Christians should therefore view their relation to each other on a biological analogy. "For as in one body we have many parts, and all the parts do not have the same function," he writes to the Roman Christians, "so we, though many, are one body in Christ and individually parts of one another" (Rom 12:4–5; cf. 1 Cor 12:27). Now if Jesus is the true Isaac, and the Church is the body of Jesus, it follows as night the day that the Church, when it turns its attention to Genesis, must see itself in the role of Isaac, that is, as the promised son of the freeborn woman who, with God's full endorsement, demands nothing less than the expulsion of the rival claimant to her husband's estate. Given the controversy in which Paul finds himself embroiled as he writes to the Galatian churches, it is natural for him to associate that rival claimant with the apostles who preached a rival Gospel to his own—a

Gospel, that is, that included the observance of the Torah and thus demanded circumcision as an entrance requirement for male converts. The expulsion of Hagar and Ishmael thus could be pressed into service in support of Paul's own uncompromising insistence that fidelity to the Christ and practice of the Torah are incompatible. Indeed, Paul's allegory is intended to make the Torah itself endorse this very message—to set the *theological message* of the Torah against its own *commandments*. "Tell me, you who want to be under the law, do you not listen to the law?" (Gal 4:21).

To attempt a comprehensive explication of the story of Jesus of Nazareth as it appears in the New Testament lies beyond the purview of our inquiry. What has been essayed here is an analysis of some of the ways in which the earliest Christian writers utilized the longstanding Jewish traditions about the beloved son to interpret the life and career of their departed master. Jesus' execution at the onset of Passover rather naturally led to an identification with the paschal lamb, and, given the already ancient associations of the aqedah with Passover and, by implication, of the same lamb with Isaac, this identification, in turn, drew in its train an ensemble of Isaac traditions that the earliest Christian authors sought in various ways to redirect to Jesus. Much early christology is thus best understood as a midrashic recombination of biblical verses associated with Isaac, the beloved son of Abraham, with the suffering servant in Isaiah who went, Isaac-like, unprotesting to his slaughter, and with another miraculous son, the son of David, the future messianic king whom the people Israel awaited to restore the nation and establish justice and peace throughout the world.

In the hands of Paul, a person whose influence on the subsequent Christian tradition it is difficult to overemphasize, the identification of Jesus and Isaac assumed an especially forceful and far-reaching statement. In one Pauline formulation, verses that in their biblical context refer with utter clarity to Isaac were reconceived as referring to Jesus exclusively. The latter thus becomes the promised seed of Abraham and the man through whose impalement the patriarchal blessing is extended to the nations. Isaac himself becomes a type of the Church, the individual members of the body of Christ, defined now in stark opposition to those obligated in the practice of Torah. In the case of Gentile Christians, this means those who would seek to change their status through circumcision and the other commandments incumbent upon Jews. The effect is to drive a hard wedge between the Abrahamic and the Sinaitic moments in the history of redemption. Sinai becomes a symbol not of freedom, but of enslavement, the destination not of the descendants of the freeborn matriarch Sarah, but of the offspring of her Egyptian slave Hagar. As the younger son Isaac displaced his older brother Ishmael, so, in Paul's thinking, does the new community, the Christian Church, displace the senior community from whom they received the Scriptures. The Jewish people are to undergo the spiritual equivalent of Ishmael's fate of expulsion into the wilderness of Sinai. It is no small irony that to argue this position, Paul had no alternative but to rely on the Jewish Scriptures—the only Bible he knew or could imagine—and to utilize exegetical procedures that the rabbis would use, with at least equal dexterity, in the defense of the inseparability of Abraham's life from subsequent Jewish experience, the continuing validity of the Torah, and the spiritual vitality of the Jewish people when they, at whatever cost, heed the voice of Sinai.

There is another sense, however, in which Paul and the ongoing rabbinic tradition stand in profound agreement. In insisting against so many of his fellow Christians that Torah in its injunctive, nomistic dimension is incompatible with the Gospel, Paul (whatever his perception at the time) helped ensure that the two communities would be separate. The community of Torah and the community of Gospel would appeal to the same Scriptures (until the New Testament documents would themselves be reconceived as biblical) and seek to practice virtues that overlap to a high degree. This is as we should expect from traditions that each revere the memory of Father Abraham. But, as we shall see in the next chapter, in laying claim to their Abrahamic status, Judaism and Christianity necessarily replicate the dynamics of the patriarchal family of Genesis seeking to establish a prime lineage in the face of an unexpected and disquieting segmentation. Their appeal to their common root in Abraham ensures that Judaism and Christianity will be mutually exclusive.

Chapter Sixteen

The Revisioning of God in the Image of Abraham

As Jesus supplants Isaac in Paul's theology, and the Church, the Jews, so does God supplant Abraham in the role of the father who did not withhold his own son from death itself:

> [28] We know that all things work for good for those who love God, who are called according to his purpose. [29] For those he foreknew he also predestined to be conformed to the image of his Son, so that he might be the firstborn among many brothers. [30] And those he predestined he also called; and those he called he also justified; and those he justified he also glorified. [31] What then shall we say to this? [32] He who did not spare his own Son but handed him over for us all, how will he not also give us everything else along with him? [33] Who will bring a charge against God's chosen ones? It is God who acquits us. [34] Who will condemn? It is Christ [Jesus] who died, rather, was raised, who also is at the right hand of God, who indeed intercedes for us. [35] What will separate us from the love of Christ? Will anguish, or distress, or persecution, or famine, or nakedness, or peril, or the sword? (Rom 8:28–35)

This highly complex meditation turns on several interlacing typologies. In one of them, Jesus is a type of the Christian. Because the members of the Church have been predestined to conform to his image, Jesus has become "the firstborn among many brothers" (v 29). The other, late-born Christians are to follow in the footsteps of the one to whom Paul here applies the highly charged terminology of the first-born son. It must not be forgotten, however, who that son is in the Hebrew Bible. He is the one who must be given to God, either through a sacrifice or through a ritual that substitutes for his literal slaughter. In some instances, as the cases of Jacob and Joseph, because he is a late-born son who has acquired the right of primogeniture through divine and parental assistance or, in addition, through his birth to the favored wife, the first-born must face the murderous rage of his older brothers. One of Paul's prime messages here is that since Jesus has already passed through the ultimate suffering—death itself—and gone on to the glory that lies beyond it, the Christians who conform to his image can have no cause for fear. The drama of the first-born having run its course, only good can now impend. As Arthur J. Droge remarks, "The life Paul lives is already a kind of postmortem existence," for having been crucified with Jesus, he lives a resurrected life (see Gal 2:19–20).[1]

The use of the word "image" (*eikōn*) in Rom 8:29 suggests that alongside the concept of the first-born or chosen son in this passage lies a distinct but related stream of tradition. This is the tradition that understands Gen 1:27–28 to mean that God created the individual man Adam in his own image (e.g., *Gen. Rab.* 8:4). Now Paul—in a move with vast implications for the history of Christian thought and Western culture as well—implies that the image of God is mediated no longer through Adam, but through Jesus—no longer, that is, through the natural means of procreation, mandated and blessed in Gen 1:28, but through the supernatural regeneration that he believes was manifested in Jesus' death and resurrection. This, Paul says, is available only to those whom God has predestined, his "chosen ones" (Rom 8:29–30, 33). That Paul thinks of Jesus as a new Adam, and the Church thus as a new and purified humanity, is apparent elsewhere in his Letter to the Romans (5:12–21). It should be noted, however, that the pictures of Jesus as first-born and as the new Adam are not at odds. For, having had no human parents, Adam was, in a certain sense, both a son of God and the first-born among all the brothers and sisters that make up the human race.

Alongside the depiction of Jesus in Rom 8:28–35 as the archetypical Christian, as the first-born, and as the eschatological Adam lies the typology most pertinent to our topic. This is, once again, Jesus in the role of Isaac, the son brought to the point of death by his loving father. It is perhaps already hinted in the prominence therein of the language of the first-born son, predestination, chosenness, and glorification, all of which, as I have noted in chapters 12 and 14, resonate profoundly with the themes of Isaac's birth, near-sacrifice, and ascent to the rank of patriarch in Genesis and even more so in later Jewish literature, where his actual sacrifice and resurrection is sometimes implied.

It is probable as well that in the background of Paul's affirmation "that all things work for good for those who love God" (Rom 8:28) lies the tradition of Abraham as the archetypical lover of God. The genesis of this tradition would seem to lie in the aqedah itself, in which Abraham chooses obedience to God over the life of his favored son, the one (the text goes out of its way to note) whom he loved (Gen 22:2). Adding to the image was the characterization of Abraham in the Book of Isaiah as the "lover [of God]" (*'ōhăbî*, Isa 41:8).[2] The tradition further developed in the forms of Judaism most germane to nascent Christianity, those of the Second Temple and Tannaitic periods.[3] It is precisely this *love* of God that Jubilees, some two centuries before Paul wrote, already identifies as that which was tested in the aqedah (Jub 17:16, 18), rather than, as one might have thought from Gen 22:12, Abraham's *fear* of God. And for Rabbi Meir, a Tanna of the second century C.E., Isa 41:8 serves as a prooftext for finding in Abraham a model for those who would observe the Torah's command to "love the LORD your God with all your heart" (Deut 6:5; *Sifre Deut.* 32). As a final illustration, an early compilation of rabbinic midrash glosses the words "those who love Me and keep My commandments" (Exod 20:6) thus: "this is our father Abraham and those who are like him" (*Mekilta de Rabbi Ishmael*, Baḥōdeš 6).[4]

The prominence of the love of God in Rom 8:28–39 alone suffices to arouse our suspicion of an allusion to the tradition of Abraham and, in particular, to the ultimate test of his love, the binding of Isaac for immolation on the altar. The suspicion is abundantly confirmed in v 32. "He who did not spare his own Son" is a transparent reworking of the angel's words to Abraham at the end of the aqedah: "since you have not withheld your son, your favored one, from Me" and "because you have done this and not withheld your son, your favored one" (Gen 22:12, 16). Paul's "spare" is the same Greek verb as the Septuagint uses for "withheld" in these two verses (*pheidomai*). His point is reminiscent of Gal 3:13–14 but far more explicit: the new aqedah, which is the crucifixion of Jesus, has definitively and irreversibly secured the blessings of which the angel there spoke. "He who did not spare his own Son but handed him over for us all, how will he not also give us everything else along with him?" (Rom 8:32)

Combined with the reference to the aqedah in Rom 8:32, the tradition of Abraham as the archetypical practitioner of the love of God sheds much light on Paul's opening claim, "that all things work for good for those who love God" (v 28). In Abraham's greatest test, his preference for the love of God over the love of his favored son enables him to have both: Abraham remains absolutely faithful yet Isaac lives. All things work out for Abraham not because, hedging his bets, he finds a middle way between his two great loves, but because God respects and rewards the uncompromising obedience—obedience even unto death—that he demands from those he has chosen. In the case of the new aqedah in which Paul believes, the crucifixion and resurrection of Jesus, God's willingness to hand over his son eventuates not in Jesus' death, but in his postmortem life. Indeed, Paul maintains that such life is possible only because God the Father follows in the path of Father Abraham and refuses to spare his son from being slain and offered. God proves faithful to the hoary imperative to slay one's first-born son, yet Jesus lives. As in the first aqedah and in the story of Joseph, the son can be enjoyed and the promise sustained only if he is exposed to death itself.

The most memorable statement of the role of love in the new aqedah of the Christian faith appears in the Fourth Gospel:

> For God so loved the world that he gave his only Son, so that everyone who believes in him might not perish but might have eternal life. (John 3:16)

The way in which God is likely to have "given" (*edōken*) his son should not be missed. The verb takes us back to where we began our inquiry, with the gruesome command of Exod 22:28b: "you shall give Me the first-born among your sons." This half-verse is not alone in its indication that the father's *gift* of the son was the way in which the ancient practice of child sacrifice was conceived. The nature of the "giving" to which John 3:16 refers merits special emphasis, for among many Christians the tendency to sentimentalize the notion of love that pervades the New Testament and attains special prominence in John is longstanding and powerful. So let it be said directly: the father's gift that the Fourth Gospel has in mind is one that necessarily entails a bloody slaying of Jesus, very much, as we have seen, along the lines of the slaughtering of the paschal lamb that Jesus becomes and also supersedes. In John's theology, the killing of Jesus, like that of the passover offering, enables those marked for death to live nonetheless. In a sense, Jesus provides those who believe in him with immortality by dying in their stead—except that, as in the cases of the beloved sons in the Hebrew Bible, Jesus' brush with death proves reversible and he is, like them, miraculously restored to those who love him but have had every reason to give up all hope for his return.

The orthodox Christian will, of course, wish to object at this point that Jesus' death is to be distinguished from those of Ishmael, Isaac, Jacob, and Joseph in being literal and not symbolic, and from that of Abel in being reversed and not final. The objection can be readily sustained, so long as the distinctiveness of the story of Jesus is not overstated (and the traditional invidious comparison with Judaism not drawn yet again). No claim is here made that the Jewish theme of the near-loss and miraculous return of the beloved son accounts for the Christian interpretation of the reported resurrection of Jesus as the pivotal moment of all history, the point at which the aeon irreversibly changes. The closest affinities of this central Christian affirmation lie, rather, in the traditions of Jewish apocalyptic, which has been aptly termed "the mother of all Christian theology."[5] But if one reckons with the importance of the doctrine of a future general resurrection in the Judaism

apocalyptic

of the Pharisees and the rabbis after them, it is not hard to see how the story of the beloved son would be transformed under the impact of the new belief. If the stories of the beloved sons in Genesis could have been told de novo in the new cultural context, it is quite likely that the averted death of the son would then have been recast as a literal resurrection from the dead. The enigmatic rabbinic references to "the ashes of Isaac," with their implication that from them he rose phoenix-like, may be an example of the conjectured effect of the new doctrine on the ancient story.

We are not, however, reduced to conjecture altogether. For there is in the narrative of the prophet Elisha and the Shunammite woman in 2 Kgs 4:8–37 (cf. 1 Kgs 17:17–24) an important biblical precedent for the changes here hypothesized. In this tale—strikingly reminiscent of the story of Sarah and Abraham—the prophet miraculously predicts the birth of a son to a childless woman with an aged husband.[6] More important for our theme, when the promised son has died—literally and not symbolically—Elisha resurrects him. The likelihood is that the tale of Elisha and the Shunammite woman represents the old pattern of the symbolic death of the beloved son in a cultural context in which a new phenomenon, unknown in Genesis, has come into being— the wonder-working prophet for whom nature presents no obstacle, not even in its cruelest and most inevitable form, death itself.[7]

It bears mention that the connection of 2 Kgs 4:8–37 to the reworking of the theme of the beloved son in the New Testament may be historical and not merely analogical. For at least in the case of the Gospel of Mark, an elaborate and intriguing case has been made that the New Testament narrative has been composed under the vivid influence of the Elijah-Elisha saga in Kings.[8] Even those unpersuaded by the case must concede this: if already in a world in which people believed in wonder-working prophets, the death of the only and promised son could be reversed by his bodily resurrection, it is all the more the case that in a world in which the resurrection of the dead is a central tenet, like that of Pharisaic Judaism, the report of the son's return from death need not be taken for a definitive break with the older pattern. The report of Jesus' resurrection is the old wine in a bottle that is relatively new but hardly unique.

It is not only the Jewish precedents to which John 3:16 bears ample witness. One can also hear in it the echoes of the old Canaanite theme of the god who, in the face of impending mass destruction, hands over his only son in the hope of averting death and securing life. The term translated as "only" (*mono-genēs*), traditionally rendered "only begotten," is the same term with which Philo of Byblos translates the name of the son the god El offered, Ieoud or Iedoud (see chapter 3). Behind Ieoud clearly stands the Phoenician equivalent of the same Hebrew word *yāḥîd*, the "favored one," which, as we have repeatedly seen, is applied to Isaac no fewer than three times in the report of the aqedah in Genesis 22 (vv 2, 12, 16). Note, however, that one version of the Septuagint renders the same term when it is applied to Jephthah's daughter in Judg 11:34 as *monogenēs*, while another version combines the two Greek expressions: *monogenēs autō agapētē* ("she was his only begotten and beloved daughter").[9]

John's statement in 3:16 that God gave his only begotten son in order to secure life for the believers thus almost certainly found rich resonance in the religiously syncretistic world of Greco-Roman antiquity. For it not only drew upon the classic Jewish elaboration of the theme of the beloved son but also recalled the ancient but persistent Canaanite story of the deity who sacrificed his only begotten son in order to eliminate a lethal menace. Here, as in Rom 8:32, the underlying identification of Jesus as the son of God has brought about a refashioning of God in the image of the father who gives his son in sacrifice. The father's gift to God has been transformed into the gift of God the Father. Despite the apparent partial return of the story to the world of the gods, however, it is the Jewish rather than the Canaanite form that dominates in John 3:16. For the father's motive is not, like El's or Mesha's (2 Kgs 3:24–27), the fear of calamity, but rather, like Abraham's, a love greater even than that for his beloved son.

Concentration upon the binding of Isaac as the text out of which important early christological reflection and reportage developed can, however, be as misleading as it is helpful. For among the tales of the beloved son in Genesis, the aqedah is unique in that in it alone the father directly and deliberately brings about the symbolic death of his favored offspring. In the other cases— Abel, Ishmael, Jacob, and Joseph—the narrative takes another course. Abel, Jacob, and Joseph die or are nearly killed by a different cause, the homicidal rage of their brother(s), jealous of the younger sibling's favored status (Gen 4:4b–8; 27:41; 37:18–35). Ishmael's story differs in that his favored brother's mother rather than the brother himself brings about his nearly fatal exposure in the desert—here, too, however, without homicidal intent, so far as we can tell (21:9–21).

In the stories of Jacob and Joseph, the reconciliation of the beloved son with the brother(s) once intent upon his murder is a major element in the dénouement. In the case of Jacob, the dynamics of his reunion with Esau are particularly complex because Jacob has assumed both his status as the first-born son and his paternal blessing by exploitation and fraud, respectively (Gen 25:29–34; 27:1–37). Yet when Jacob returns from his long, painful exile in Paddan-aram, where he has himself been the victim of repeated exploitation and significant fraud, he is generous to the brother whom he grievously wronged and who once plotted his murder (33:1–17). What is more, Esau, too, is magnanimous to a fault, demanding no recompense for his victimization: "I have enough, my brother; let what you have remain yours" (v 9). Similar dynamics can be detected in the story of Joseph, who insists to his brothers even after their father's death that even their evil plot was part of a higher and benevolent plan: "although you intended me harm, God intended it for good, so as to bring about the present result—the survival of many people" (50:20; cf. 45:5). Like Abraham's aborted attempt to slay Isaac, the brothers' evil design actually eventuated in the blessing of the chosen family. The proof of this happy ending is the reconciliation of the beloved son with his would-be slayers. Joseph's refusal in the end to engage in recrimination and retaliation derives from an acknowledgment that, however unwittingly, his brothers were advancing the wishes of God.

In addition to what we might call the Isaac christology in early Christian literature, we also find what we can, with due qualification, term a Joseph christology—that is, a pattern in which the emphasis lies on the malignancy of the slayers rather than on the pious intentions of the father who gave up his beloved son. The qualification is this: in this stream of early christology there is no reconciliation with the Jews accused (almost certainly inaccurately) of doing Jesus in but much recrimination and angry talk of retaliation.[10] The best illustration is the final New Testament text to mention the beloved son that we shall investigate, traditionally known as "The Parable of the Wicked Husbandmen":

> [1]He began to speak to them in parables, "A man planted a vineyard, put a hedge around it, dug a wine press, and built a tower. Then he leased it to tenant farmers and left on a journey. [2]At the proper time he sent a servant to the tenants to obtain from them some of the produce of the vineyard. [3]But they seized him, beat him, and sent him away empty-handed. [4]Again he sent them another servant. And that one they beat over the head and treated shamefully. [5]He sent yet another whom they killed. So, too, many others, some they beat, others they killed. [6]He had one other to send, a beloved son. He sent him to them last of all, thinking, "They will respect my son." [7]But those tenants said to one another, "This is the heir. Come, let us kill him, and the inheritance will be ours." [8]So they seized him and killed him, and threw him out of the vineyard. [9]What [then] will the owner of the vineyard do? He will come, put the tenants to death, and give the vineyard to others. [10]Have you not read this scripture passage:

The stone that the builders rejected
has become the cornerstone;
[11]by the Lord has this been done,
and it is wonderful in our eyes'?" [Ps 118:22–23]

[12]They were seeking to arrest him, but they feared the crowd, for they realized that he had addressed the parable to them. So they left him and went away. (Mark 12:1–12; cf. Matt 21:33–46; Luke 20:9–19)

The parallels to this passage show it to have undergone a complex process of editorial expansion. For example, Matt 21:45 and Luke 20:19 explicitly identify the parable as directed at "the chief priests and the Pharisees" and "the scribes and chief priests," respectively, though Mark 12:12 does not specify those who sought Jesus' arrest. The Gospel of Thomas, an early Christian work that has not become canonical, seems to preserve a form of the parable more original than any of its canonical versions. There, the man only owns a vineyard and does not plant it, put a hedge around it, dig a wine press, or build a tower. He sends two servants instead of three and "many others" as in Mark, and the son sent in Thomas is not characterized as "beloved." The Gospel of Thomas also omits all mention of the owner's response to the murder (Mark 12:9), only paraphrases Psalm 118:22 (omitting v 23), and exhibits no parallel to the narrative frame of Mark 12:1 and 12. It ends with the scriptural paraphrase (Gospel of Thomas 65–66).[11]

Whether Jesus originated the Parable of the Wicked Husbandmen or even used it is unknown, and the meaning of the passage in its pristine form is a matter of considerable speculation.[12] Some scholars, for example, take the point to be that the rich have by their vice forfeited their lofty status to the poor. Others believe the parable refers to the execution of John the Baptizer, who is presented in the preceding Markan passage as standing in a line whose next figure is Jesus himself (Mark 11:27–33). Impressive arguments can be mustered in defense of both of these interpretations and still others, but certainty necessarily eludes us.

What is more secure is the direction in which the Synoptic Gospels have shaped the parable, a direction of supersessionism on the one hand, and intense indebtedness to the scriptures of the superseded Jewish people on the other. The details about the man's planting the vineyard, digging a wine press, and building a tower are a transparent play on the "Song of the Vineyard" in Isa 5:1–7 (see esp. v 2). The differences, however, are most illuminating. In Isaiah 5, the difficulty lies with the *vineyard*, which yields only wild grapes, whereas in the Parable of the Wicked Husbandmen, the problem is the *tenants*, who refuse to pay the owner his due and murder his agents. Behind the image of the serial killings lies the tradition that Israel has done in the prophets whom God has continually commissioned to admonish them (e.g., Neh 9:26; cf. Matt 5:12; Luke 6:23). The thinking of the tenants as they formulate their conspiracy—"This is the heir. Come, let us kill him and the inheritance will be ours" (Mark 12:7)—is also rich in echoes from the Hebrew Bible. It recalls, for example, the parable of the wise woman of Tekoa (2 Sam 14:4–11), who complains to King David that, one of her two sons having murdered the other, "the whole clan confronted your maidservant and said, 'Hand over the one who killed his brother, that we may put him to death for the slaying of his brother, even though we wipe out the heir' " (v 7). That the potential homicides are of the same "clan" (*mišpāḥâ*) and designate their victim as "the heir" (*yôrēš*) demonstrates that their motivation is mercenary and not the selfless pursuit of justice. By eliminating the only remaining son of the widowed mother, they hope to make the family's inheritance their own, as she puts it to David, "leav[ing] my husband without name or remnant upon the earth" (v 7).

The parable of the wise woman of Tekoa suggests, in turn, other narratives that bear upon the Parable of the Wicked Husbandmen in ways that are more distant but hardly incidental. That "the two [brothers] came to blows out in the fields where there was no one to stop them, and one of them struck the other and killed him" (2 Sam 14:6) is distinctly and strikingly reminiscent of the tale of Cain and Abel ("and when they were in the field, Cain set upon his brother Abel and killed him" [Gen 4:8]). It may be pertinent that some rabbinic midrashim attribute the quarrel of the primal brothers to debates over inheritance, such as how the two will divide up the world and which of them should assume Eve after Adam had divorced her (*Gen. Rab.* 22:7). Within the Hebrew Bible itself, however, the wise woman of Tekoa's parable is most reminiscent of Sarah's insistence that Ishmael be expelled, "for the son of that slave," as she puts it, "shall not share in the inheritance with my son Isaac" (Gen 21:10). In both cases, a mother pleads that her only son's rights to the legacy be upheld against the plausible claims of others.

If the conflict of Ishmael and Isaac lies in the background of the Parable of the Wicked Husbandmen, then it makes eminent sense that the victim of the climactic murder, slain so that the tenants could grab his inheritance, should be the "beloved son." Indeed, it may well have been precisely the affinities of the parable with the tale of Ishmael and Isaac, the archetypical beloved son of Jewish tradition, that caused the "son" in Thomas to become the "beloved son" of the Synoptic Gospels. Alternatively, if the point of the parable was—or became—to tell the story of the execution of Jesus and its consequences, the language of the "beloved son" so prominent in the accounts of the baptism and the Transfiguration (Mark 1:11; 9:7 and parallels) could rather easily metastasize to the parable. In truth, we need not decide between these two scenarios, as they are intrinsically related: the Church's identification of Jesus as the "beloved son" is inextricable from its belief that he was the new Isaac, the consummative antitype to whom the archetypical Isaac actually pointed and whose life was dimly pre-enacted in that of the promised and chosen son of Abraham.

That the beloved son in the parable, like the owner's servants before him, was put to death by the tenants about to be dispossessed is also a point deeply indebted to the Israelite legacy. Jacob (Israel), who foreshadowed and per-sonified the fate of the entire nation, was, it will be recalled, the son beloved of his mother and his God in contradistinction to Esau, the favorite of his earthly father alone (Gen 25:28; Mal 1:3). Here again, it is the beloved son who inherits the status of the first-born, originally the possession of his older brother (Gen 25:23, 29–34; 27:28–29), and here again, the older brother's determination to murder the beloved son is an important feature of the story (27:41). Although the details of the narrative of Jacob and its sequence differ in important ways from those of the Parable of the Wicked Husbandmen, the two share crucial features—not only the beloved son, but also the issues of murder and property. And in both cases, the Israelite and the Christian, the overriding objective is the same: to explain the anomalous situation by which the late-born have assumed the privileges of the first-born; the new commu-nity, the unique status of the old.

If our allegorical decoding of the Parable of the Wicked Husbandmen is accurate, then its affinities with Paul's allegory of Hagar and Sarah, Ishmael and Isaac (Gal 4:21–5:1) is striking. For in each case, the objective is to validate the Church's claim to the patrimony of Israel, the new community's right to the inheritance of the old. In Paul's allegory, this is accomplished by equat-ing the Church with Isaac, and the Jews (and those Gentile Christians who join them) with Ishmael, the son of the slave woman whom Paul associates with Sinai. This makes the community of the Torah into usurpers and the community of the Pauline Gospel into the rightful claimants of the Abrahamic legacy. If we further recall that earlier in the same letter, Paul interprets the promise of a son to Abraham as really referring to Jesus (3:16), then it is but a stone's throw to the point of the Parable of the Wicked Husbandmen: those who killed Jesus have, by the very act, forfeited their claim to the status of Israel, represented by the vineyard. They have not only passed a capital sentence upon themselves. They have also, in the process, inadvertently founded the Church (Mark 12:9 and parallels).

Both of these classic statements of Christian supersessionism are articulated in terms redolent of the Jewish theme of the son beloved of his father and resented by his brothers. Their very effort to dispossess the community of the Torah bears eloquent and enduring witness to the indispensability of the Torah to the early Church and to the thoroughly intertextual, indeed midrashic character of the most basic elements of the Christian message—a point with which most Christians, even most New Testament scholars, have failed to reckon. There is, however, also a revealing difference between the anti-Judaic theologies of Paul and of the Parable of the Wicked Husbandmen in its canonical forms, and this can best be seen in what each omits.

For all his fulminations against the observance of Jewish law, Paul never blames the Jews for the death of Jesus or ascribes the founding of the Church to God's wrath against the people of the old covenant. Indeed, he does not attribute Jesus' demise to the Jews at all—an extraordinary datum in light of the reports of the trial and execution of Jesus in the canonical Gospels.[13] The Parable of the Wicked Husbandmen, for its part, shows no trace of the language of child sacrifice that we pointed out in Rom 8:32 and John 3:16, language that relates subtly but potently to the typologies of Isaac and the lamb so crucial to some early christologies, especially Paul's. The owner of the vineyard never intends to give up his son; he only wants to collect his share of the crop. This, typologically, resembles the story of Joseph more than the aqedah. For whereas Abraham obeys God's command to slay Isaac (Gen 22:2, 9–10), Jacob only sends Joseph to his would-be murderers in order to find out "how [his] brothers are and how the flocks are faring" (37:12–14). News of his beloved son's death shocks him (vv 32–37). The relationship between the story of Joseph and the New Testament efforts to pin the responsibility for Jesus' execution on the Jews may be more than typological. Here again one can reasonably suspect that the betrayal of Jesus by Judas is a midrashic play on the sale of Joseph by Judah, with Judas, as his name suggests, perhaps typifying the Jews as the homicidal opponents of the beloved son of God. The father's gift has been recast as the brothers' crime.

If doubt remains about the midrashic character of the Parable of the Wicked Husbandmen or its pronounced participation in the intertextuality of the Jewish Scriptures, the following rabbinic midrash should help dispel the doubt and shed light on the Jewish-Christian debate to which the parable bears witness:

> "For the LORD's portion is his people" [Deut 32:9]. A parable: A king had a field which he leased to tenants. When the tenants began to steal from it, he took it away from them and leased it to their children. When the children began to act worse than their fathers, he took it away from them and gave it to (the original tenants') grandchildren. When these too became

worse than their predecessors, a son was born to him. He then said to the grandchildren, "Leave my property. You may not remain therein. Give me back my portion, so that I may repossess it." Thus also, when our father Abraham came into the world, unworthy (descendants) issued from him, Ishmael and all of Keturah's children. When Isaac came into the world, unworthy (descendants) issued from him, Esau and all the princes of Edom, and they became worse than their predecessors. When Jacob came into the world, he did not produce unworthy (descendants), rather all his children were worthy, as it is said, "Jacob was a mild man who stayed in camp" [Gen 25:27]. When did God repossess His portion? Beginning with Jacob, as it is said, "For the LORD's portion is His people / Jacob His own allotment" [Deut 32:9], and, "For the LORD has chosen Jacob for Himself" [Ps 135:4] (*Sifre Deut.* 312).[14]

As in the Synoptic parable, so in this rabbinic midrash, the climactic act of election is the final one, the one occasioned by the arrival of the son. In both passages, the point is to justify the preference for the latecomers at the expense of those whom they dispossess, the non-Israelite descendants of Abraham in the case of the midrash, the Jews in the Christian parable as we have interpreted it. That rabbinic culture transmitted a parable on these matters so similar to the Synoptic text and its alloform in Thomas suggests that the prominence of the "beloved son" in the canonical Gospels—or at least of the concept underlying it—is not incidental to the meaning of the Gospel passage. Rather, both texts would seem to have had their origins in the dispute of Jews and early Christians over the identity of the beloved son and the community that harks back to him.[15] The only way in which a dispute of this sort could be carried on was through the exegesis of the only scripture either community knew—the Hebrew Bible.

The biblical texts on which the two contending groups focused are, in each case, those that speak of the origins of the faithful community and the legitimation of its separation from its unworthy competitor, and, in each case, the legitimation derives from God's new and definitive act of election. It is this that repudiates the previous beneficiaries of his gracious acts of preference. In the rabbinic midrash, the objective is to replace Abraham and Isaac with Jacob: only the last produces entirely worthy offspring, that is, the people Israel. As in the Pauline literature discussed above, so here Isaac is displaced in the crucial position of the beloved son—not, however, by Jesus and the Church but by Jacob and the Jews.

This rabbinic analogy to Christian supersessionism provides further evidence for the deeply Jewish character of the parallel New Testament exegetical moves and for the similarity of the ways in which the two communities laid a midrashic claim to the patrimony of Abraham. It is revealing that for all their dependence upon Genesis, both the Jewish and the Christian texts offer scenarios of complete dispossession. In the Christian parable, the former tenants of the vineyard are executed; in its Jewish parallel, Jacob's cousins and nephews (the Ishmaelites and Edomites) are only dispossessed. Neither version presents a counterpart to the poignant secondary blessings upon the dislodged first-born that appear in Genesis itself (16:10–12; 17:20; 27:39–40). Instead, all affinity between the old tenants on the divine estate and the new is implicitly repudiated. The break is total: contrary to what the biblical archetype might have suggested, the Jews and the Church are not even related, and the discord between them is, by both accounts, something very different from a squabble within the family.

The language of sonship common to these two parables, the one Jewish and the other Christian, discloses a critical insight about the relationship of the two traditions. That relationship, usually characterized as one of parent and child, is better seen as a rivalry of two siblings for their father's unique blessing. Judaism and Christianity are both, in substantial measure, midrashic systems whose scriptural base is the Hebrew Bible and whose origins lie in the interpretive procedures internal to their common Scripture and in the rich legacy of the Judaism of the late Second Temple period. The competition of these two rival midrashic systems for their common biblical legacy reenacts the sibling rivalry at the core of ancient Israel's account of its own tortured origins. In light of the universalistic dimension of that legacy (e.g., Gen 9:1–17), it is not surprising that both Judaism and Christianity have proven able to affirm the spiritual dignity of those who stand outside their own communities. But the two traditions lose definition and fade when that universalistic affirmation overwhelms the ancient, protean, and strangely resilient story of the death and resurrection of the beloved son.

Notes

Chapter One
Child Sacrifice in the Hebrew Bible

1 Roland de Vaux, *Studies in Old Testament Sacrifice* (Cardiff: University of Wales, 1964) 71.
2 Ibid.
3 See also Jer 7:31 and 32:35.
4 See Paul G. Mosca, "Child Sacrifice in Canaanite and Israelite Religion: A Study in *Mulk* and *mlk*," Ph.D. diss., Harvard University, 1975, 229. But note that the absence of any mention of Baal in Jer 7:31 and of any mention of sacrifice to Baal in Jer 32:35 suggests the expansionistic character of this verse. The absence of ʿōlôt labbāʿal in the Septuagint speaks to the same point.
5 John Day, *Molech* (University of Cambridge Oriental Publications 41; Cambridge: Cambridge University Press, 1989) 68.
6 I have departed from the NJPS at the beginning of v 25 because *gam* here intensifies *ʾānî* and is not adverbial. Correctly translated, the verse can readily be seen as the condign response to the situation described in v 21.
7 E.g., Exod 4:21 and 7:3.
8 De Vaux, *Studies*, 72.
9 Ronald M. Hals, *Ezekiel* (The Forms of Old Testament Literature 19; Grand Rapids: Eerdmans, 1989) 141.
10 Ezek 16:20–21 and 23:36–39. See George C. Heider, *The Cult of Molek* (JSOT Sup 43; Sheffield, U.K.: JSOT Press, 1985) 365–75.
11 Moshe Greenberg, *Ezekiel 1–20* (AB 22; Garden City, N.Y.: Doubleday, 1983) 368.
12 Ibid., 369.
13 I. Tzvi Abusch, "Hammurabi," *Harper's Bible Dictionary* (ed. Paul J. Achtemeier; San Francisco: Harper & Row, 1985) 371.
14 Roland de Vaux, *Ancient Israel* (New York: McGraw-Hill, 1961) 1.176–77.
15 As we shall soon see, there is ample evidence for the occasional sacrifice of the first-born son in ancient Israel. It is most unlikely that Exod 22:28b is only a secondary expression of an old law about the firstling of animals, as argued by Otto Kaiser, "Den Erstgeborenen deiner Söhne sollst du mir geben," in *Denkender Glaube: Festschrift Carl Heinz Ratschow* (ed. Otto Kaiser; Berlin and New York: de Gruyter, 1976) 24–48.
16 Mosca, "Child Sacrifice," 212. See, more generally, 199–212.
17 But see Heider, *The Cult*, 323, who renders here "for the king it has been established," which seems most unlikely.
18 Mosca, "Child Sacrifice," 212.
19 E.g., cf. Isa 34:5–8.

20 Cf. Heider, *The Cult*, 326.

21 De Vaux, *Studies*, 69.

22 Mosca, "Child Sacrifice," 225.

23 Heider, *The Cult*, 318.

24 Greenberg, *Ezekiel*, 369.

25 Shalom Spiegel, *The Last Trial* (New York: Behrman House, 1967) 64.

26 Mosca, "Child Sacrifice," 85. See also Day, *Molech*, 85: "Gen. 22 is rather to be seen as directed against the offering of human sacrifice to YHWH." Heider (*The Cult*, 273–77) is indecisive on the point.

27 *'ôlâ*, Judg 11:31.

28 *Yĕḥîdâ*, Judg 11:34. Cf. Gen 22:2,12,16, wherein Isaac is characterized as Abraham's *yāḥîd*. On the technical meaning of this term in child sacrifice contexts, see below pp. 26–31.

29 For a balanced discussion, see David Marcus, *Jephthah and his Vow* (Lubbock, Tex.: Texas Tech University Press, 1986), especially the conclusion on 50–55.

30 Judg 11:31, 39.

31 *Gen. Rab.* 60:3. It is interesting that this midrash attributes the sacrifice of the daughter to divine providence.

32 I have removed the brackets around "their own" in v 27 in the NJPS because I endorse the versional reading, *lĕ'arṣām*.

33 *Wayya'ălēhû 'ōlâ* in 2 Kgs 3:27 is to be compared with *wĕha'ălēhû šām lĕ'ōlâ* in Gen 22:2 and *wĕha'ălîtîhû 'ôlâ* in Judg 11:31.

34 For a discussion, see Mordechai Cogan and Hayim Tadmor, *II Kings* (AB 11; Garden City, N.Y.: Doubleday, 1988) 47–48.

35 See John Barclay Burns, "Why Did the Besieging Army Withdraw? (II Reg 3,27)," *ZAW* 102 (1990) 187–94, esp. 191–92.

36 See, e.g., M. Weinfeld, "The Worship of Molech and the Queen of Heaven and Its Background," *UF* 4 (1972) 133–54. Weinfeld is rebutted in Morton Smith, "A Note on Burning Babies," *JAOS* 95 (1975) 477–79, but attempts to answer Smith in "Burning Babies in Ancient Israel," *UF* 10 (1978) 411–13. See also Domenico Plataroti, "Zum Gebrauch des Wortes *mlk* im Alten Testament," *VT* 28 (1978) 286–300.

37 See M. Tsevat, "*BKWR, bekhôr*," *Theological Dictionary of the Old Testament* (ed. Johannes Botterweck and Helmer Ringgren; Grand Rapids: Eerdmans, 1977) 121–27.

Chapter 2
YHWH Versus Molech

1 The dissociation of the gift of the first-born from the cult of Molech is common in the secondary literature, though, as will become clear, I find this a bit too simple. See Paul G. Mosca, "Child Sacrifice in Canaanite and Israelite Religion: A Study in *Mulk* and *mlk*," Ph.D. diss., Harvard University, 1975, 235–38; George C. Heider, *The Cult of Molek* (*JSOT* Sup 43; Sheffield, U.K.: *JSOT*, 1985) 252–58, especially

p. 254; and John Day, *Molech* (University of Cambridge Oriental Publications 41; Cambridge: Cambridge University Press, 1987) 67.

2 John Milton, *Paradise Lost* I:392–93. See also "On the Morning of Christ's Nativity," 205–210:

> And sullen *Moloch* fled,
> Hath left in shadows dread
> His burning Idol of blackest hue;
> In vain with Cymbals' ring
> They call the grisly king,
> In dismal dance about the furnace blue.

3 Otto Eissfeldt, *Molk als Opferbegriff im Punischen und Hebräischen und das Ende des Gottes Moloch* (Beiträge zur Religionsgeschichte des Altertums 3; Halle: Max Niemeyer, 1935).

4 Heider, *The Cult*, and Day, *Molech*, both defend the idea that "Molech" was a god's name.

5 I here depart from the NJPS in the interest of accuracy.

6 See Day, *Molech*, 12.

7 See Weinfeld, "The Worship of Molech and the Queen of Heaven and Its Background," *UF* 4 (1972) 136–37; Heider, *The Cult*, 32–34, 91; Day, *Molech*, 46–52. But see the attempted rebuttal in the review of Heider by Saul M. Olyan and Mark S. Smith in *RB* 94 (1987) 273–75. Against Olyan and Smith, it must be noticed that the existence of child sacrifice to YHWH in pre-Josianic Israel (a point accepted by both Eissfeldt and Heider) constitutes no proof whatsoever that there were not also child sacrifices dedicated to Molech. That the Canaanite god El is the most likely recipient of the Phoenician and Punic child sacrifices (*pace* Day, *Molech*, 31–40) no more requires that the biblical *mōlek* be other than a god's name than it requires the same of Phoenician Baal-Hammon. The precise relationship between El, Molech, Baal-Hammon, and the Baal to whom Jer 19:5 says the Judeans sacrifice children remains murky.

8 See M. Almagro-Gorbea, "Les reliefs Orientalisants de Pozo Moro (Albacete, Espagne)," in *Mythe et Personification* (ed. Jacqueline Duchemin; Paris: Société D'Edition "Les Belles Lettres," 1980) 123–36; and "Pozo Moro y el influjo fenico en el periodo orientalizante de la Peninsula Ibérica," *Rivista di Studi Fenici* 10 (1982) 231–72 and the illustrations on L–LVI..

9 Heider, *The Cult*, 191.

10 Ibid., 190. The quote is from Charles Kennedy, "Tartessos, Tarshish, and Tartarus: The Tower of Pozo Moro and the Bible," unpublished paper presented to the First International Meeting of the Society of Biblical Literature, Salamanca, Spain, 1983, p. 8.

11 Lawrence E. Stager and Samuel R. Wolff, "Child Sacrifice at Carthage—Religious Rite or Population Control?" *BARev* 10:1 (Jan.-Feb., 1984) 31–51. See also Law-

rence E. Stager, "Carthage: A View from the Tophet," in *Phönizer im Westen* (ed. Hans Georg Niemeyer; Mainz am Rhein: Philipp von Zabern, 1982) 155–66.

12   Stager and Wolff, "Child Sacrifice," 32.

13   Stager, "Carthage," 158.

14   Stager and Wolff, "Child Sacrifice," 39.

15   Stager and Wolff may well be right that, from the vantage point of the social system, child sacrifice addressed the issue of overpopulation. But their analogy to infanticide ("Child Sacrifice," p. 51) fails to do justice to the meaning of the rite in the minds of the parents who carried it out.

16   Stager and Wolff, "Child Sacrifice," 40–41.

17   Ibid., 42.

18   See Day, *Molech*, 8–9, especially p. 9, n 24.

19   See Jeanne and Prosper Alquier, "Stèles votives à Saturne découvertes près de N'gaous (Algérie)," *CRAI* (1930) 21–27; Jérôme Carcopino, "Survivances par substitution des sacrifices d'enfants dans l'Afrique romaine," *RHR* 106 (1932) 592–99; James G. Février, "Le Rite de substitution dans les textes de N'gaous," *Journal Asiatique* 250 (1962) 1–10.

20   This is Day's translation of Stela III (*Molech*, 8, n 23). For the original publication of the Latin text, see Alquier, "Stèles votives," 22–24.

21   See Carcopino, "Survivances," 599.

Chapter Three
The Sacrifice of the Son as the Imitation of God

1   Tertullian, *Apology* (ed. T. R. Glover and W. C. A. Kerr; Cambridge, Mass.: Harvard University Press, 1977) 47 (IX:2–4).

2   *Edōken* in John 3:16 is to be compared to *titten* in Exod 22:28b.

3   The passage is from the *Praeparatio evangelica* I.10.40. The translation is that of Edwin Hamilton Gifford, *Eusebius, Preparation for the Gospel* (Grand Rapids: Baker Book House, 1981) 1.45. Gifford's translation was first published in 1903. I have changed his "Iedud" to "Iedoud" to reflect the spelling of Eusebius' Greek. A more recent critical edition and translation is Jean Sirinelli and Edouard des Places, *Eusèbe des Césarée, La Préparation Evangélique* (Paris: Les Editions du Cerf, 1974). Our passage appears on pp. 204–05.

4   Cristiano Grottanelli, "Cosmogonia e Sacrificio, II," *Studi Storico Religiosi* 5 (1981) 185.

5   See below, pp. 176–87, 206–10.

6   Lawrence E. Stager and Samuel R. Wolff, "Child Sacrifice at Carthage—Religious Rite or Population Control?" *BARev* 10:1 (January-February 1984) 45.

7   See William L. Holladay, *Jeremiah 1* (Hermeneia; Philadelphia: Fortress, 1986) 226.

8   "But" at the end of v 24 is a departure from NJPS intended to bring out the likely adversative effect of the word order here.

9 See P. Kyle McCarter, *II Samuel* (AB 9; Garden City, N.Y.: Doubleday, 1984) 303.
10 See C. H. Turner, "*HOYIOS MOY HO AGAPĒTOS*," *JTS* 26 (1926) 113–29. The notion that *agapētos* in this context means nothing more than "only" and has no affective connotation is effectively countered by Alfredo Scattalon, "L'AGAPĒTOS sinnotico nella Luce della Tradizione Giudaica," *RevistB* 26 (1978) 5.
11 I depart from the NJPS in order to retain the Hebrew word order.
12 The "A" text.
13 See Raymond E. Brown, *The Gospel According to John* (AB 29; Garden City, N.Y.: Doubleday, 1966) 147. For Usaac as *yādîd*, see Rashi to *b.Shab.* 137b.
14 See below, pp. 200–02.
15 See below, pp. 223–25.

Chapter Four
El and the Beloved Son

1 Frank Moore Cross, *’L, ’ēl, Theological Dictionary of the Old Testament* (ed. Johannes Botterweck and Helmer Ringgren; Grand Rapids: Eerdmans, 1977) 1.245–48.
2 Cristiano Grottanelli ("Cosmogonia e Sacrificio, II," *Studi Storico Religiosi* 5 [1981] 194–95), noting the expressions *mdd ilm* and *ydd il* used of Mot, argues that Mot and the beloved son who is sacrificed may once have been one and the same, so that Mot would have been "the First Victim of a human sacrifice, as a son sacrificed by his father, the god El." At present, this must remain at best a tantalizing speculation. Grottanelli's effort to connect his speculation to Job 18:11–14 (p. 196, n. 52) is forced.

For an argument that there is textual evidence for the sacrifice of the first-born son at Ugarit, see A. Herdner, "Nouveaux Textes Alphabétiques de Ras Shamra, XXIVe Campagne, 1961," in *Ugaritica VII* (Paris: Paul Geuthner; Leiden: Brill, 1978) 31–39, esp. 37–38, and Baruch Margalit, "A Ugaritic Prayer for a Time of Siege (RS 24.266)" (Hebrew), in *Proceedings of the Seventh World Congress of Jewish Studies* (Jerusalem: The Perry Foundation for Biblical Research and World Union of Jewish Studies, 1981) 63–83.

3 Cross, *’L, ’ēl*, 245–48. The reference is to the *Praeparatio evangelica* I.10.26.
4 Michael David Coogan, *Stories from Ancient Canaan* (Philadelphia: Westminster, 1978) 86.
5 Ibid., 112–13.
6 Below, pp. 149–50.
7 See chapter 13.
8 Cross, *’L, ’ēl*, 253, 258.
9 I have left the actual divine names in the translation in order to make the point about their synonymy.
10 Cross, *’L, ’ēl*, 260.

11 See the chapter on "YHWH and El" in Frank Moore Cross, *Canaanite Myth and Hebrew Epic* (Cambridge: Harvard University Press, 1973) 44–75.

12 See chapter 2, n 1.

Chapter Five
The People Israel as the Son of God

1 See Jon D. Levenson, "Liberation Theology and the Exodus," *Midstream* 35:7 (October 1989) 30–36 and *Reflections* 86:1 (Winter-Spring 1991) 2–12; and "Exodus and Liberation," *HBT* 13(1991) 134–74. A revised form of the last article appears as chapter 6 of *The Hebrew Bible, the Old Testament, and Historical Criticism* (Louisville: Westminster/John Knox, 1993).

2 The appearance of *bēn* and *běkōr* in adjacency is rare. A "canonical reading" would have to note that the initial challenge to Pharaoh of Exod 4:22 is echoed in the law of the redemption of the first-born son in Exod 13:15 and 34:20, two other texts that display the same adjacency.

3 I have left this difficult text as it is translated in the NJPS, except that I have rendered the *hapaxlegomenon tirgaltî* in v 3 as "I was a guide to," following the reasoning of Francis I. Andersen and David Noel Freedman, *Hosea* (AB 24; Garden City, N.Y.; Doubleday, 1980) 579.

4 See below, chapter 8.

5 See Robert R. Wilson, *Genealogy and History in the Biblical World* (Yale Near Eastern Researcher 7; New Haven: Yale University Press, 1977).

6 Isaac and Joseph are, however, the first-born of their mothers, each of whom is her husband's favorite wife. See pp. 55–58.

Chapter Six
The Sacrifice of the First-Born Son

1 On this, see George C. Heider, *The Cult of Molek* (JSOT Sup 43; Sheffield, U.K.: JSOT, 1985), 378–82. How long the practice survived among the Jews depends on the dating of Isa 57:5 and 66:3, about which there is no compelling consensus.

2 Jer 7:31; 19:5; 32:35.

3 Cf. Deut 12:6, 17; 14:23.

4 For convenience, I use the familiar term "paschal lamb" throughout, though the reader should note that even Exodus 12 allows a kid to be offered (v 5).

5 See Brevard S. Childs, *The Book of Exodus*, OTL (Philadelphia: Westminster, 1974) 183.

6 "Formally assigned" in v 16 is *nětûnîm nětûnîm*, from the verb *nātan*, "to give."

7 The translation is from Joseph H. Hertz, *The Authorized Daily Prayer Book*, rev. ed. (New York: Bloch, 1948) 1037.

8 See Jacob Milgrom, *Numbers*, (Philadelphia and New York: Jewish Publication Society, 5750/1990) 355–58.

9 E.g., ibid., 355. On the Nazirite identity of Samuel, see the text critical notes in P. Kyle McCarter, *1 Samuel* (AB 8; Garden City, N.Y.: Doubleday, 1980) 53–54, 56.

10 Thus, the NJPS and the New English Bible (Oxford University and Cambridge University Presses, 1970), respectively.

11 See above pp. 22–23.

12 James G. Février, "Le rite substitution dans les textes de N'gaous," *Journal Asiatique* 250 (1962), esp. p. 8.

13 The translation is from Jacob Z. Lauterbach, *Mekilta de-Rabbi Ishmael* (Philadelphia: Jewish Publication Society of America, 5694/1933). 1. 33–34, though I have adjusted the biblical quotations to the NJPS, except where so doing would obscure Rabbi Matia ben Heresh's point. On the Tannaitic association of the two bloods, see Lester A. Segal, "R. Mattiah ben Ḥeresh of Rome on Religious Duties and Redemption: Reaction to Sectarian Teaching," *Proceedings of the American Academy for Jewish Research* 58 (1992) 221–41.

14 Note the statement in *Pirqe R. El.* 29 that on the night of the original Passover, the Israelites "would take the blood of circumcision and the blood of the paschal lamb and put them on the lintel of their houses," with Ezek 16:6 as the prooftext.

15 On this, see Childs, *The Book of Exodus*, 95–101.

16 On some possible connections of circumcision to sacrifice, see Howard Eilberg-Schwartz, *The Savage in Judaism* (Bloomington and Indianapolis: Indiana University Press, 1990) 175.

Chapter Seven
First-Born and Late-Born, Fathers and Mothers

1 See above, pp. 5–8.

2 See M. Tsevat, "*Bekhôr*," in *Theological Dictionary of the Old Testament* (ed. G. Johannes Botterweck and Helmer Ringgren; Grand Rapids: Eerdmans, 1977) 2.125.

3 The translation is taken from Herbert Danby, *The Mishnah* (London: Oxford University Press, 1933) 539.

4 On the problems with this interpretation, see Tsevat, "*Bekhôr*," 125–26.

5 Ibid., 126.

6 See above, pp. 45–52.

7 See chapter 5.

Chapter Eight
The Loved and the Unloved

1 I have departed from the NJPS at the beginning of v 3 in order to capture the adversative sense of the Hebrew word order.

2 I have departed from the NJPS in order to convey the resonance of the Hebrew use of the term "brother."

3 On the replication of Jacob's experience in Joseph's life, see *Gen. Rab.* 84:6.

4   Isaac's name has been inserted in v 29 with the Hebrew and against NJPS.
5   Note that the word translated "enough" here (*rāb*) subtly draws attention to the inversion of the status of the two brothers: "and the older [*rab*] shall serve the younger" (Gen 25:23).

Chapter Nine
Favor and Fratricide

1   See chapter 15.
2   "Along with their fat" in v 4 and "look/looked with favor" in vv 4–5 have been added to the NJPS for reasons of accuracy. In v 8, *nēlēkâ haśśādeh* (or the like) has been added on the basis of a number of ancient versions.
3   Ibn Ezra to Gen 4:3.
4   Nahum M. Sarna, *Genesis* (The JPS Torah Commentary; Philadelphia: Jewish Publication Society, 5449/1989) 31.
5   E.g., Lev 10:1–2; Num 12:1–15; Deut 24:8–9.
6   E.g., Gen 32:23–33.
7   E.g., E. A. Speiser, *Genesis* (AB 1; Garden City, N.Y.: Doubleday, 1964) 31.
8   E.g., Lev 26:3–5, 10; Deut 28:4–5, 11–12.
9   William G. Dever, "Palestine in the Second Millennium BCE: The Archaeological Picture," in *Israelite and Judean History* (ed. John H. Hayes and J. Maxwell Miller; London: SCM, 1977) 106. See also M. B. Rowton, "Urban Autonomy in a Nomadic Environment," *JNES* 32 (1973) 201–15, and "Enclosed Nomadism," *Journal of the Economic and Social History of the Orient* 17 (1974) 1–30.
10 Claus Westermann, *Genesis 1–11* (Minneapolis: Augsburg, 1984) 297.
11 See chapter 10.
12 *Testament of Abraham*, trans. E. P. Sanders, in *The Old Testament Pseudepigrapha* (ed. James H. Charlesworth; Garden City, N.Y.: Doubleday, 1983) 1. 889–90.
13 See Wolfgang Roth, "Jesus as the Son of Man: The Scriptural Identity of a Johannine Image", in *The Living Text: Essays in Honor of Ernest W. Saunders*, ed. Dennis E. Groh and Robert Jewett (Lanham, Md.: University Press of America) 11–26, esp. pp. 21–22.
14 Whereas NJPS puts the quotation marks after "Abel," it seems more likely to me that the last clause is still part of Eve's speech.
15 E.g., Gen 16:11 (J) and 16:15 (P); 17:17 (P) and 18:12 (J).
16 I thank my colleague, Professor Theodore Hiebert, for drawing my attention to this likelihood.
17 Cf. the underlying conception of the law of Levirate marriage in Deut 25:5–10.

Chapter Ten
"Let me not look on as the child dies"

1   Michael Fishbane, *Biblical Interpretation in Ancient Israel* (Oxford: Oxford University Press, 1985) 372–73.

2   Ibid., 375–76.
3   Arnold B. Ehrlich, *Randglossen zur Hebräischen Bibel* (Leipzig: J. C. Hinrichs, 1908) 1.53.
4   E. A. Speiser, *Genesis* (AB 1; Garden City, N.Y.: Doubleday, 1964) 97.
5   Cf. e.g., Gen 34:9; Deut 7:3.
6   Joel Rosenberg, *King and Kin* (Bloomington and Indianapolis: Indiana University Press, 1986) 94.
7   See Jo Ann Hackett, "Rehabilitating Hagar: Fragments of an Epic Pattern," in *Gender and Difference in Ancient Israel*, ed. Peggy L. Day (Minneapolis: Fortress, 1989) 12–27.
8   See Jon D. Levenson, "Liberation Theology and the Exodus," *Midstream* 35:7 (October 1989) 30–36, and *Reflections* 86:1 (Winter-Spring 1991) 2–12, and idem., "Exodus and Liberation," *HBT* 13 (1991) 134–74. A revised version of the last essay appears as chapter 6 in Jon D. Levenson, *The Hebrew Bible, the Old Testament, and Historical Criticism* (Louisville: Westminster/John Knox, 1993).
9   On the pathos of Hagar's status, see Phyllis Trible, *Texts of Terror* (OBT 13; Philadelphia: Fortress, 1984) 9–35. For a different and less sympathetic interpretation of Hagar, see Devora Steinmetz, *From Father to Son* (Literary Currents in Biblical Interpretation; Louisville; Westminister/John Knox, 1991) 72–78.
10 Nahum M. Sarna, *Genesis* (JPS Torah Commentary; Philadelphia: Jewish Publication Society, 5749/1989), 343. On the importance of sight in the Abraham cycle, see Steinmetz, *From Father*, 72–74; 76–85.
11 See Speiser, *Genesis*, xxx–xxxi.
12 See above, n. 1.
13 See chapter 7.
14 Søren Kierkegaard, *Fear and Trembling* (Garden City, N.Y.: Doubleday, 1954) 57. The book was first published in 1843.
15 Ibn Ezra to 21:14.
16 On the text-critical problems in Gen 21:14, see Ehrlich, *Randglossen*, 1. 88–89.
        My student Larry L. Lyke has pointed out in a seminar paper (spring, 1991) that the placement of *wĕ'et-hayyeled* yields a structure for Gen 21:14 suggestively similar to that of 22:3: "So early next morning, Abraham saddled his ass and took with him two of his servants and his son Isaac."
17 See Shadal to 21:19.
18 See pp. 22–23.
19 See above, pp. 96–97.
20 E.g., Gen 18:2; 19:1; Judg 13:16; Zech 1:8, 11.
21 E.g., 2:133, 136.
22 Chapters 15 and 16.
23 Hugh C. White, "The Initiation Legend of Isaac," *ZAW* 91 (1979) 2.
24 Idem., "The Initiation Rite of Ishmael," *ZAW* 87 (1975) 305.
25 See pp. 45–52.

Chapter Eleven
The Aqedah as Etiology

1   See pp. 20–24; 32–35.

2   See pp. 20–24.

3   Shalom Spiegel, *The Last Trial* (New York: Behman House, 1967) 64.

4   Alberto R. W. Green, *The Role of Human Sacrifice in the Ancient Near East* (ASORDS 1; Missoula, Mont.: Scholars, 1975) 174, 158.

5   Paul G. Mosca, "Child Sacrifice in Canaanite and Israelite Religion: A Study of *Mulk* and *mlk*," Ph. D. diss., Harvard University (1975) 237.

6   See pp. 12–13.

7   See pp. 5–8.

8   E.g., see Hermann Gunkel, *Genesis*, Göttinger Handkommentar zum Alten Testament 1 (Göttingen: Vandenhoeck and Ruprecht, 1910) 242.

9   Ibid., 240–42.

10 Rudolf Kilian, *Isaaks Opferung* (Stuttgarter Bibelstudien 44; Stuttgart: Verlag Katholisches Bibelwerk, 1970) 45–46.

11 Ibid., 36.

12 Ibid., 22, 48.

13 Gunkel, *Genesis*, 241; Kilian, *Isaaks Opferung*, 36.

14 Gunkel, *Genesis*, 241.

15 See J. Wellhausen, *Die Composition des Hexateuchs und der historischen Bücher des Alten Testaments* (3rd ed., Berlin: Walter de Gruyter, 1963) 18–19. The book was originally published in 1899.

16 See Arnold B. Ehrlich, *Randglossen zur hebräischen Bibel* (Leipzig: J. C. Hinrichs, 1908) 1.64–65.

17 Royden Keith Yerkes, "The Location and Etymology of *YHWH yr'h*, Gn. 22:14," *JBL* 31 (1912) 136–39.

18 Henning Graf Reventlow, *Opfere deinen Sohn* (Biblische Studien 53; Neukirchen-Vluyn: Neukirchener, 1968) 30.

19 *Ibid.*, 37, 35.

20 See Moshe Garsiel, *Midrashic Name Derivations in the Bible* [Hebrew] (Ramat-Gan: Revivim, 1987) 153.

21 See Garsiel, *Midrashic*, 134.

22 Martin Noth, *The History of Israel* (New York and Evanston: Harper & Row, 1960) 126. See also n 1 on the same page.

23 Martin Noth, *A History of Pentateuchal Traditions* (Englewood Cliffs, N.J.: Prentice-Hall, 1972) 154.

24 See Nahum M. Sarna, *Genesis* (JPS Torah Commentary; Philadelphia: Jewish Publication Society of America, 5749/1989) 110.

25 Kilian, *Isaaks Opferung*, 45.

26 Reventlow, *Opfere*, 30.

27 E.g., Exod 17:15.

See Joel Rosenberg, *King and Kin* (Bloomington and Indianapolis: Indiana University Press, 1986) 85, fig. 3.

Chapter Twelve
Isaac Unbound

Gerhard von Rad, *Das Opfer des Abraham* (Munich: Chr. Kaiser, 1971) 23.
Gerhard von Rad, *Genesis* (OTL; Philadelphia: Westminster, 1972) 244.
Ibid.
Ibid., 238–39.
See E. A. Speiser, *Genesis* (AB 1; Garden City, N.Y.: Doubleday, 1964) 162.
I have departed from the NJPS by putting "Isaac" last in the sequence of four designations of the son, in order to mirror the Hebrew word order and to capture the climactic pattern. "Forth" has been added to reflect the connection of the Hebrew to Gen 12:1.
"Kinsmen" has been added to the NJPS in the interest of accuracy and to aid in the understanding of this midrash.
See pp. 26–30.
Bachya ben Asher, *Commentary on the Torah* (Hebrew; ed. Charles B. Chavel; Jerusalem: Mossad Harav Kook, 5726/1966) 1. 193.
Note Royden Keith Yerkes, "The Location and Etymology of *YHWH yr'h*," *JBL* 31 (1912) 136 n 1, in which it is speculated that Aquila derived *'ōmar* in Gen 22:2 from a root meaning "to be evident, prominent," perhaps cognate with Akkadian *amāru*, "to see."
See also *b. Mo'ed Qaṭ*. 18a.
Søren Kierkegaard, *Fear and Trembling* (Garden City, N.Y.: Doubleday, 1954) 46–47. The book was written in 1843.
The citation from Gen 21:12 is taken from the NJPS rather than the NAB.
See e.g., Bekhor Shor, Chizquni, and Seforno to Gen 22:5.
Bachya ben Asher to Gen 22:5.
Erich Auerbach, *Mimesis: The Representation of Reality in Western Literature* (Princeton: Princeton University Press, 1953) 11–12.
I have departed from the NJPS in rendering "and the two of them walked together" identically in vv 6 and 8, for reasons that my discussion will soon make evident. The Hebrew supports my rendering.
I have replaced "proceeded" (NJPS) with "came" to facilitate the understanding of the midrash that follows.
See also *Gen. Rab.* 54:6 and Rashi to Gen 21:34.
See E. Nestle, "Wie alt war Isaak bei der Opferung?" *ZAW* 26 (1906) 281–82.
See Shalom Spiegel, *The Last Trial* (New York: Behrman, 1979).
See Arthur J. Droge and James Tabor, *A Noble Death* (San Francisco: Harper San Francisco, 1992), esp. 114–20.
Kierkegaard, *Fear and Trembling*, 46.

24 See Ibn Ezra to Gen 22:4.

25 See n 6, above.

26 See n 5, above.

27 I have rendered the first word as a present perfect rather than an imperative (as in the NJPS) in order to bring out the historical reference presupposed in the midrash.

28 See R. W. L. Moberly, "The Earliest Commentary on the Akedah," *VT* 38 (1988) 302–23, esp. 318–23.

29 See part III, below.

30 On the implications of the aqedah for Jewish theology, see Emil L. Fackenheim, *Quest for Past and Future* (Boston: Beacon, 1970) 52–65.

31 Arnold B. Ehrlich, *Randglossen zur hebräischen Bibel* (Leipzig: J. C. Hinrichs, 1908) 1. 98. The first to notice this connection seems to have been Rabbi Joseph Kara (late eleventh-early twelfth century). See Rashbam to Gen 24:60.

32 Hugh C. White, "The Initiation Legend of Isaac," *ZAW* 91 (1979) 23, 17.

Chapter Thirteen
The Beloved Son as Ruler and Servant

1 E.g., see "The Code of Hammurabi" (trans. Theophile J. Meek) in *Ancient Near Eastern Texts Relating to the Old Testament* (3rd ed; ed. James B. Pritchard; Princeton: Princeton University Press, 1969) 164.

2 See *Exod Rab.* 2:3, on Exod 3:1 but with most direct reference to David: "The Holy One (blessed be He) said to him: You have proven yourself faithful with the flock. Come, shepherd *My* flock."

3 The NJPS restores the material in brackets from the Septuagint.

4 See Moshe Weinfeld, "The King as Servant of the People—The Source of the Idea," [Hebrew], in *'Ēšel Bĕ'ēr Šeba'* 2 (5740/1980) 19–25.

5 See chapter 12, n 6.

6 See Edward L. Greenstein, "An Equivocal Reading of the Sale of Joseph," in *Literary Interpretations of Biblical Narratives*, vol. 2 (ed. Kenneth R. R. Gros Louis; Nashville: Abingdon, 1982) 114–25.

7 Note also the observation of Devora Steinmetz (*From Father to Son* [Literary Currents in Biblical Interpretation; Louisville: Westminster/John Knox, 1991] 116, 122) that the courtier to whom Joseph is handed over is the *śar haṭṭabbāḥîm*, literally, "the Chief of the Slaughters" (Gen 37:36; 39:1). Is the presence of *ṭebaḥ* in the genealogy that follows the aqedah (22:24) coincidence?

8 See pp. 32–34.

9 See *Gen. Rab.* 85:3 (end).

10 See Jon D. Levenson and Baruch Halpern, "The Political Import of David's Marriages," *JBL* 99 (1980) 507–18.

11 E. A. Speiser, *Genesis* (AB 1; Garden City, N.Y.: Doubleday, 1964) 299.

12 Claus Westermann, *Genesis 37–50* (Minneapolis: Augsburg, 1986) 49.

3   Walter Brueggemann, *Genesis* (Interpretation; Atlanta: John Knox, 1982) 307.
4   Bruce Vawter, *On Genesis: A New Reading* (Garden City, N.Y.: Doubleday, 1977) 390.
5   E.g., Speiser, *Genesis*, 299.
5   On the methodological issues, see Jon D. Levenson's untitled response in *The State of Jewish Studies* (ed. Shaye J. D. Cohen and Edward L. Greenstein; Detroit: Wayne State University Press, 1990) 47–54, esp. pp. 51–52.
7   Robert Alter, *The Art of Biblical Narrative* (New York: Basic Books; Philadelphia: Jewish Publication Society, 1981) 6.
8   Ibid., 10–11.
9   Ibid., 10.
    Because of the identification of Potiphar, Pharaoh's chief steward, with Poti-phera, Priest of On, whose daughter Joseph marries (Gen 41:45).
    Alter, *The Art of Biblical Narrative*, 6.
    On this, see also James S. Ackerman, "Joseph, Judah, and Jacob," in *Literary Interpretations of Biblical Narratives*, vol. 2 (ed. Kenneth R. R. Gros Louis with James S. Ackerman; Nashville: Abingdon, 1982) 85–113, esp. pp. 103–05.
    On *nāśā' rō'š* as "pardon," compare 2 Kgs 25:27 and the very similar expression *nāśā' pānîm*, as in Gen 19:21. Gen 40:20 plays on another sense of *nāśā' pānîm*, "to count." On this, see Rashi, Rashbam, and Ibn Ezra to 40:13, where Qimchi would still seem to have the more contextually appropriate interpretation.
    Radaq to Gen 37:7.
    This observation was suggested to me by Professor James Nohrnberg.
    The translation is taken from *Mekilta de Rabbi Ishmael* (ed. Jacob Z. Lauterbach; Philadelphia: Jewish Publication Society of America, 5694/1933) 2. 229–30, except that I have rendered all three instances of the clause *'emlôk 'ălêkem* as questions, whereas Lauterbach, presumably as a result of misguided theological scruples, translates the last as a declarative.

Chapter Fourteen
The Rewritten Aqedah of Jewish Tradition

See pp. 114–17.
For a survey, see Geza Vermes, *Scripture and Tradition in Judaism* (2d rev. ed.; Studia Post-Biblica; Leiden: Brill, 1973) 193–227; Robert J. Daly, "The Soteriological Significance of the Sacrifice of Isaac," *CBQ* 39 (1977) 45–75; James Swetnam, *Jesus and Isaac* (An Bib 94; Rome: Biblical Institute, 1981) 4–80; and Alan F. Segal, " 'He Who Did Not Spare His Only Son . . . ' (Romans 8:32): Jesus, Paul, and the Sacrifice of Isaac," in *From Jesus to Paul* (ed. Peter Richardson and John C. Hurd; Waterloo, Ontario: Wilfred Laurier, 1984) 169–84; rpt. as "The Sacrifice of Isaac in Early Judaism and Christianity," in *The Other Judaisms of Late Antiquity* (BJS 127; Atlanta: Scholars, 1987) 109–30. A critique of the more maximal claims about the role of the

aqedah as background for the New Testament appears in P. R. Davies and B. D. Chilton, "The Aqedah: A Revised Tradition History," *CBQ* 40 (1978) 514–46, and Philip R. Davies, "Passover and the Dating of the Aqedah," *JJS* 30 (1979) 59–67. Davies and Chilton's objections are answered in Swetnam, *Jesus and Isaac*, 18–21; Segal, "The Sacrifice," 113–14; and C. T. R. Hayward, "The Sacrifice of Isaac and Jewish Polemic against Christianity," *CBQ* 52 (1990) 292–306.

3   All translations from Jubilees herein are taken from that of O. S. Wintermute in *The Old Testament Pseudepigrapha* (ed. James H. Charlesworth; Garden City, N. Y.: Doubleday, 1985) 2.35–142.

4   See Mircea Eliade, *Myth and Reality* (New York and Evanston: Harper & Row, 1963) 21–38.

5   The alternative is to attribute the onset of Abraham's journey to the fifteenth of the first month (three days after Mastema's accusation) so that the dates of the episode coincide with those of Passover. If so, then the association of the aqedah with the paschal sacrifice is more remote. What this otherwise reasonable alternative does not explain is the reason that the whole episode begins on the twelfth of the month. On the chronological problem, see James C. Vanderkam, "The Origin, Character, and Early History of the 364-Day Calendar: A Reassessment of Jaubert's Hypotheses," *CBQ* 41 (1979) 393–94. My thinking on these matters has been clarified through discussions with my student Fook-Kong Wong in connection with his seminar paper on the etiologies of the holidays in Jubilees (fall, 1992).

6   Davies and Chilton point out in rebuttal that "every major event in the lives of the patriarchs is dated to a major Jewish festival" in Jubilees ("The Aqedah," 519; see also Davies, "Passover," 62–63). This argument, however, begs the question of why the author matches a given event to one particular festival and not another, and it overlooks the crucial point that Jub 17:15–18:19 is explicitly etiological.

7   See pp. 22–23.

8   "These things," a more literal translation than appears in the NJPS, better captures the source of the rabbis' wonderment.

9   In this connection, note the expression *śāṭān hammašḥît* (Satan the Destroyer) in a prayer ascribed to Rabbi Judah the Patriarch, a figure of the late second century c.e. (*b. Ber.* 16b).

10   E.g., Jacob Z. Lauterbach in his edition of the *Mekilta de-Rabbi Ishmael* (Philadelphia: Jewish Publication Society, 1933) 1.57 n 7.

11   See Shalom Spiegel, *The Last Trial* (New York: Behman House, 1967) 54–55, esp. n 14.

12   See also *b. Roš. Haš.* 10b–11a, where it is asserted, even in the name of Rabbi Eliezer (first century c.e.), who generally prefers Tishri to Nisan, that "Isaac was born on Passover." Note, however, that Tishri is eventually said to be the month in which the aqedah took place. See, e.g., *Lev. Rab.* 29:9.

13   The text can be found in *Neophyti* (ed. Alejandro Díez Macho; Madrid and Barcelona; Consejo Superior de Investigaciones Científicas, 1971) 3.161. On this, see

Roger Le Déaut, *La Nuit Pascale* (Rome: Biblical Institute, 1963), esp. pp. 170–74; Vermes, *Scripture*, 211; Daly, "Soteriological Significance," 53–54; and Swetnam, *Jesus and Isaac*, 64.

The translation of Lev 1:11 here departs from the NJPS to bring out the reasoning of the midrash.

Cf. Gal 3:28–29.

See Robert J. Daly, *Christian Sacrifice* (Washington, D.C.: Catholic University Press, 1978), esp. pp. 498–508.

See the comments of H. Anderson in *The Old Testament Pseudepigrapha* (ed. James H. Charlesworth) 2.533–37.

All translations from 4 Maccabees are taken from Anderson (see the previous note).

The translation of Deut 33:3 is Anderson's and conforms to the Greek better than the NJPS does.

See Leonard J. Greenspoon, "The Origin of the Idea of Resurrection," in *Traditions in Transformation* (ed., Baruch Halpern and Jon D. Levenson; Winona Lake, Ind.: Eisenbrauns, 1961) 247–321.

See the remarks of D. J. Harrington in *The Old Testament Pseudepigrapha* (ed., James H. Charlesworth) 2.298–300. All quotations from the *Biblical Antiquities* are taken from Harrington's translation.

See chapter 1.

The italicized material is from Judg 11:36.

The translations from the *Jewish Antiquities* are those of H. St. J. Thackeray, *Josephus* (Cambridge: Harvard University Press; London: William Heinemann, 1978), vol. 4,; except that I have modernized the second-person pronouns.

On the connection of joy with consent in ancient Judaism, see Gary A. Anderson, *A Time to Mourn, A Time to Dance* (University Park, Pa.: Penn State University Press, 1991) 101–07.

See E. Nestle, "Wie alt war Isaak bei der Opferung?" *ZAW* 26 (1906) 281–82.

See above, pp. 182–83.

See D. Hoffmann, *Mechilta de Rabbi Simon b. Jochai* (Frankfurt: J. Kauffmann, 5665/1905) 4. Cf. *Tanḥ. wayyērā'* 23.

The Hebrew expression *běnê těmûtâ* can also be rendered "those who are dead" and may have been so understood by the rabbis. On the association of Isaac with resurrection, see below.

See Spiegel, *The Last Trial*, 40–41.

See Spiegel, *The Last Trial*, 126–31.

Ibn Ezra to Gen 22:19.

The text can be found in *Pesikta de Rav Kahana* (ed. Bernard Mandelbaum; New York: Jewish Theological Seminary, 5722/1962) 2.451.

Spiegel, *The Last Trial*, 148–49. The non-italicized lines are adapted from biblical verses.

Chapter Fifteen
The Displacement of Isaac and the Birth of the Church

1   Given the explicit reference to Abraham's love for Isaac in Gen 22:2 and such later
    texts as Jub 17:16 and 18, it would seem unwise to interpret *agapētos* in this verse or
    in texts under its influence as meaning "only," without any connotation of affect or
    preference, as advocated by C. H. Turner, *"HOYIOS MOY HO AGAPĒTOS," JTS*
    26 (1926) 113–29. See Alfredo Scattolon, "L'AGAPĒTOS Sinottico Nella Luce
    della Tradizione Giudaica," *RivistB* 26 (1978) 3–32, esp. p. 5. See also Eduard Nor-
    den, *Die Geburt des Kindes* (Studien der Bibliothek Warburg 3; Leipzig and Berlin: B.
    G. Teubner, 1924) 131–33.

2   See Geza Vermes, *Scripture and Tradition in Judaism* (Studia Post-Biblica; Leiden:
    Brill, 1973) 221–23.

3   See Beryl Smalley, *The Study of the Bible in the Middle Ages* (New York: Philosophical
    Library, 1952) 164–65, 173–74.

4   Vermes (*Scripture*, 203) finds an identification of Isaac with the servant in a Job Tar-
    gum (3:18), but this does not establish the pre-Christian origin of the equation.

5   On the conception of the twelve disciples as the twelve tribes of Israel, see E. P.
    Sanders, *Jesus and Judaism* (Philadelphia: Fortress, 1985) 95–106.
        Judas's identification of Jesus by means of a kiss (Matt 26:48–49 and parallels)
    may hark back to another Israelite story of a brother who sought to do in a beloved
    son, Esau, who kisses Jacob in Gen 33:4. Note the midrash to the effect that Esau
    did not intend to "kiss" Jacob (*lĕnaššĕqô*) but to "bite" him (*lĕnaššĕkô*) (*Gen. Rab.* 78:9).

6   See Jon D. Levenson, *Sinai and Zion* (Minneapolis: Winston, 1985) 97–101.

7   For the Egyptian background, see Jan Assmann, "Die Zeugung des Sohnes," in
    Funktionen und Leistungen des Mythos (ed. Jan Assmann et al.; OBO 48; Göttingen:
    Vandenhoeck and Ruprecht, 1982) 13–61. See also Norden, *Die Geburt*.

8   Note the dependence of the Magnificat (Luke 1:46–55) upon the Song of Hannah (1
    Sam 2:1–10).

9   See Norden, *Die Geburt*, 129–34.

10 Note that God promotes David in Ps 89:28 to the rank of his first-born son. It is
    possible that the humiliation of the Davidic king was part of a ritual process that
    eventuated in his exaltation and the legitimization of his authority. See. G. W.
    Ahlström, *Psalm 89* (Lund: Haakan Ohlsson, 1959).

11 See 1 Cor 16:8. I thank Professor John T. Townsend for drawing my attention to
    this point.

12 I have substituted "in" for "through" (NJPS) in order to convey the midrashic un-
    derstanding of the verse.

13 See David Daube, *The New Testament and Rabbinic Judaism* (London: Athlone, 1956)
    438–44.

14 Nils A. Dahl, "The Atonement—An Adequate Reward for the Akedah?", in *The
    Crucified Messiah and Other Essays* (Minneapolis: Augsburg, 1974) 153–54. Dahl sees
    Gal 3:13a–14 as "a fragment of pre-Pauline tradition" (p. 154). On the influence of

the aqedah on Paul, see, more generally, Hans Joachim Shoeps, "The Sacrifice of Isaac in Paul's Theology," *JBL* 65 (1946) 385–92, and *Paul* (London: Lutterworth, 1961) 141–49. Note also the works listed in chapter 14, n 4.

5 See David Lerch, *Isaaks Opferung* (BHT 12; Tübingen: J. C. B. Mohr [Paul Siebeck], 1950).

6 E.g., *M. 'Abot* 6:2 and *b. Qidd.* 22b. See Jon D. Levenson, *The Hebrew Bible, the Old Testament, and Historical Criticism* (Louisville: Westminster/ John Knox, 1993), 146–49.

7 E.g., *Gen. Rab.* 53:11.

8 See Gerson D. Cohen, "Esau as a Symbol in Early Medieval Thought," in *Studies in the Variety of Rabbinic Cultures* (Philadelphia and New York: Jewish Publication Society, 5751/1991) 243–69, esp. 251–52.

In the anglophone world, New Testament scholars now more than occasionally argue that Paul was not a supersessionist and intended his negative remarks about Jewish law to apply only to its observance by Gentiles. Its observance by Jews was, in this view, altogether unexceptionable to him. In the more extreme formulations, Paul is presented as adhering to something approaching Franz Rosenzweig's theology of the dual covenant or even as altogether relativizing Torah and Christ (as Rosenzweig did not). See John G. Gager, *The Origins of Anti-Semitism* (New York and Oxford: Oxford University Press, 1983) 193–264, and Lloyd Gaston, *Paul and the Torah* (Vancouver: University of British Columbia Press, 1987). On the inadequacies of the theory, see Arthur J. Droge's review of Gager in *JR* 66 (1986) 99–101. Droge points out that the "wild olive shoot" that is the Gentiles has been engrafted *in place of* the branches broken off, that is, the Jews (note *en autois* in Rom 11:17), not *alongside* them. The re-engrafting of the Jews will occur only when they give up their unbelief (vv 20, 23). In context, the unbelief in question can be safely presumed to refer to the claims Christians make on behalf of Jesus. On the broader problems in the non-supersessionist interpretation of Romans 9–11, see Alan F. Segal, *Paul the Convert* (New Haven and London: Yale University Press, 1990) 276–84.

The point of Paul's highly involved reflections on the Jewish question in Romans 9–11 seems to me to be that the election of the Jews has not been revoked, but only suspended pending the eschatological consummation. There is no good reason to doubt that in Paul's mind that eschatological consummation would be thoroughly christocentric and thus a decisive refutation of Jewish skepticism about Jesus.

Chapter Sixteen
The Revisioning of God in the Image of Abraham

Arthur J. Droge and James D. Tabor, *A Noble Death* (San Francisco: HarperSanFrancisco, 1992) 120. (Droge is the principal author of this chapter).
I depart here from the NJPS in the interest of the literalism with which the midrashim discussed below reflect this text.

3 See Samuel Sandmel, *Philo's Place in Judaism* (augmented ed.; New York: KTAV, 1971), esp. pp. 125, 151, 195.

4 The association was undoubtedly aided by the fact that *'ōhăbay* in Exod 20:6 and *'ōhăbî* in Isa 41:8 are consonantally identical.

5 Ernst Käsemann, "The Beginnings of Christian Theology," *JTC* 6 (1969) 40.

6 The resemblance must account for the fact that 2 Kgs 4:1–37 became the prophetic lection for *wayyērā'* (Gen 18:1–22:24), which includes the aqedah (22:1–19). This match would seem to presuppose the midrashim about Isaac's resurrection. I owe this point to Rabbi Joel Poupko.

7 See 2 Kgs 13:20–21, in which mere contact with the bones of Elisha is reported to have effected another resurrection.

8 Wolfgang Roth, *Hebrew Gospel* (Oak Park, Ill.: Meyer-Stone, 1988).

9 These are the B and A versions, respectively.

10 There is widespread consensus among critical scholars of the New Testament that the reports therein of the trial of Jesus have been shaped so as to reinforce certain theological and political convictions, among the most important of which is the anti-Judaism of the early Church. See the carefully reasoned discussion in E. P. Sanders, *Jesus and Judaism* (Philadelphia: Fortress, 1985) 294–318.

11 See the translation by Helmut Koester and Thomas O. Lambdin in *The Nag Hammadi Library* (ed. James M. Robinson; San Francisco: Harper and Row, 1978) 125–26.

12 See, e.g., Joachim Jeremias, *Recovering the Parables* (New York: Charles Scribner's Sons, 1966) 57–63; Malcolm Lowe, "From the Parable of the Vineyard to a Pre-Synoptic Source," *NTS* 28 (1982) 257–63; and David Stern, "Jesus' Parables from the Perspective of Rabbinic Literature," in *Parable and Story in Judaism and Christianity* (ed. Clemens Thoma and Michael Wyschogrod; New York: Paulist Press, 1989) 42–80, esp. pp. 51–69. A revised version of parts of Stern's essay, which is rich in methodological observations, appears in his *Parables in Midrash* (Cambridge: Harvard University Press, 1991) 188–206.

13 1 Thess 2:14–16 is almost certainly a non-Pauline interpolation. See Birger A. Pearson, "1 Thessalonians 2:13–16: A Deutero-Pauline Interpolation," *HTR* 64 (1971) 79–84, and Daryl Schmidt, "1 Thess 2:13–16: Linguistic Evidence for an Interpolation," *JBL* 102 (1983) 269–79.

14 The translation of the midrash is that of Reuven Hammer, *Sifre: A Tannaitic Commentary on the Book of Deuteronomy* (New Haven and London: Yale University Press, 1986) 318; the biblical quotes are from the NJPS. The citation from Gen 25:27 is premised upon the notion that Jacob was a blameless man who lingered in houses of traditional learning (see, e.g., *Gen. Rab.* 63:10).

15 See Eugene Mihaly, "A Rabbinic Defense of the Election of Israel," *HUCA* 35 (1964) 103–43, and Stern, "Jesus' Parables," 59–66.

Scripture Index

Author Index